PLAGUE,
PESTILENCE
AND
PANDEMIC

Hans Holbein the Younger, 'The Bridal Pair', from the woodblock series
The Dance of Death, c. 1526.

PLAGUE, PESTILENCE AND PANDEMIC

VOICES FROM HISTORY

EDITED BY

PETER FURTADO

CONTENTS

Plague in 1665.

S. Wale del.   N. Parr sculp.
Publish'd June 6.1747. by T. Astley.

Victims of the City of London's Great Plague of 1665 are lifted onto a death cart. Engraving by Nathaniel Parr after Samuel Wale, 1747.

INTRODUCTION

Disease has always been with us. Epidemics and pandemics, less so.

To cause an epidemic, an infectious pathogen requires a population sufficiently settled and tightly grouped to allow it to spread from person to person. Yet settled populations eventually become familiar with the dangers that surround them; they acquire a degree of physical immunity to, or develop behaviours that mean they do not come into contact with, the most threatening pathogens. This means it is rare for a sudden epidemic of these local infective agents to sweep through them. Instead, epidemics – plagues in the most general sense of the term, a sense that was established by the men who translated the Bible into English in the 16th and 17th centuries – occur where enough people move far enough to encounter unfamiliar bacteria, viruses or parasites. They are historical events.

Even more so, a pandemic that causes widespread disease and death, bringing serious disruption to societies and their economies regionally or even globally, is not just a human tragedy or a medical event. It is one of historical importance. This will surprise no one who has seen how Covid-19, which has killed well over a million people and infected scores of millions, has also significantly affected the lives of the vast majority of the eight billion people on the planet, even those who have not been directly touched by the virus itself. Covid-19 will change history.

By contrast, the most deadly pandemic of modern times, which killed an estimated fifty million worldwide – equivalent to the entire population of England in 2020, and somewhat more than that of California – left surprisingly little trace on history. Its peak, in Europe at least, coincided with the final weeks of the First World War, and brought fear and tragedy to countless households, many of which had already suffered the loss of husbands, sons, brothers and lovers. It almost killed British prime minister David Lloyd George, and it permanently weakened the constitution of US president Woodrow Wilson, at a critical juncture of the Paris Peace Conference, which was reshaping Europe in the hopes of preventing another war. Yet the so-called Spanish flu of 1918–20 was a strangely private affair. Its hundreds of thousands of individual miseries took place behind closed doors and the press was restrained in its coverage. Health care workers and bus conductors wore masks and cinemas spaced out their performances to allow the air to be refreshed, but workplaces and town centres remained busy and there was no 'lockdown'. No one blamed the flu for causing recession. No one suggested that those hundreds of thousands who died from flu were 'our glorious dead', or should be commemorated as the men blown apart on the Western Front were to be commemorated. The whole pandemic was soon forgotten, little more than a sad footnote to the more public tragedy of the Great War.

Even at the time of the flu epidemic, however, the men and women at the heart of the battle recognized that it was not an 'act of God' but a product of a modern, industrialized world in which people moved at speed right across the globe, and often mixed in close proximity and – under war conditions at least – in considerable squalor. This disease, which is now thought to have been incubated in the military camps of the United States and northern France, was a product of historical forces closely related to those that had brought about the war itself. There was much to be learned from it – not only what caused it (the flu virus was not isolated until the 1930s), how to treat it, how it spread and how to prevent or slow that spread, but also how a pandemic was becoming part of 20th-century life, something for which governments and medical authorities increasingly could and should plan.

Thus, in December 1918, American physician George Price described the Spanish flu as 'both destroyer and teacher'. While those with a professional interest in public health, like Price, have sought to learn the lessons from past pandemics and prepare, with stuttering, intermittent success, for the next, they have not always had the consistent moral, logistical and financial backing of their political bosses, who have often paid less heed to what past pandemics might have taught them. When, in April 2020 and in the heat of the Covid-19 pandemic, US president Donald Trump defunded the World Health Organization, he gave the most dramatic instance of the short-sightedness of some elected politicians in preparing for, and understanding, the unpredictable but massive impact of the arrival of a novel pathogen within their borders.

The 20th and 21st centuries have produced great medical and scientific advances. Pathogens (bacteria and viruses) are understood in extraordinary detail, their life cycles, genetic structures, biochemistry and infection pathways quickly identified, their effects on those who are infected soon mastered. Antibiotics or antivirals to defeat the pathogens or mitigate their impact, vaccines to prevent infections and treatments to alleviate symptoms are widely available or are developed with astonishing speed. In parallel with this scientific progress has been the development of public health, nationally and internationally, which has brought unparalleled cooperations between countries and means that some diseases, such as smallpox and polio, have been, or are close to being, wholly eradicated in the wild.

In the light of this amazing explosion of understanding, one might have thought that pandemics would be a thing of the past. Indeed, in 1972 the Australian virologist Sir Macfarlane Burnet, who had won the Nobel Prize in Physiology or Medicine in 1960 for his work on immunology, argued that the likely future of infectious disease would be 'very dull'. He acknowledged there might possibly be 'some wholly unexpected emergence of a new and dangerous infectious disease, but nothing of the sort has marked the last fifty years'. The field, he implied, was basically done and dusted.

Burnet was mistaken. In the half-century since 1972 the world has suffered more, and more diverse, pandemics than any comparable period in history. As products of an ever-more interconnected world, of cheap travel for ever-larger numbers of people, of factory farming and deforestation, of species loss and increasing pressure on the natural world, new pathogens have found ways to escape from their reservoirs in the animal kingdom into human society, and then to spread alarmingly from person to person. From HIV to Ebola, from Mad cow disease to Zika, from Legionnaires' disease to Covid-19, the array of novel and frightening pathogens has only grown, and our ability to understand them and resist their spread has scrambled to catch up. As the US National Academy of Medicine acknowledged in 2016: 'Despite extraordinary advances in medical science, we cannot be complacent about the threat of infectious diseases; the underlying rate of emergence of infectious diseases appears to be increasing.'

And we have been forced to take increasingly drastic action to resist them. In 1957–58, the flu killed about two million people worldwide; another pandemic eleven years later killed another million. Yet no state at that time felt impelled to counter its spread by forcing its citizens indoors for weeks, at untold cost to the economy and jobs. By early 2020, when the coronavirus that caused Covid-19 was beginning to expand out of China and to cross the globe, only extreme libertarians railed against such measures. The difference was not so much in the virulence of the virus as in the complexity of the 21st-century world; we live in a social and economic system that is so tightly bound together, so dependent on ceaseless movement of goods and people, on 'just-in-time' planning, that the disruption of an unchecked pandemic – especially on overstretched health care systems – would be even worse than the deep economic depression that the necessary countermeasures bring with them.

As a result, in 2020, we learned what it means to be stuck in our homes for months, when families and friends are unable to meet and it is forbidden for people to gather together for relaxation, when workplaces are closed down and unemployment soars, when schools and colleges stop offering education, when we are forcibly quarantined after travelling abroad. We discovered what it's like when streets are emptied, when we go out masked and nervous while buying our groceries and other necessities; when we can plan nothing, when we don't know – even when this is all over – whether there will be jobs to go back to or shops to buy what we need. We witnessed what real tragedy is when doctors and nurses are close to being overwhelmed and short of basic equipment, when people die without their loved ones, when morgues are full, when weddings and funerals are lonely, private ceremonies, when neighbours' houses fall silent and we don't know why.

All this was a huge shock, although certain aspects were alleviated to some extent by the electronic media available to us: if a lockdown of this kind had been necessary just twenty years ago, in the days before Netflix, Amazon and Zoom, before Facebook and digital news, it would have been even harsher in its psychological and economic impact.

Like the Spanish flu, Covid-19 is both destroyer and teacher. As well as causing a huge loss of life and upsetting many institutions and ways of behaviour we have taken for granted, it has also taught us a great deal about ourselves and the way we live. Like any pandemic, it makes visible previously invisible tensions at the heart of society. It has, at the very least, given us a new perspective on the kind of world we have made, and offered some challenges for the future. Do we offer adequate community support for vulnerable neighbours? Is there an adequate safety net for anyone in need? Should health and care services – and their workers – be better valued in future? What is the relationship between the generations in our society? How important is consumption to us, and what are the implications of that for the natural world? These and many other questions have been raised by Covid. They will not be simple or quick to answer.

As we think about these questions and, more generally, process the emotional shock of the Covid-19 pandemic, history may offer some helpful insights. Pandemics have happened for thousands of years. Many of those who lived through them have written about what they saw, what they felt, what they did.

Reading about the pandemics of the past, we see that most of the challenges that appear new to us in 2020 have already been faced by others, centuries or millennia ago. It is a curious fact that even the most familiar history can always surprise us. Before Covid, to read Samuel Pepys's or Daniel Defoe's accounts of the 1665 Great Plague – with their scenes of woe and despair, empty streets, quarantined houses, closed businesses, overflowing graveyards, heroic doctors and carers, quack remedies and masked figures – was to enter a disturbing and unfamiliar world. Today, however, we are hit by a jolt of recognition and understanding – the history has not changed, but we have.

It is not always a matter of *plus ça change, plus c'est la même chose*. While basic public health measures have been practised for centuries, their effectiveness in the past was limited by insufficient knowledge of pathogens, disease and individual responses to disease. Scientists know incomparably more about pathogens and their means of transmission than even a century ago, and our medical knowledge is equally advanced. Yet our understanding of the wider context of a pandemic, why it begins and why it hits particular people at a particular time, has not advanced in the same way. Most of us, just like people at the time of the Black Death, ask why this invisible, deadly enemy suddenly appears in our midst, and strikes down some and not others. Whatever explanations may be provided by the scientists may cut little ice with the mass of people, and the popular response will reveal much about existing tensions in society. The Black Death was blamed by some on God punishing humankind for its carnal excesses, and they tried to allay that anger by public flagellation; others attributed it to hated outsiders – notably the Jews, who were scapegoated and suffered terrible pogroms in much of Europe. Today social media gossip blames Covid on supposedly unhygienic Chinese people, or on a virus engineered by the Chinese military or by mobile phone companies; claims are made that the race to find a vaccine is 'really' an attempt to microchip – and thereby forever control – every last person in the world.

Pandemics, and the suffering they bring and the actions taken to alleviate them, therefore throw a complex, penetrating light on the times and places they affect. The way that people of the time thought and wrote about them says much about how they experienced a crisis that was probably unique within their lifetime. Some presented sober facts laced with anecdote, while others produced emotional outpourings, at times very personal. Moralists explained the origins of the horror and poets distilled the suffering. Physicians tried to explain what they saw, and how they were able to advance their understanding of the disease and cure it. Survivors and the families of victims gave the inside story of the nightmare that developed when a long-feared disease entered their homes or bodies. It is notable that, at least until very recent times, the heads of government, monarchs, prime ministers and presidents have had little to say publicly in the face of a pandemic – realizing, perhaps, that they have little to offer and much to lose. On this score, Covid-19 marks a distinct break with much that has gone before.

This book looks at twenty-two pandemics and the pathogens that caused them, from ancient times to the present, through the words of the men and women who lived through them. The authors include victims and their families, medics, researchers, public health campaigners, commentators, statesmen and women, and imaginative writers. None knew all that we know today about the dangers they faced, and they interpreted what they encountered in language that made sense to them.

We cannot look to these contemporary narratives to provide a complete account of all that is known about the pandemics they describe. Nor is this collection of writings an encyclopaedia – it does not cover every infectious pathogen that has caused historic pandemics or every outbreak of a particular disease mentioned here. Many infectious diseases, such as tuberculosis or malaria, have been endemic in society, accepted and managed in such a way that, though they may cause huge personal suffering, they do not threaten sudden social, political or economic breakdown. Then there are other types of epidemic – for example, diseases of civilization like obesity or heart disease – which do damage a society but are not directly infectious. Both kinds have been omitted, but without any intention to imply a lack of importance. Instead, this anthology offers a series of impressionistic pictures of moments when infectious diseases have swept over a region or the world, where the authorities have found themselves suddenly and desperately up against the limits of their knowledge and understanding. Read together, I believe that they offer both historical and human context as we face our own, similar, challenges.

Not all pandemics are equal, and there is a huge difference between a pestilence from the ancient world, where little could be done other than locking the doors and waiting for the unseen, unknown killer to pass, and a 21st-century pandemic, potentially global in scale and the subject of frantic attention by scientists in many disciplines and many countries, with daily reports in the media and expensive interventions by governments. Between these extremes came, in turn, the Christian world that saw pandemics as an act of God, a punishment or a teaching; the age of European expansion that produced a catastrophic exchange of pathogens between the Old World and the New; and the emergence of a rational approach that led to our modern scientific understanding of diseases and their causes, and the discipline of public health. While these categories are not watertight, their differences can be seen in the ways in which people acted, thought and wrote at the time.

The history of pandemics has been closely associated with that of military activity. From the plague of Athens in the early years of the Peloponnesian War, to the spread of syphilis among soldiers in 15th-century Italy, to the creation of the first vaccine against yellow fever by the US Army in Cuba: armies and troop movements, and refugees from the violence they bring, have meant that the histories of war and disease are intertwined. Even today, the threat of aggressive pathogens being released as biological weapons haunts our nightmares. And because pandemics often result from the exposure of a susceptible population to a pathogen that may have been long familiar in a different part of the world, imperial expansion has inevitably been associated with the spread of disease, sometimes disastrously so. The bubonic plague was spread across Asia by the marauding Mongols; cholera only became a global killer in the early 19th century when the British Army in north-eastern India encountered it.

The history of pandemics is, in part, the history of efforts made to counter them, whether public health measures – perhaps in the form of public prayers, or, more prosaically, the development of quarantine measures against the plague, medieval hospitals to isolate lepers or mass vaccination against smallpox – or medical advances. Some governments have made important changes that have saved lives, such as improved sanitation to counter cholera, for example, while others (like Thabo Mbeki, president of South Africa in the AIDS crisis) have intervened less happily or, perhaps more commonly (like US president Ronald Reagan, faced with the same AIDS crisis), waited too long.

For much of history, doctors were working in the dark, ignorant of the true nature of the pathogen and left guessing at the conditions in which it thrived, hampered in their efforts to cure the disease or treat the symptoms by their inadequate understanding of bodily processes. It was only in the later 19th century that Louis Pasteur and Robert Koch demonstrated that bacteria can cause diseases, and more decades passed before the first virus pathogens were identified. Although some earlier doctors proposed a 'germ theory of disease', the idea persisted into the 20th century that epidemics were the product of something much more nebulous, such as an imbalance in the bodily humours, a rare conjunction of the planets or a miasma, the so-called 'bad air' that gave malaria its name. Patients have not always trusted the efforts of medical men, and one recurrent theme in the accounts of the pandemics involves anger at those who, whether through ignorance or cynicism, promoted and sold 'cures' that were worse than useless.

Some people, not always professional medics, have faced the conceptual and practical challenges presented by an epidemic on their doorstep, and in doing so have advanced knowledge or developed treatments that have benefited humanity. Yet many – among them Lady Mary Wortley Montagu, who introduced the practice of inoculation to Europe; Robert Koch, who identified the bacillus responsible for cholera; even Dr Li Wenliang, who first spread the word about Covid-19 in Wuhan in January 2020 – have found their work initially rejected and even ridiculed both by the general public and the medical establishment.

One question often asked about pandemics is how they changed the course of history. Did Woodrow Wilson's attack of flu in 1919 affect the terms of the Treaty of Versailles? It may be impossible definitively to answer such counter-factual questions, but we are culturally programmed to ask them. The first 'plagues' that many of us encountered in our lives were the 'Plagues of Egypt' described in the biblical Book of Exodus. This is a story that teaches us that widespread suffering is not random, but carries meaning on many levels, including the historical one: the suffering inflicted on the Egyptians for the Pharaoh's refusal to release the enslaved Israelites is a foundational event to the entire story of the Jews. Without these (mythical) plagues, we infer, the history of the world would have been very different.

The impact of pandemics is often long-term – the Black Death may have killed more than half the people of western Europe, but that did not prevent England and France raising armies for the Hundred Years' War; on a longer view, however, it is often credited with causing a labour shortage that changed the relationship between landlord and tenant. In the New World, the inadvertent arrival of smallpox with the conquistadors weakened Aztec resistance and killed several of their leaders, making Spanish military ambitions infinitely easier to achieve, and changing the shape of world history. Covid-19 may bring an equivalent sea change to our world, perhaps by influencing the course of important elections or reshaping economies and attitudes to society or the natural world. But we cannot ourselves see what that change will be, nor how it may come about, and contemporary accounts of similar historical events can rarely offer the kind of insight that comes from historical perspective.

Finally, pandemics have always challenged the imagination. Extreme events of love and loss, sudden changes to the way we behave, urgent questions about the meaning and value of a human life – these are the purlieu of the spirit as much as the archive. New forms and expression are sometimes needed. Faced with a new sexually transmitted disease around 1500, Girolamo Fracastoro, a natural scientist and physician, resorted to the forms of epic poetry to express (and name) the nightmarish impact of syphilis. Though the horrors of mass death through disease were perhaps seen as too squalid for many 19th-century writers, the more genteel suffering brought on by tuberculosis became a staple of 19th- and early 20th-century literature. In recent decades, creative writers have again found pandemic a topic to grapple with, and Covid-19 may come to be seen as the blogger's pandemic. The 'destroyer and teacher' has done huge damage, but may have taught us ways of being, and helped us find new forms to express them.

Note

The extracts in this volume date from many periods and places. Some are translated, others written in an English that seems more or less archaic to us now. Where possible, we have sought to present the translated texts in reasonably modern idiom, whereas archaic English has been left intact in most respects, except for some simplification in the phrasing, spelling and punctuation. Even so, there are marked inconsistencies in spelling between the different extracts. This can be irritating when it's a question of American or British English spellings, but is far worse with regard to the spelling of place names and the transliteration of foreign words into English. This is, however, surely better than imposing some rigorous and spurious standardization on the diversity of human history.

HIPPOCRATE SAUVANT LES ATHÉNIENS DE LA PESTE.

'Hippocrates saves the Athenians from the plague.' Engraving by an
unnamed artist published in *La médecine Populaire*, 1881.

PART I
THE ANCIENT WORLD

Today we understand that many pathogens (a parasite, a bacillus or a virus) may long be endemic in one part of the world, where the population acquires a degree of immunity or learns to live with its effects; an epidemic only occurs when that pathogen comes into contact with a different population that has no such immunity or experience – especially a dense population among whom it can spread easily. Warfare, trade or migration – all features of developing urban civilizations – are among the likely mechanisms for this transmission between populations. The very word 'epidemic' was coined in the 5th century BC by the Greek physician Hippocrates.

The huge, overcrowded city of Rome, heart of an aggressive empire and visited by people from across Eurasia, was certainly an unhealthy place to live and a natural centre for early epidemics. Indeed, its most famous historians mention regular – and sometimes severe – pestilence, though little is known of most of these instances. The worst epidemic to devastate it occurred in the mid-2nd century AD, the so-called 'Antonine plague'. Athens, similarly overcrowded in the late 430s BC, had been devastated by a 'plague' that helped to bring an end to its Golden Age. (The pathogen for either event is still unknown, but it is unlikely that bubonic plague itself was involved.) Early imperial China, too, had its large cities, but whether they suffered epidemics is not known, though bacteriological study of ancient skeletons, both in China and in Europe, is starting to offer light on the prevalence of particular pathogens in the ancient world.

Beyond these two pandemics was a further major event, the Plague of Cyprian, in the mid-3rd century AD, which added significantly to the social, economic and political chaos in the Roman Empire of that period. Both the Antonine and Cyprian plagues contributed to the hollowing out of the Mediterranean population relative to that of more distant parts of the empire, allowing others to take over the vacuum that developed.

ATHENIAN PLAGUE

The Athenian plague of 430 BC is the first in history for which a detailed account is available. Thought to have killed 100,000 in the city of Athens yet barely spreading to the rest of Greece, it was the most lethal epidemic of the ancient Greek world. It significantly weakened Athens in the long and ultimately disastrous Peloponnesian War (431–403 BC) with Sparta, perhaps robbing it of a quarter of its army.

At the time, Athens, which had a tradition of naval power but an army that was no match for the Spartans, had adopted a strategy of retreating behind its famous long city walls while focusing its war effort on the sea. It was also filled with tens of thousands of refugees from its unprotected hinterland. In his history of the war, Thucydides notes that the disease may have previously broken out on the Aegean island of Lemnos but may have reached there from Ethiopia via Egypt. The effects were first felt in Piraeus, the city's port through which much of its food supplies arrived. Although his account is full of detail as to its spread through the population and the range of symptoms experienced by those who caught it (Thucydides himself was one), there has long been doubt as to the pathogen: plague, measles, typhoid and smallpox have all been suggested, while some scholars think it was a virus unknown today.

It made no difference whether men worshipped the gods or not

THUCYDIDES, *The History of the Peloponnesian War, Book II*
   (*c.* 425–410 BC)

Thucydides (c. 460–c. 400 BC) fought for Athens as a general; his vivid and dramatic account of the epidemic in The History of the Peloponnesian War, *like all his writing about the war, takes a pragmatic view, refusing to side with those who ascribed the disaster to divine intervention. Nevertheless, it carries a strong, though implicit, moral message. Thucydides described how, a few months before the plague struck, the Athenians had held a lavish traditional funeral for all those who had died in the fighting, at which the civic leader Pericles gave a powerful oration, praising the fallen for their honour and selflessness, and asserting the values of the Athenian state. Yet just a few months later, to*

*Thucydides the contrast is stark: Athenian civic values have collapsed,
traditional rites are forgotten or mocked, and, he says, those who tried
to act with honour on behalf of their suffering neighbours were seen to
pay for it with their lives. Indeed, Pericles himself and his entire family
died during a revisitation of the disease the following year.*

In the early summer [of 430 BC] the Spartans and their allies invaded Attica
and laid waste the country. Not long after their arrival the plague began
to show itself among the Athenians. It was said that it had broken out
previously in the neighbourhood of Lemnos and elsewhere; but nowhere
had seen a pestilence of such extent and mortality.

The physicians were of little use, as they were ignorant of the proper
way to treat it, but they themselves died in the largest numbers, as they
visited the sick most often. But no other art fared any better. Supplications
to the gods in the temple and divinations were equally futile; in the end
the overwhelming nature of the disaster put a stop to them altogether.

The sickness first began, it is said, in the parts of Ethiopia above
Egypt, and descended from there into Egypt and Libya and into most of
the king's country.

When it arrived in Athens, it first attacked Piraeus, whose inhabitants
claimed that Peloponnesians had poisoned the reservoirs, since there were
no wells there. From there it spread to the upper city, where the mortality
became much higher.

I leave it to other writers, professional or lay, to speculate about its
origin and causes – if causes sufficient to explain so great a disaster could
ever be found; for myself, I shall simply set down its nature, and explain
the symptoms by which it may be recognized, in case it ever breaks out
again. I can do this well, as I had the disease myself and watched its progress in many others.

Generally, there was no ostensible cause; people in good health were
all of a sudden attacked by violent fever in the head, and redness and
inflammation in the eyes, the inward parts such as throat or tongue,
becoming bloody and emitting an unnatural and fetid breath. These
symptoms were followed by sneezing and hoarseness, after which the
pain soon reached the chest and produced a hard cough. When it fixed
in the stomach, it caused an upset and discharges of bile of every kind

ensued, accompanied by very great distress. In most cases an ineffectual retching followed, producing violent spasms which in some cases ceased soon after, in others much later.

Externally the body was not very hot to the touch, nor pale in its appearance, but reddish, livid and breaking out into small pustules and ulcers. But internally it burned so that the patient could not bear to have on him clothing or linen even of the very lightest description; or indeed to be otherwise than stark naked. What they would have liked best would have been to throw themselves into cold water, as some of the neglected sick did indeed do, plunging into the rain tanks in their agonies of unquenchable thirst, though it made no difference whether they drank little or much.

Besides this, they were endlessly tormented by a miserable feeling of being unable to rest or sleep.

The body did not waste away while the sickness was at its height, but held out against its ravages, so that when they succumbed, typically on the seventh or eighth day to the internal inflammation, they had still some strength in them. But if they passed this stage, and the disease descended further into the bowels, inducing a violent ulceration accompanied by severe diarrhoea, this was generally fatal.

For the disorder first settled in the head, then ran through the whole of the body, and, even where it did not prove mortal, it still left its mark on the extremities; for it settled in the privy parts, the fingers and the toes, and many escaped with the loss of these, some also lost their eyes. Others who survived endured a complete loss of memory and did not know either themselves or their friends.

But while the disease defied all description, and its attacks were almost too grievous for human nature to endure, it was very different from all ordinary disorders, as the following observations clearly show. All the birds and beasts that usually prey upon human bodies abstained from touching them (even though there were many lying unburied), or died after tasting them... In fact, carrion birds actually disappeared. But these effects could best be observed in domestic animals like dogs.

The various symptoms of particular cases were many and peculiar, but these were the general features of the disease.... Some people died in neglect, others in the midst of every attention. No specific remedy was found, for what seemed to help in one case, caused harm in another. Both strong constitutions and weak ones proved susceptible, and all were swept away, even those who dieted with great care.

By far the most terrible feature was the dejection that ensued when any one felt himself sickening, for the despair into which he fell removed any power of resistance, and left him easy prey to the disorder; besides which, there was the awful spectacle of men dying like sheep, through having caught the infection in nursing each other. This caused the greatest mortality of all.

Those who were afraid to visit each other, perished from neglect – indeed many houses were left empty of their inmates for want of a nurse – but for those who did venture to visit the sick, death was often the result. This was especially the case for people with pretensions to goodness: their honour made them selfless in their attendance in their friends' houses, where even the members of the family were at last worn out by the moans of the dying, and succumbed to the force of the disaster.

The sick and dying found the greatest compassion from those who had recovered from the disease. These knew, from personal experience, what it was like, and they had no fear for themselves, for the same man was never attacked twice – at least fatally. And such persons not only received the congratulations of others, but they themselves, in the elation of the moment, half-entertained the vain hope of being safe from any disease ever.

The calamity was exacerbated by the influx from the country into the city, and new arrivals suffered the worst. There were no houses to receive them, so they had to be lodged at the hot season of the year in stifling cabins where the mortality raged unchecked. The bodies of dying men lay one upon another, and half-dead creatures reeled about the streets and gathered round the fountains, desperate for water.

The sacred places where other refugees quartered themselves were also full of corpses, for as the disaster became overwhelming, men, not knowing what was to become of them, became utterly careless of everything, sacred or profane.

All the traditional burial rites were abandoned, and the citizens buried the bodies as best they could. Many people, unable to make the proper arrangements, had to resort to shameless ways of burying their loved ones: some, taking advantage of those who had already built a pile, threw their own dead body upon the stranger's pyre and ignited it; others tossed a corpse on the top of another while it was burning.

Nor was this the only form of lawlessness. Men coolly behaved in public in a manner they had formerly done only in secret, seeing how quickly things were changing. So they resolved to spend and enjoy themselves, regarding both their lives and their riches as things of a day. No one persevered with what men called honour, as it was so uncertain if they would be spared to attain the object; instead present enjoyment, and all that contributed to it, was seen as both honourable and useful. None was restrained by fear of the gods or of human law.

Men judged it to make no difference whether they worshipped the gods or not; nor did they expect to live to be brought to trial for any offences they committed. Rather, they felt a far more severe sentence had been already passed upon them all and hung over their heads, and it was only reasonable to enjoy life before the inevitable befell.

Such was the nature of the calamity, and it weighed heavily on the Athenians as death raged within the city and devastation without.

One thing they did remember was the following ancient verse: 'A Dorian war shall come and, with it, death.'

Some claimed that *dearth,* and not *death,* was the correct word, but now it was of course decided in favour of the latter, for people make their recollection fit with their sufferings. I suspect that if another Dorian war should ever happen, and a dearth should accompany it, the verse will probably be read accordingly.

The oracle given to the Spartans was now remembered. When the god Apollo had been asked whether they should go to war, he had answered that if they put their might into it, victory would be theirs, and that he would himself be with them. Events were now supposed to tally with this oracle. For the plague broke out as soon as the Peloponnesians invaded Attica; it never entered the Peloponnese (to any extent worth noticing), and committed its worst ravages at Athens and the largest other towns.

Such was the history of the plague.

A deadly pestilence is on our town
SOPHOCLES, *Oedipus Rex*, 429 BC
The tragedy Oedipus Rex, *by the playwright Sophocles (c. 496–406 BC),*
was performed for the first time in about 429 BC. Set in the city of Thebes,
it begins with the description of the disasters that had befallen the city
because of a curse. This description surely resonated with its Athenian
audience still reeling from the effects of the plague the previous year.

> A blight is on the fruitful plants of the earth,
> a blight is on the cattle in the fields,
> a blight is on our women that no children
> are born to them; a god that carries fire,
> a deadly pestilence, is on our town,
> strikes us and spares not, and the house of Cadmus
> is emptied of its people while black Death
> grows rich in groaning and in lamentation.

ANTONINE PLAGUE

The pandemic that hit the Middle East and Roman world in the AD 160s
is named after the family Antoninus, for the emperors Lucius Verus, who
may well have died of it in 169, and Marcus Aurelius, who did die of the
disease in 180. The great medical writer Galen lived through the pandemic
but frustratingly (considering the enormous extent of his writings on all
kinds of medical matters) provides little more than cursory allusions to it in
what remains of his work. These (and similar references in other writers) are
not sufficient to make an unambiguous diagnosis, although many modern
scholars consider this to have been one of the earliest outbreaks of smallpox.

Modern scholars have estimated that five million may have died,
up to a third of the population in some affected areas, and the disease
returned several times over the succeeding two decades. It was thought
at the time to have originated in the East – indeed, it may have originated

in an epidemic in China earlier in the 160s, which then moved westwards along the Silk Road – and introduced to the Mediterranean world by a Roman army returning from Mesopotamia.

With the medical knowledge of the time unable to provide help, many turned to amulets and superstitions to protect themselves. The disease particularly ravaged the army, and the resulting manpower shortage meant that Marcus Aurelius needed to recruit wherever he could – including accepting slaves and gladiators into the army – to sustain his war against the incursions of Germanic tribes (although these, too, were affected by the epidemic). The plague was also responsible for a significant fall in tax revenues for the Roman state as a result of the decline in both agricultural output – the disease struck rural regions as well as towns – and general trade. Despite this, the Antonine plague was not, as has sometimes been claimed, the start of the fall of the Roman Empire.

Disease escapes from the temple of Apollo

AMMIANUS MARCELLINUS, *The Roman History, Book XXIII*, chapter VI (*c.* AD 385)

The soldier Ammianus Marcellinus (AD 330–c. 391), from the eastern provinces of the Roman Empire, wrote a major record of the empire, The Roman History, *of which only the portion about the 4th century AD survives. This contains a discourse on the earlier history of Persia, from which this extract about the spread of the Antonine plague derives.*

When Seleucia in Mesopotamia was stormed by the generals of Verus Caesar, the statue of Apollo Comaeus was torn from its place and taken to Rome, where the priests set it up in the temple of the Palatine Apollo. And it is said that, after this statue had been carried off and the city burned, the soldiers who were ransacking the temple found a narrow crevice; this they widened in the hope of finding something valuable, but from a kind of shrine, closed by the occult arts of the Chaldaeans, what came out was the germ of that pestilence, which generated the virulence of an incurable disease, and in the reigns of Verus and Marcus Antoninus polluted everything with contagion and death, from the frontiers of Persia all the way to the Rhine and to Gaul.

Nursed by Athena

AELIUS ARISTIDES, *Sacred Tales II* (c. AD 170)

Aelius Aristides (AD 117–181) was a Greek orator and philosopher, who suffered throughout his life from a variety of ailments, which he recounted in detail in his Sacred Tales. *A pagan, he sought respite in the faith of Asclepius, the healing god, who repeatedly appeared to him in dreams. In 165 he narrowly escaped death from the sickness that was to become known as the Antonine plague.*

At the height of the summer [of AD 165] a plague infected nearly all of my neighbours. First two or three of my servants grew sick, then one after another. Then all were in bed, both the old and the young. I was last to be attacked. Doctors came from the city [Smyrna] and we used their attendants as servants. Even certain of those who cared for me acted as servants. The livestock too became sick. And if anyone exerted himself, he was immediately laid out dead before the front door.... Everything was filled with despair, ailing, groans and thorough gloom. There was also terrible sickness in the city. Meanwhile, I persisted in my concern for the safety of others, no less than for my own.

Then the disease increased and I was attacked by a terrible burning of a bilious mixture, which troubled me continuously day and night, and I was prevented from taking nourishment and my strength failed. The doctors gave up and finally despaired entirely, and it was announced that I would die immediately. However, even here you might invoke Homer's phrase, 'Still his mind was firm.' Thus I was conscious of myself as if I were another person, and I perceived my body slipping away until I was nearly dead. I happened to turn to the inside of my bed, and it seemed it was then the end. But Asclepius the Saviour turned me suddenly to the outside. Then not much later Athena appeared with her aegis and the scent of the aegis was as sweet as could be, and marvellous in beauty and magnitude.... I pointed her out to those present – two of my friends and my foster sister – and I named her Athena, saying she stood before me. They did not know what to do but were afraid I had become delirious until they saw my strength was restored and heard the words which I heard from the goddess. Thus the goddess consoled me and saved me while I was on my sick bed.

Thereupon I took an enema of Attic honey, and there was a purge of the bile. After this came curatives and nourishment. First I think goose liver after frequent refusal of all food, then some sausage. Then I was brought to the city in a long covered carriage, and little by little, with trouble and difficulty, I recovered. The fever, however, did not completely leave me until the most valued of my foster children had died – on the same day as my disease ended. Thus I was given a new life by the gods.

The physician's view

GALEN OF PERGAMON, various sources (*c.* AD 165–180)

Galen of Pergamon (AD 129–c. 216) is the best-known physician and writer on medical matters of the ancient world. As much admired during his lifetime as after his death, he studied anatomy and physiology as well as medicine. His writings proved extremely influential both in the Byzantine and the Islamic world, from which they passed to medieval Christendom where they were treated as unchallengeable until the Renaissance. Probably the most prolific writer of the ancient world, less than half of his output survives, yet what remains of his five hundred treatises amounts to more than three million words. Curiously, despite living through its worst years, he did not write extensively on the Antonine plague, although a recently discovered (2005) text, 'Avoiding Distress', offers his view on the symptoms.

On my arrival in Aquileia [city in north-eastern Italy], the plague attacked more destructively than ever before, so the emperors fled immediately to Rome with a small force of men. For the rest of us, survival became very difficult for a long time. Most, indeed, died, and the effects were exacerbated by the fact that all this was occurring in the middle of winter....

I discovered the cure of them, in that place, at the time of the great plague (would that it will at some point cease), when it first came upon us. A young man broke out in ulcers all over his whole body on the ninth day, just as did almost all the others who were saved. On that day there was also a slight cough. On the following day, immediately after he bathed, he coughed more violently and brought up with the cough what they call a scab....

Those easily restored to health from the plague seem to have been previously dried and purged in respect to the whole body, for vomiting occurred in some of them and the stomach was disturbed in all. And, in the same way, in those already purged who were going to be saved, dark pustules appear over the whole body, in most ulcerous, in all dry. It was obvious to the observer that what was left of the blood which had been putrefied during these fevers, had, like a kind of ash, been forced through the skin by nature, just like many other superfluities.

A plague laid waste all Italy

PAULUS OROSIUS, *Seven Books of History Against the Pagans,*
   Book VII (c. AD 417)

The priest Paulus Orosius (c. AD *375–c. 418) was probably born in Iberia, studied under St Augustine, Bishop of Hippo, and travelled to Palestine late in life. His major work* History Against the Pagans *is a universal account that aimed to demonstrate how Christianity had improved the world. This extract emphasizes the devastating effect of the plague on the Roman armies fighting the Germans who were beginning to invade the empire.*

After the death of Verus in 169, Marcus Aurelius alone ruled the state. But in the days of the Parthian War [AD 161–66], severe persecutions of Christians on his order broke out, for the fourth time since Nero in Asia and in Gaul, and many of the saints received the martyr's crown.

A plague which broke out over many provinces followed and so laid waste all Italy that everywhere country estates, fields and towns were left without a cultivator or inhabitant and gave way to ruins and forests. Indeed it is reported that the Roman army and all its legions stationed far and wide in winter quarters were so used up that the war against the Marcomanni, which broke out immediately, could not have been carried on without a new levy of troops which Marcus Aurelius Antoninus held continuously at Carnuntum [capital of Pannonia (in present-day Austria)].

Putting trust in the 'unshorn Phoebus'

LUCIAN OF SAMOSATA, *Alexander the False Prophet* (*c.* AD 180)

The prolific satirist Lucian of Samosata (AD 125–c. 180) was a popular writer from Asia Minor who frequently used sarcasm to ridicule the superstitions and pretensions of the religious. In Alexander the False Prophet, *Lucian presents his contemporary Alexander of Abonoteichus as a complete charlatan. Alexander was a genuine figure who claimed to be a priest of the god Glycon, whose cult he invented. In 2014, a pewter amulet bearing the Phoebus motto mentioned in this extract was discovered on the Thames foreshore in London.*

No sooner did Alexander get Italy in hand than he began to devise ever more ambitious projects, and sent oracle-mongers everywhere across the empire warning the cities to be on their guard against plagues and conflagrations and earthquakes; he promised that he would himself afford them infallible aid so that none of these calamities should befall them. There was one oracle which he despatched to all the nations during the pestilence; it was just a single line of verse:

> 'Phoebus, the god unshorn, keepeth off plague's nebulous onset.'

This verse could be seen everywhere, written over doorways as a charm against the plague; but in most cases it had the opposite result to that intended. By some chance it was those very houses on which the verse was inscribed that suffered the worst. I don't mean that they were stricken specifically on account of the verse – but by some chance or other that's what happened. Perhaps the residents neglected the usual precautions because of their confidence in the oracle and so carelessly didn't help the oracle in combating the disease. They just trusted the syllables to defend them and 'unshorn Phoebus' to drive the plague away with his arrows.

Hans Holbein the Younger, 'The Abbot', from the woodblock series
The Dance of Death, c. 1526.

PART II
THE CHRISTIAN WORLD

The late Roman world and the European Middle Ages saw two extended pandemics (the Plague of Justinian and the Black Death) that caused as much devastation as any prior to those of the 20th century. Both were outbreaks of bubonic plague, and both apparently caused huge depopulation of towns and countryside. People did what little they could to protect themselves against the unseen killer, fleeing its advance or introducing quarantines to keep the infection away.

Such efforts, however, were seen as of limited use. Preachers brought up on the story of the plagues of Egypt understood that disease was neither a natural nor an arbitrary destruction, but a lesson sent from God: a statement of the awesome power of the divine will and his judgment to which people had to submit; a punishment for sin, to be atoned for; a message on living better; or even, as Martin Luther emphasized, as an opportunity to learn the true meaning of Christian love. Such moralizing was not, of course, restricted to medieval Christianity; similar arguments were seen in the Islamic world, and continued for many centuries in Christendom, recurring as recently as the AIDS epidemic of the late 20th century (see page 254).

Both bubonic plague and the sweating sickness (which was far less impactful in terms of numbers and geographical spread, but equally devastating as it caused death within hours) gave people two choices – social distancing or praying for miracles. This contrasts with the epidemic of skin diseases that the Middle Ages called leprosy, again taking its cue from the Bible, this time from Jesus' healing ministry. Though incurable at the time, leprosy was addressed by neither fatalism nor moralizing, but through establishing networks of hospitals and other institutions that managed to protect both the sick and the rest of society.

PLAGUE OF JUSTINIAN

In the early 540s, during the reign of the Byzantine Emperor Justinian (r. 527–65) in Constantinople, a true pandemic struck the Mediterranean world, the Middle East and western Europe. It was first recorded in Egypt, spreading disastrously throughout the Eastern Roman Empire and reaching the capital in 542, where it laid waste the population. Thousands died daily, and one contemporary writer estimated that perhaps 300,000 died in the city; if correct, this would have represented at least 60 per cent of the population. The Emperor himself was said to have become severely ill, but survived. From Constantinople the disease spread west to Italy, Spain, France and Britain, as well as south to Arabia and east to Persia; it did not die out until the mid-8th century, by which time it may have killed 50 million or more people, including a third of the population of the Mediterranean world.

It is clear from contemporary graphic descriptions of the symptoms that this was the first appearance of bubonic plague, the disease that brought equivalent devastation on several occasions, notably the Black Death of the mid-14th century (the so-called 'second pandemic' that continued for more than three centuries; see page 56); and the 'third pandemic' (see page 183) that broke out in China in the 1880s. Bubonic plague (now known to be caused by the bacterium *Yersinia pestis*, which lives in the gut of fleas that normally live on rats and other rodents) has been the deadliest of all diseases and responsible for the deaths of hundreds of millions of people through the last fifteen hundred years.

The plague – never previously seen in the 6th-century Mediterranean world, and probably brought from China by traders from India – appeared inexorable and devastating on a large scale, yet random in its impact on individuals. This is the first epidemic with multiple significant accounts written by eyewitnesses, their graphic details of horrific suffering echoed by all the writers. Some attention was given to practical efforts by civic authorities to deal with the impact, but most of the focus was on the difficult choices made by individuals facing up to the calamity that was overwhelming them. While some writers, such as Procopius, wrote their histories in the tradition of Thucydides, describing events and seeking to discern human motivations in the actions they were describing, this was a Christian age in which churchmen were more inclined to ascribe the plague to the wrath of God and the failure of the people to seek forgiveness for their sinful way of life. They therefore used dramatic anecdotes – of which there was no shortage – to stress the moral message of living a godly life and accepting the will of God.

The Plague of Justinian has been relatively little studied by modern historians, but is often credited with contributing to the decline of Byzantine power in the Balkans and across the Mediterranean, and to deepening the social and economic collapse of western Europe in the wake of the fall of the Western Roman Empire. This is often argued in generalized terms and by analogy with the better-known effects of the Black Death. Yet recently it has been suggested that evidence for any such breakdown of administration, civic life or demographic, agricultural or economic prosperity is lacking.

Despite this, the plague unarguably played an important role in the narrative of early medieval writers. Gregory of Tours, whose History of the Franks is an important source for the history of western Europe in this period, several times mentioned the pandemic and also described one of its important cultural legacies. When the plague was finally passing from Rome in the 590s, Pope Gregory the Great saw a vision of the Archangel Michael sheathing his sword. In recognition of this, he renamed the Roman tomb of Hadrian the Castell Sant'Angelo (Castle of the Holy Angel), and since medieval times it has been topped with a statue of the saint sheathing the sword.

No cause that human reasoning could see

PROCOPIUS, *History of the Wars, Volume II* (c. 545)

Born around 500 in Palestine, Procopius, a lawyer, travelled with Justinian's armies in the western Mediterranean and spent the second half of his life in Constantinople. He wrote a well-regarded History of the Wars, *which described the campaigns of the 530s. The account of the plague in Constantinople provided in the history, based on his own experience, was less alarmist than in his* Secret History *(page 39) and showed the influence of Thucydides' writing on the Athenian plague nine hundred years earlier (see page 20). It is probably the best-known source for the Justinian plague.*

During these times there was a pestilence that brought the whole human race close to annihilation. Now when other scourges are sent from Heaven some explanations might be made up by the kind of clever men who love to conjure up incomprehensible theories and fabricate outlandish concepts of natural philosophy, knowing well that they are saying nothing sound, but just like to deceive people and persuade them to their view. But for this calamity, the only explanation can be to refer it to God, for the pestilence embraced the entire world, and blighted the lives of all, of every status, sex and age. Now let each man, whether sophist and astrologer, express his own opinion, but for my part, I shall tell where this disease originated and how it destroyed men.

It started in Pelusium on the Nile delta. Then it moved west and south towards Alexandria and the rest of Egypt, and east to Palestine; and then over the whole world.... Typically an outbreak began at the coast, and then moved into the interior. And in the spring of the second year [542] it reached Byzantium, where I happened to be staying.

Supernatural apparitions in human guise appeared, and on encountering them, people thought that they had been struck by a man in one or other part of the body, but immediately after they went down with the disease. At first those who met these demons tried to turn them aside by uttering the holiest of names and exorcizing them, but this accomplished nothing. People shut themselves in their rooms and refused to answer the door to their friends, fearing that one of the demons was calling. Others dreamed that the creature stood over them, or heard a voice saying that they were written down in the number of those who were to die. But most were seized by the disease without warning. The fever came on suddenly, for some when just roused from sleep, for others while walking about or otherwise engaged. The body showed no change from its previous colour, nor was it hot as with a usual fever, nor did any inflammation set in, and for the first day the fever was so mild that neither they themselves nor their physician would raise any suspicion of danger. But on the following day or not many days later, a bubonic swelling developed in the groin, but also inside the armpit, and in some cases also beside the ears and on the thighs.

Some now fell into a deep coma, others a violent delirium. For those who were under the coma seemed to be sleeping constantly; if anyone cared for them, they would eat without waking, but some were neglected and died through lack of sustenance. But those who were seized with delirium suffered from insomnia and a distorted imagination; they imagined men were coming upon them to destroy them, and fled crying at the top of their voices. Those who were attending them were in a state of constant exhaustion; people pitied them as much as the sufferers, less because they were threatened by the pestilence in going near it (for neither physicians nor other carers seemed to contract this malady simply through contact with the sick or with the dead), but because of the hardships which they had to undergo. When their patients fell out of bed, they had to put them back, and when they tried to flee their homes, they had to restrain them and force them back. And many sufferers tried to jump into nearby water, not because of thirst but because of the diseased state of their minds. They could not easily take food. Many perished through lack of care, and were either overcome by hunger or threw themselves down from a height. And in those cases where neither coma nor delirium came on, the bubonic swelling became mortified and often the pain was such that the sufferer died; some though were unable to feel any pain as their minds were so troubled that they lost all sense of feeling.

In some cases death came quickly, in others after many days, and with some the body broke out with black pustules the size of a lentil; these cases did not survive even one day. Many vomited blood before dying. Now some physicians decided to investigate the bodies of the dead, and on opening the buboes or swellings, they found a strange sort of carbuncle inside. Even the most illustrious physicians would predict that people would die, who then unexpectedly recovered; and they declared that many would be saved, who were carried off almost immediately. In this disease there was no cause that human reasoning could see; in all cases the issue tended to be in some way unaccountable. Methods of treatment had different results with different patients. Some were helped by bathing, others harmed by it. Even some of those who received no care were saved. Essentially, people found no way to save themselves, whether by taking precautions against catching the disease, or by treating it; suffering came without warning and recovery was due to no external cause....

Now the disease in Byzantium ran a course of four months, and its peak lasted about three. And at first the mortality was a little higher than the normal, then it rose until the tally of the dead reached 5,000 a day, then 10,000 or more. At first each man attended to the burial of the dead of his own house, though they sometimes threw them into the tombs of others whether by stealth or using violence; but afterwards confusion and disorder everywhere became complete. Many slaves became masterless, while prosperous men lost their domestics, and many houses became completely abandoned. As a result, even some of the notable men of the city remained unburied for many days.

It fell to the emperor to make provision for the trouble. He therefore distributed money, commanding Theodorus [his servant] to take charge of this work.... While those who had not as yet fallen into complete destitution buried their own households, Theodorus used the emperor's money and some from his own purse, to bury the bodies of any who were not cared for. And when it came about that all the tombs were full, then they dug new cemeteries. Later unable to keep up with the number of the dying, they climbed the towers of the fortifications in Galata, tore off the roofs and threw in the bodies in complete disorder, piling them up until they had filled all the towers with corpses, and then put the roofs back on. As a result of this an evil stench pervaded the city and distressed the inhabitants still more, and especially whenever the wind blew fresh from that quarter....

Those who previously had devoted themselves to shameful pursuits, now changed their ways and diligently took up their religious duties, not because they had seen the light or suddenly become lovers of virtue, but because they were utterly terrified and, expecting to die very soon, felt they must learn respectable behaviour for a season. But any who were rid of the disease or supposed that they were safe, since the curse had moved on elsewhere, these soon enough reverted to their old ways, surpassing themselves in villainy and in lawlessness. In truth this disease, whether by chance or by providence, chose the very worst men and let them escape.

The streets were deserted. Anyone fortunate enough to be healthy was indoors, attending the sick or mourning the dead. The only people on the streets were carrying the dead. Work of every description ceased, and all the trades were abandoned by the artisans, and all other work as well. Though this city held dominion over the whole Roman Empire, the *clamys* [uniform of public service or authority] was nowhere to be seen, for every man was now wearing private clothes and staying quietly at home. Such was the course of the pestilence in the Roman Empire at large as well as in Byzantium. And it fell also upon the land of the Persians and visited all the other barbarians besides.

Justinian – a second pestilence sent from heaven
PROCOPIUS, *Secret History* (*c.* 500)
Procopius also wrote the more scurrilous and scathing Secret History *in which he revealed his deep dislike of Justinian and Empress Theodora. In it, he claimed that whereas the plague proved a dreadful blight on half the citizens of the empire, the emperor's overwhelming impositions were even worse in that not one citizen could escape them (he even claimed Justinian was responsible for the deaths of a trillion people).*

Justinian, while still a youth, was the virtual ruler, and the author of more and worse calamities to the Romans than any one man in all their previous history. He had no scruples against murder or seizing other peoples' property; and it was nothing to him to make away with myriads of men, with no cause. He had no care for established customs, but was always eager for experiments, and, in short, was the most prodigious corrupter of all noble traditions.

Though the plague attacked the whole world, just as many men escaped as died of it; for some never were taken by the disease, while others recovered from it. But not one of all the Romans could escape Justinian; like a second pestilence sent from heaven, he fell on the nation and left no man untouched. Some he slew without reason, and some he released into penury, and their fate was worse than that of those who had perished, so that they prayed for death to free them from their misery; and others he robbed of both their lives and their property.

The sickness waxed hot
EVAGRIUS SCHOLASTICUS, *Ecclesiastical History* (*c.* 593)
Evagrius Scholasticus (536–594) was a lawyer from Antioch who, in his great Ecclesiastical History *written towards the end of his life, described his own first-hand experience of being stricken with the plague as a child, and mentioned three other encounters with the disease during his lifetime.*

The greatest mortality of all fell upon mankind...and I myself was troubled with an impostume or swelling about the privy members or secret parts of the body: moreover, in process of time, when the sickness waxed hot and dispatched diversely and sundry kinds of ways, it fell out to my great grief and sorrow that God took from me many of my children, my wife also with divers of my kinsfolk, some of whom dwelled in the city and some in the country. Such were my adventures and the calamities which the course of those lamentable times distributed unto me.

Pitilessly trampled like grapes in a wine press

JOHN OF EPHESUS

John of Ephesus (c. 507–588), a Syriac churchman, lived in Constantinople in the 530s, where he won the confidence of the emperor, and acted as a missionary in Asia Minor in the 540s. After the death of Justinian in 565, the new emperor Justin II followed a different religious policy and attacked the Monophysite church, of which John was a leading member. He described his imprisonment in his Ecclesiastical History, *which also included extended coverage of the plague and its effects, from a strongly Christian point of view.*

Ecclesiastical History (*c.* 585)

During the peak of the pestilence, we journeyed from Syria to the capital. Day after day we, too, used to knock at the door of the grave along with everyone else. We used to think that if it was evening, death would come upon us in the night. Although the next morning would come, we used to face the grave during the whole day as we looked at the devastated and moaning villages in these regions, and at corpses lying on the ground with no one to gather them.

Fertile fields of wheat in all the regions through which we passed, from Syria to Thrace, were white and standing but there was no one to reap them and store the grain. Vineyards whose picking season had come and gone, shed their leaves since winter was severe, but kept their fruits hanging on the vine as there was no one to pick them and press them.

Lives of the Eastern Saints (560s)

Now, the blessed prophet Jeremiah is most helpful to us, being versed in raising songs of lamentation amid groans over the afflictions and the ruin of his people. He is a model for the present writer in putting down the story of this terrible scourge over the many cities which have been changed, by the wrath of God, into a wine press and all their inhabitants pitilessly trampled and squeezed like grapes.

Over the whole earth upon which the command of God went out, like a reaper upon standing corn, to mow and cut down innumerable people of all ages, all sexes and all ranks, a Jeremiah would have to lament:

- corpses split open and rotten on the streets with nobody to bury them;
- houses large and small, beautiful and desirable, became tombs and where servants and masters together suddenly fell, mingling their rottenness together in their bedrooms, and not one escaped to remove their corpses;
- people perished in the streets, their bellies swollen and their mouths wide open, vomiting pus in torrents, their eyes inflamed and their hands stretched out;
- ships whose sailors were attacked by the sickness, drifting on the waves, carrying the corpses of their owners;
- other ships forever in harbour, never again to be untied by their owners;
- girls in their wedding finery suddenly became lifeless and terrifying corpses;
- roads empty of traffic;
- villages where all the inhabitants perished together;
- and many other things, which defeat the power of speech.

When the chastisement came upon Byzantium, the abundant benignity and grace of God appeared with it. Although this chastisement was very frightening, grievous and severe, we should see it not only as a sign of threat and wrath but also a sign of grace and a call to repentance. For the scourge used patience and moderation until it arrived at a place. Just as a king gives orders to his captains saying, 'Prepare yourself, assemble your arms and your provisions, and we will march to war on such and such a day', and likewise tells the neighbouring cities, 'I am coming; be prepared, for when I have come there will be no lingering', so this scourge sent clear messages from one country to another, and from city to city, as if to say, 'Turn back and repent and beg for forgiveness, and prepare alms from your goods, for behold I am coming, and shall make your property irrelevant.'

God's providence ensured that news was sent to every place, before the scourge arrived there. And only when what has been ordered against one city had been accomplished, did the scourge pass on to the next. This is what happened to Byzantium: the city had news of the visitation for one or two years before it arrived. God's grace was both eager and encouraging, and in some people in Byzantium it was truly active.

As in the days of Noah, so now some people managed speedily to build ships to transport both themselves and people in need; others achieved salvation by giving alms and distributing their possessions to the needy; still others by lamentation and humility, vigils, abstinence and woeful calling upon God. In this way many people bought for themselves the kingdom of God.

When the scourge weighed heavy upon this city, first it began to assault the poor, who lay in the streets. As many as 16,000 died in a single day. Since these were early days, men stood by the harbours, at the crossroads and at the gates counting the dead. They were diligently shrouded and buried; they departed this life clothed and followed to the grave by everybody....

Among the horrors, people found one house all closed up and stinking, so that they trembled at its smell. They entered and found about twenty people dead and rotten, with worms creeping all over them. Although terror seized them, they paid people to pick them up in cloaks and remove them on carrying poles.

In another, all were found dead but the babies which were crying; elsewhere, the mothers lay dead in their beds but their babies were alive and sleeping beside them, holding and sucking their dead mother's breasts....

The imperial palace was overwhelmed by sorrow. The emperor and the empress to whom tens of thousands of commanders and the whole senate had bowed and paid honour every day, now were like all their subjects, sunk into a deep grief....

Many people's riches, their gold, silver and other possessions, were left unguarded, their gates stood open and treasures abandoned, their houses full of everything one could desire in the world; for if somebody wished to steal it, on the very same day the sentence – the disease and death – would come upon him. This was another sign of God's just sentence....

There were, however, some people who thought: 'Perhaps we shall escape death, so why not ask a dying man if he is willing to give us something, and if he is, then accept the gift? We won't break into a house and take something from those who have died, but simply ask for a favour.' And they came to a shop of a moneylender who was sitting on his doorstep; the whole of the rest of his family had perished. They approached him and said: 'Grant us a gift. Perhaps we shall live and then we can commemorate you.' And he said: 'My sons, see, the whole shop is before you. Enter and take whatever your soul desires, and do not fear. Take as much as you can carry, and go in peace.'

So they entered, and looked and were astonished. They cast their eyes on many things, especially on gold, and picked it up and left. But when two crossed the threshold to go out, it was as if a sword came between them and cut both of them down. Their souls fled and their load was scattered. Terror fell upon the rest of the people; from now on gold, silver and all material goods were despised in everybody's eyes. A frightful and zealous power laid hold of all and nobody relied on either gold or other riches, but the faces of all were turned toward the grave....

In one city on the border of Palestine, demons appeared in the shape of angels. These deceived the inhabitants, making them worship a bronze statue, which had been a pagan idol and was still secretly worshipped by those still caught up in paganism. The demons made the whole city worship it, saying: 'If you worship this idol, death will not enter this city.'

The words of the psalm would also apply to these wretches: 'They reel to and fro, and stagger like a drunken man and are at their wits' end.' Yet they could not avert the wrath of God. Forgetting the second death after this one, they all fell down and worshipped that idol. But the power of the Lord revealed itself: when they were gathered before the statue, a whirlwind as it were entered into this idol and lifted it up, as far up as the eye could see, and threw it down with force upon the surface of the earth. It was broken into pieces and scattered like water on the surface of the earth.

And the sword of death now fell upon them and by evening no living soul could be found in the city, but it was as is written in the prophet, 'Now all of them have perished since they did not remember the name of the Lord.'

The great city was ruined

MICHAEL THE SYRIAN, *World Chronicle* (*c.* 1180)

Living and writing well after the pandemic was over, Michael the Syrian (1126–1199), a monk and church leader, wrote many works on Christian liturgy and canon law. He also wrote a World Chronicle, *covering the history of the world from Adam to Michael's own time, in which he described the initial outbreak of plague in Constantinople, and later recurrences across the empire, such as that of 704–5 when, he claimed, a third of the known world's population died, and that of 743–44, when 100,000 died in Mesopotamia alone. His figures, though, are inevitably exaggerated – as was his claim that fewer than one in two thousand inhabitants of Constantinople survived the 540s visitation described in this extract.*

John of Ephesus speaks of the great plague which occurred in the Year of Alexander 855 [AD 543–44]. The whole world was struck by this cruel scourge, unequalled since the beginning of the world. It began at first among the peoples inland of the countries to the south-east of India; then spread to the regions of the West, which are called 'upper', the peoples of the Romans, the Italians, the Gauls and the Spanish. Men became enraged like dogs, became mad, attacked one another, went into the mountains and committed suicide. The scourge reached the lands of Kush on the borders of Egypt, and from there spread to Egypt itself.... When the greater part of the people had perished, to the extent that Egypt was deprived of its inhabitants, ruined and deserted, it fell upon Alexandria, and consumed a multitude of people. Those who escaped a quick death were struck with a terrible disease: that of buboes in the groin; some on one side, others on both sides. The groin swelled, swelled again, filled with water, and then there were great and deep ulcers, which leaked blood, pus and water, night and day. By this plague the scourge fell upon them, by which they were promptly removed.

The poor died first, and thereby the mercy of God was shown them: the wealthier inhabitants of the cities, displaying their faith and seeking spiritual advantages for themselves, buried their bodies; for if the calamity had taken the poor at the same time as the better-off, their putrefying corpses and their bare bones could never have been removed from public places. So they died first, while others were still healthy enough to carry them away and bury them.

If the evil began with the youngest of a house, the house was reduced to despair because all would die. Men lost all hope of living, and feared to go out, saying: 'I shall die in my own house.' If someone had to go out, he wrote a tablet that he hung on his arm, saying: 'This is my name, and that of my father, this is my neighbourhood; if I die, for God's sake, let them know at my house, and let my people come to bury me.' The great city was ruined; men feared to go into the streets because of the stink of corpses and of bodies being eaten by the dogs.

Prodigies in the sky

GREGORY OF TOURS, *History of the Franks* (c. 585)

Gregory (538/9–c. 594), the bishop of Tours, wrote the History of the Franks, *an important source for Merovingian France. The plague of the 540s was a recurring theme in many of the incidents he described.*

Book 4 Before the plague arrived at Clermont great prodigies terrified that region. For three or four great shining places frequently appeared about the sun and the rustics used to call them suns, saying: 'Behold, three or four suns in the sky.' In October the sun was so darkened that it looked hideous and discoloured, like a sack. Moreover a comet with a ray like a sword appeared over the country. Many other signs were seen. A lark flew into the church at Clermont, flapping its wings above the candles, extinguishing them as quickly as if a man had plunged them into water. The bird flew on into the sanctuary and tried to put out the candle there too, but was prevented from doing so and killed. And then the plague came, and such a carnage took place through the whole district that the numbers that fell could not be counted.... At that time Cato the priest died. For when many had fled from the plague he never left, but remained courageously burying the people and celebrating mass. He was a priest of great kindliness and a warm friend of the poor. But the bishop Cautinus ran from place to place in fear of this plague; when he returned to the city, he caught it and died the day before Passion Sunday. At that very hour too, his cousin Tetradius died. At the same time Lyons, Bourges, Cahors and Dijon were seriously depopulated from this plague....

Book 9 The city of Marseilles was sick with a deadly plague at a time when Bishop Theodore was there. A ship from Spain put in at the port with its usual wares but also brought the seed of this disease. Many citizens bought merchandise from her, and were infected – one household in which were eight souls was quickly left empty, its inmates all dying. But the fire of the plague did not at once spread through all the houses, but after a time it swept the whole city like a fire in standing grain. However the bishop shut himself within the walls of St Victor's church and devoted himself to prayer and watching, praying for God's mercy that the deaths might at length cease and the people be allowed to rest in peace. The plague passed away in two months, but when the people, now reassured, had returned to the city the disease came on again and those who had returned now perished.

Pestilence in the British Isles

VENERABLE BEDE, *Ecclesiastical History of the English People* (c. 731)

The Venerable Bede (672–735) spent his life as a monk at Jarrow, Northumbria, where he wrote his Ecclesiastical History of the English People. *In it he described the arrival of the plague in Britain, and its spread to Ireland, in 664; perhaps surprisingly, he did not present it as a curse from God but more as part of God's plan in contributing to the development of a Roman-focused church. Some twenty years later Bede himself, aged about twelve, survived another outbreak that killed many of the monks at Jarrow.*

In the same year of our Lord 664, there happened an eclipse of the sun, on the third day of May, about the tenth hour of the day. In the same year, a sudden pestilence depopulated first the southern parts of Britain, and afterwards attacking the province of the Northumbrians, ravaged the country far and near, and destroyed a great multitude of men. By this plague the aforesaid priest of the Lord, Tuda, was carried off, and was honourably buried in the monastery called Paegnalaech.

Moreover, this plague prevailed no less disastrously in the island of Ireland. Many of the nobility, and of the lower ranks of the English nation, were there at that time, who, in the days of the Bishops Finan and Colman, forsaking their native island, retired thither, either for the sake of sacred studies, or of a more ascetic life; and some of them presently devoted themselves faithfully to a monastic life, others chose rather to apply themselves to study, going about from one master's cell to another. The Scots willingly received them all, and took care to supply them with daily food without cost, as also to furnish them with books for their studies, and teaching free of charge.

LEPROSY

The archetypal image of the leper, clothed in rags that disguise his wasted limbs and carrying a bell and crying 'unclean, unclean' to warn away those who might catch his shameless and contagious sickness, peering into church through the narrow slit windows known as lepers' squints, is a persistent one. In fact, much of this is Victorian fantasy: the 12th–14th centuries saw hospitals or refuges for lepers – called leprosaria or lazar houses after the biblical figure of Lazarus – built in or on the outskirts of hundreds of towns and cities across the Western world.

The term is probably applied in historical sources to a wide variety of skin diseases, an epidemic of which occurred in the Middle Ages, but leprosy proper is a disease caused by the bacterium *Mycobacterium leprae* and today known as Hansen's disease. It was apparently recognized in both India and China in ancient times, while the renowned Greek doctor Hippocrates (*c.* 460–370 BC) called it the Phoenician disease. The Bible describes Jesus healing lepers by touch – but for those not fortunate enough to encounter him, the most effective treatment in the ancient world was said to be bee stings or snake bites, or bathing in the blood of animals, children or virgins. Leprosy was endemic in the Byzantine Empire from about the 4th century AD, but only became common in Western Christendom in about 1100, perhaps introduced by soldiers returning from the First Crusade.

While leprosy was sometimes seen as God's punishment on a sufferer for his or her sins, modern medievalists stress the more compassionate responses that meant that the leprosaria were often well endowed and run, offering (at least in principle) a surprising level of comfort and care for the inmates.

There are many forms of the disease but it can cause skin tumours and lesions, and the loss of fingers and toes. It was sometimes known as elephantiasis (though modern elephantiasis is a quite different disease). In medieval times efforts were concentrated on isolating sufferers and relieving their symptoms. It remained incurable until the later 20th century when the widespread availability of antibiotics was found to be an effective way to combat the disease.

Although it is highly contagious, most people have a natural immunity to leprosy, which means it does not cause devastating pandemics but remains endemic in a society for a long time.

We cannot walk on by

GREGORY OF NAZIANZUS, *Oration 14* (4th century AD)

Gregory of Nazianzus (d. AD 374), a Christian convert who became a bishop and flourished in the Eastern Roman Empire, left a series of influential Orations on religious topics, including one (Oration 14) on the treatment of the poor in general, and lepers in particular. In it, he stresses the importance of a compassionate response to those who suffer an appalling bodily affliction that leaves them to endure a kind of living death.

Those whose plight stands in contrast to their former state arouse even greater sympathy than those whose misfortune is chronic. I am referring to those wasted with the sacred disease that devours their flesh and bones and marrow clear through – the visitation that Scripture threatens certain individuals and leaves them betrayed by this wretched, vile and faithless body....

While confronted with the suffering of others, I have been dwelling on the infirmity of my own flesh. We must, my brothers, look after it as being our kinsman and fellow-servant.... And we must look after the physical needs of our neighbours, both the healthy and those consumed by the same ailment, no less than we look after our own persons....

Before our eyes is a pathetic sight, one that no one would believe who has not seen it: human beings alive yet dead, disfigured in every part of their bodies, barely recognizable for who they once were or where they came from; the pitiful wreckage of what had once been human beings.... Mutilated, stripped of their possessions, their families, their friends, their very bodies, they hate themselves and feel pity for themselves at the same time, yet know not whether they should grieve more for the limbs they have lost or for those they have left....

We are so poor in our obligations to look after our fellow man that we actually believe that avoiding these people assures the well-being of our own persons.... Who could be more loyal than a father? Who more devoted than a mother? Yet the natural care of parents has been denied these people. The father grieves over his son whom he regarded as the light of his life, yet is forced to drive him away. The mother relives the pain of giving birth and her heart is wretched; yet with piteous cries she laments for him as though he were dead....

Sufferers are driven out of cities, away from home, from the market-place, from public gatherings, from the streets, from festivities, from parties, even from water itself. They neither share the springs with others nor are they permitted to rinse away their contamination in the rivers. But strangest of all, we drive them away as pariahs on the one hand, yet on the other we bring them back, claiming that they are really harmless, but all the while denying them shelter and failing to provide basic sustenance or dressing their sores. And so they wander about day and night, helpless, naked, homeless, exposing their sores for all to see, invoking the Creator, leaning on each other's limbs in place of those they have lost, begging for a crust or some tattered rag to hide their shame or provide relief for their wounds....

What will our attitude towards these people be? What shall we do? Shall we neglect them? Walk on by? Dismiss them as execrable corpses, the vilest of beasts and creatures that crawl? Most certainly not, my brothers! These actions neither become ourselves, the flock of Christ the Good Shepherd, nor do they become our human nature which, learning piety and kindness from our common weakness, has given compassion the force of law.

The Leper King

Wᴵᴸᴸᴵᴀᴹ ᴏꜰ Tʏʀᴇ, *A History of Deeds Done Beyond the Sea* (c. 1170s)

The chronicler William of Tyre (c. 1130–1186) was born in the Crusader Kingdom of Jerusalem and became tutor to the future King Baldwin IV (r. 1174–1185), known as the Leper King. Baldwin, who inherited the throne aged thirteen, repeatedly led his forces into battle against Saladin, fighting on horseback despite a right arm withered by the disease. In 1182, unable to walk, he appointed his brother-in-law Guy de Lusignan as regent, but the following year resumed his position and remained king until his death aged twenty-four.

William wrote an extensive and much-praised History of Deeds Done Beyond the Sea *on the creation and fate of the Kingdom of Jerusalem. As the archbishop of Tyre, he attended the Third Lateran Council in 1179, which established Church policy on the treatment of lepers.*

Book XXI When I was Archdeacon of Tyre, King Amalric, anxious about the education of his son, about nine years old, prevailed upon me to undertake the task of tutor.... He was playing one day with his companions when they began, as playful boys will often do, to pinch each other's arms and hands with their nails. The other boys gave evidence of pain by their cries, but Baldwin, though his comrades did not spare him, endured it altogether too patiently, as if he felt nothing. At first I supposed it proceeded from his capacity for endurance and not from lack of sensitiveness. But when I called him and began to inquire what it meant, I discovered that his right arm and hand were partially numb, so that he did not feel pinching or even biting in the least. I began to be uneasy, remembering the words of the wise man [Hippocrates], 'There is no question that a member which is without feeling detracts greatly from the health of the body, and one who does not realize that he is sick is in danger.'

The lad's father was informed of his condition, and physicians were consulted. Repeated fomentations, oil rubs and even poisonous remedies were employed without result in the attempt to help him. For, as we recognized in process of time, these were the early symptoms of a most serious and incurable disease which later became plainly apparent.

It is impossible to keep back my tears while speaking about this great misfortune. For as he began to reach years of maturity, it became apparent that he was suffering from the terrible disease of leprosy. Day by day his condition became worse. His extremities and the face were especially attacked, so that his faithful followers were moved with compassion when they looked at him. Nevertheless he continued to make progress in the pursuit of letters and gave ever-increasing promise of developing a lovable disposition....

Book XXII While the army was waiting at the fountain of Sephorie, the king was suffering from a severe attack of fever at Nazareth. In addition, the leprosy which had begun to trouble him in very early youth became much worse than usual. His sight failed and his extremities became completely deadened so that his hands and feet refused to perform their office. Yet up to this time he had declined to heed the suggestion that he lay aside his kingly dignity and give up the administration of the realm, so that he could lead a tranquil life in retirement.

Although physically weak and impotent, mentally he was vigorous, and, far beyond his strength, he strove to hide his illness and to support the cares of the kingdom. However now, when attacked by the fever, he lost hope of life. He summoned his nobles and, in the presence of his mother and the patriarch, he appointed as regent of the realm Guy de Lusignan, Count of Jaffa and Ascalon, his sister's husband. He retained the royal dignity, however, and kept for his own use only the city of Jerusalem, with an annual revenue of ten thousand gold pieces.

Mass of Separation

EDMOND MARTÈNE, *De Antiquis Ecclesiae Ritibus* (1700)
Alice of Schaerbeek (fl. 1240), a Cistercian lay sister, became known as Alice the Leper. Her life, written in the 17th century by Edmond Martène, included the description of a mass held outside a leper's hut, which laid down strict rules for the leper's isolation from wider society. Despite living in the manner set out here, her holiness was recognized in her life; she became patron saint of the blind.

I forbid you to enter the church or monastery, fair, mill, marketplace or any assembly of people. I forbid you ever to leave your house without your leper's costume and shoes. I forbid you to wash your hands or your clothes in any stream or fountain, unless using your own barrel or dipper. I forbid you to touch anything you buy or barter for until it becomes your own. I forbid you to enter a tavern, and if you wish for wine, have it funnelled into your keg. I forbid you to share house with any woman but your own wife. I command you, if you go on the road and you meet some person who speaks to you, to put yourself downwind of him before you answer. I forbid you to go into a narrow lane such that if you should meet anyone he might catch the affliction from you. I forbid you ever to touch children or give them anything. I forbid you to eat or drink from any dishes but your own. I forbid you to eat or drink in company except with other lepers.

Leprosy and intercourse

BERNARD DE GORDON, *Lilium Medicinae* (1303)

A French scholar and doctor from Montpellier, Bernard de Gordon (1270–1330), wrote Lilium Medicinae *in which he described a number of diseases including leprosy. His account combined several different, even contradictory, suggestions of its cause, ranging from sexual indulgence to hereditary factors, to an imbalance in the traditional four humours of the body.*

Leprosy results from great corruptions at conception; it is either caught within the womb, or after birth. If within the uterus, it is either because the baby was conceived during menstruation, or because the mother is a leper, or because a leper has intercourse with a pregnant woman. If it happens after birth, this can be because the air is bad, corrupted and pestilential, or because of prolonged use of melancholic foods such as lentils and other legumes, and from such melancholic meats as that of foxes, wild boars, hares and other quadrupeds such as asses and the like, since in some regions all wild animals are eaten.

Leprosy also can result from too much company with lepers and from coitus with a leprous woman. And it can also result if a man has intercourse with a woman who has previously lain with a leper and whose seed still remains in her womb. The woman is not infected unless she continues a long time, because of the density of the womb; but if a healthy man lies with a woman with whom a leper has recently lain such that the leper's semen still remains in her womb, he will necessarily become leprous because the pores are loose in the male and the infection readily moves to the whole body. As a result exceptional precautions are required, and a woman should try to expel the seed by dancing, sneezing, bathing and rinsing the womb.

There are many other means which need not be rehearsed, of expelling the received semen. Without these, one should be prepared for the beggar's cup, life under the stars and everlasting disgrace. Everyone should guard against having intercourse with a leprous woman, as I have myself seen: a certain countess came leprous to Montpellier and in her end was under my treatment. A young physician who attended to her also lay with her and she fell pregnant, while he was made completely leprous. Fortunate therefore is the man who is made cautious by the disasters of others....

There are other ways leprosy can be induced. For example, by eating fish with milk, or by the nauseous surfeit of warm foods that burn the blood or of cold, dry melancholic foods. Therefore, people who are weakened by choler, who are very warm and adust [burning up] with a warm liver, should beware because they are in an intermediate stage. Even though the immediate cause of leprosy is melancholic matter and a bad dry complexion, and though in this respect there is only one kind, in view of the antecedent causes there are four kinds.

The five signs of leprosy

JORDAN OF TURRE, *The Symptoms of Lepers* [*c.* 1313–30?]
Little is known of Jordan of Turre other than that he was a colleague of Bernard de Gordon at Montpellier in the 1320s, but his study of leprosy combined some ancient and Islamic ideas with observations of his own.

Leprosy can be recognized by five signs: by the urine, by the pulse, by the blood, by the voice and by the different members. Whoever wants to determine whether someone has leprosy should first make him sing. If his voice is harsh it may be a sign of leprosy but if it is clear, it is a good sign....

The urine of lepers must be white with a certain transparency, clear and thin. The contents will be clotted and should look like flour or ground bran.... It is also possible to recognize lepers by the pulse, which should be weak. Avicenna [Persian philosopher and physician, *c.* 980–1037] gives the reason for this, that it has little force because of the resistance of the artery which is almost entirely dried up.

Similarly, they can be recognized by the blood. You should bleed the patient from a vein in any part of the body and collect it in a clean vessel, leave it until a residue is formed, which should be put into a linen cloth and shaken in fresh water; squeeze it gently until the water is no longer appreciably tinted. Then take what is left in the cloth and if you see brilliant white corpuscles looking like millet or panicum, it is a sign of leprosy.... Finally, pour urine onto the blood; if it sinks and mixes, it is a sign of leprosy; if not, not.

It is also possible to recognize lepers by examining the different members. Lepers have thin, fine hairs that thicken at the roots; their hairs are pale and grey. It is advisable to examine the hairs in sunlight to see if they are thin and straight like pigs' bristles.

They are also recognized by the skin of the head, which is lumpy so that one area is higher than the next; by the lack of hair on the eyebrows; and by the roundness of the eyeballs which seem to be staring from their sockets, so that a leper's face is horrible to see, its natural expression being distorted, it is a terrible sight. The disease can also be recognized by a wound inside the nostrils...or by the bridge of the nose where there should be a depression like a thread stretched lengthways along it for the cartilage which joins the two parts is eaten away leaving a furrow.

The veins around the eyes and the veins of the chest are very red. Or draw out the tongue, and if you see white corpuscles at its root like grains of millet, it is a sure sign of leprosy. Having done these things, examine the patient completely naked to see if the skin is darkened and its surface feels rough with a certain smoothness at the same time. Then sprinkle cold water on the shoulders; if it is not retained, it is a sure sign of leprosy. Or make the patient cover his eyes and say 'I'm going to prick you', but do not prick him, but tell him, 'I pricked you on the foot'; if he agrees, it is a sure sign. Likewise prick him with a needle from the little finger and the flesh next to it up to the arm. These fingers are the weakest and therefore the ones first lost to the natural state.

How to run a leper hospital

ARCHBISHOP BIRGER OF UPPSALA, Sweden, 14th century

The Enköping leper hospital in Sweden was established by the archbishop of Uppsala, probably in the 1370s. The regulations, which are typical of those of similar institutions across Western Christendom, provide an insight into the care with which the archbishop sought to balance looking after the bodies and souls of the lepers with safeguarding the citizenry of the town.

Men and women afflicted with leprosy must be carefully sought out and found by the wardens of the hospital throughout the diocese of Uppsala. If they are poor they must be admitted to the hospital without charge. Those that have movable possessions are to be admitted with their possessions, which are to be used for the common good under the warden's supervision. They or their heirs can be compelled if they resist. So far as immovable assets are concerned, the same usage applies as is normally followed relating to other goods given or bequeathed to the churches or other holy places.

The following rules are to be observed in the hospital. Each of them is to receive every day two pure barley loaves and at special festivals each is to have two barley loaves and one wheaten loaf.... On every fourth day in summer they are to share an urn of soured milk. Every week they are to share a jar of freshly brewed good beer between five and eight people....

Every year at Martinmas each person is to have eight ells of cloth; at Christmas and on John the Baptist's day everyone is to be given a pair of shoes....

No one, however powerful or from whatever condition or class he comes, once he has dedicated himself to God in the hospital, is to leave the gates of the hospital for churches, meetings or any gatherings, if he does not wish to lose the rations due to him.... But for the begging of alms, mazers [bowls] should be placed around the chapel...where there are bystanders...so that they may receive alms from passers-by or visitors.

Men and women living in the hospital who are strong enough and able to work ought to help and work together with their own hands in summer and autumn to bring in the hay and to harvest the grain in wagons to the granary.

THE BLACK DEATH

The Black Death – the return of the bubonic plague to Europe in 1347–51 for the first time in some 600 years (see page 34) – was part of history's deadliest pandemic: some scholars estimate that it killed up to 200 million people worldwide, and as much as 60 per cent of the population in some areas.

Caused – although this was in no way imagined at the time – by a bacterium residing in fleas that normally infest rats but could easily transfer to humans if no rats were available, it was carried speedily from place to place on ships or in bales of wool or other merchandise. Mortality was worst in towns, but the countryside was also badly affected, with many rural areas depleted and some villages abandoned entirely.

The plague is thought to have been endemic in East Asia but expanded its range in the 1330s, carried across Asia by the Mongol armies. It had already killed tens of millions in Asia by the time it reached the West in 1347. From Italy it spread through the peninsula and northwards to the rest of Europe.

The high death rate – from both bubonic plague and its even more lethal counterpart pneumonic plague – caused major social and political disruption, with a reduction in land under cultivation, labour shortages and rising wages, which led to greater social fluidity and accelerated the long-term reduction in serfdom.

The search for explanations led many to blame the plague on sinfulness. Some sought expiation by public displays of flagellation; others went in search of scapegoats and the Black Death saw a rise in attacks on Jewish communities across central Europe.

Although the Black Death itself passed in the early 1350s, the threat from plague remained, both in Europe and across the Middle East. In 1377 the Adriatic city of Ragusa (now Dubrovnik) introduced a policy of isolating any ship for thirty days before allowing goods or people to enter the city. Seeing its success, Venice later adopted a similar policy, extending the isolation period to forty days, giving rise to the term 'quarantine'.

The so-called 'second plague' pandemic that had begun in the early 14th century continued to rumble on for more than four hundred years, being particularly threatening again in the 17th century (the Great Plague; see page 119).

Mountains of dead were thrown into the city

GABRIELE DE' MUSSI, narrative of the Siege of Kaffa, *c.* 1348/9

Gabriele de' Mussi (1280–1356), a lawyer from Piacenza in Italy, described the 1346 Mongol siege of Kaffa (present-day Feodosiya, Ukraine) and ascribed the entire Black Death to a Mongol action. However, this was, in his view, only the immediate cause; the real cause of the disaster was the wrath of God at the manifold sins of humanity.

The dying Tartars, stunned and stupefied by the immensity of the disaster brought about by the disease, and realizing that they had no hope of escape, lost interest in the siege. But they ordered corpses to be placed in catapults and lobbed into the city in the hope that the intolerable stench would kill everyone inside. What seemed like mountains of dead were thrown into the city, and the Christians could not hide or flee or escape from them, although they dumped as many bodies as they could into the sea.

And soon the rotting corpses tainted the air and poisoned the water supply, and the stench was so overwhelming that hardly one in several thousand was in a position to flee the remains of the Tartar army. More-over, one infected man could carry the poison to others, and infect people and places with the disease by look alone. No one knew, or could discover, a means of defence.

Devotion of the holy sisters

JEAN DE VENETTE, *The Chronicles of Jean de Venette* (c. 1348–49)

The French Carmelite friar Jean de Venette (c. 1307–c. 1377) wrote a chronicle of the early decades of the Hundred Years' War, which included a description of the Black Death in France. He saw the disaster as a result of 'unbelief'.

At Paris and in the kingdom of France, as in the other parts of the world, there was in this same year (1348) and the year following so great a mortal-ity of people of both sexes, of the young rather than of the old, that it was scarcely possible to bury them. They were only ill for two or three days and died suddenly, their bodies almost sound; and he who one day was in good health, was dead and buried on the morrow.... Soon in many places out of every twenty inhabitants there were only two alive. The mortality was so great at the Hôtel-Dieu in Paris that for a long time more than five hundred dead were carried daily on wagons to be buried at the cemetery of St Innocent of Paris. The holy sisters of the Hôtel-Dieu, having no fear of death, discharged their task to the end with the most perfect gentleness and humility. These sisters were wiped out by death and were replaced more than once; and they now repose in peace with Christ.

This plague, it is said, began among the infidels, and then came to Italy. Crossing the mountains, it reached Avignon, where it struck down several cardinals and decimated their suites. Then by degrees it passed across Spain and Gascony, from town to town, from village to village, finally from house to house and from person to person till it arrived in France, and spread on to Germany, though it was less terrible there than it was among us.

Triple wages

CATHEDRAL PRIORY OF ROCHESTER, ENGLAND, CHRONICLE OF THE
    BLACK DEATH, 1348

This extract comes from a chronicle of the Black Death years, written at the priory of Rochester, England.

A great mortality destroyed more than a third of the men, women and children. As a result, there was such a shortage of servants, craftsmen and workmen, and of agricultural workers and labourers, that a great many lords and people, although well endowed with goods and possessions, were yet without service and attendance. Alas, this mortality devoured such a multitude of both sexes that no one could be found to carry the bodies of the dead to burial, but men and women carried the bodies of their own little ones to church on their shoulders and threw them into mass graves, from which arose such a stink that it was barely possible for anyone to go past a churchyard.

Such a shortage of workers ensued that the humble turned up their noses at employment, and could scarcely be persuaded to serve the eminent unless for triple wages. Instead, because of the doles handed out at funerals, those who once had to work now began to have time for idleness, thieving and other outrages, and thus the poor and servile have been enriched and the rich impoverished. As a result, churchmen, knights and other worthies have been forced to thresh their corn, plough the land and perform every other unskilled task if they are to make their own bread.

Some shut themselves away
GIOVANNI BOCCACCIO, *The Decameron* (1349–53)
The Decameron, the most famous work by the Florentine poet Giovanni Boccaccio (1313–1375), purports to be a suite of one hundred stories told by a group of young Florentines who had left the city to escape the Black Death. Its introduction includes a famous description of the epidemic, heavily influenced by Thucydides' account of the Athenian plague (see page 20).

In the year 1348 after the Son of God's fruitful incarnation, into the distinguished city of Florence, that most beautiful of Italian cities, there entered a deadly pestilence. Whether one believes it came through the influence of the heavenly bodies or that God, angered by our iniquities, sent it for our correction, it had begun several years earlier in the East and killed innumerable people, spreading steadily and growing as it moved west.

No human wisdom or provision was of any help. Huge amounts of filth were removed from the city; sick people were forbidden to enter; advice was given on how to stay healthy; the devout made many humble supplications to God, in processions and by other means; nonetheless in the spring the sad effects of the plague began to appear in an almost miraculous manner. It was not as it had been in the east, where nosebleeds had signalled that death was inevitable. Here the sickness began in both men and women with swelling in the groin and armpits. The lumps varied in size, some reaching the size of an ordinary apple and others that of an egg, and the people called them *gavoccioli*. Having begun in these two parts of the body, the *gavoccioli* soon began to appear at random all over the body. After this point the disease started to alter in nature, with black or livid spots appearing on the arms, the thighs, everywhere. Sometimes they were large and spaced out, other times small and numerous. These were a certain sign of impending death, but so was the swelling.

No doctor's advice, no medicine, seemed to be of any help. Either the disease was actually incurable or the doctors simply didn't know how to cure it. Many tried, though. A multitude of people, men and women with no medical training whatsoever, took their place alongside those who were properly trained. But no one knew the cause of the pestilence and thus no one could do much about curing it, so not only were few people healed but most died by the third day after the signs appeared, some a little sooner or a little later....

The pestilence spread from the sick to the healthy like fire among dry or oily materials. It was so bad that it could be communicated not only through speaking or associating with the sick, but even by touching their clothing or anything else they had touched....

There were some who thought they could avoid the illness by moderate living and avoiding excess, so they lived apart from others in small groups. They shut themselves in houses where no one had been sick, partaking moderately of the best food and the finest wine, avoiding excess in other ways as well, trying their best not speak of or hear any news about the death and illness outside but occupying themselves with music and whatever other pleasures they had available.

Others were of the opposite opinion. They believed that heavy drinking, enjoying themselves, singing and having fun, satisfying all their appetites as much as they could, laughing and joking was sure medicine for any illness. They spent day and night going from one tavern to the next, drinking without measure, or doing the same thing in people's homes, engaging only in those activities that gave them pleasure. This was easy for them because many people had just abandoned their possessions as if they no longer had to cope with the problem of living, and many houses had become common property where complete strangers made use of whatever they contained, if they owned them. And they combined this bestial behaviour with as complete an avoidance of the sick as they could manage....

Many took a middle way between these two extremes, neither restricting themselves like the first group nor engaging in dissolute behaviour as the second did. This third group used things as they felt the need of them and, rather than shut themselves away, they went about carrying flowers, herbs or various spices which they held to their noses, imagining that the best thing for the brain was to comfort it with such odours, since the air was filled with the stench of dead bodies and illness and medicine.

Some...believed the best medicine against the plague was to escape from it. Caring for nothing except themselves, many men and women abandoned their city, houses, families and possessions in order to go elsewhere, at least to the countryside, imagining that the wrath of God punishing humankind with this pestilence would not follow them there, but would content itself with oppressing only those found within the city walls, or that no one at all would remain there and that the city's final hour had come.

But whatever their approach, not all of these people died but not all survived by employing these measures, either. And, having given an example to others while they were healthy, when they themselves fell sick they were abandoned by all. Citizens avoided each other, neighbours took little care of one another, and family members rarely visited one another, preferring to stay far apart. Brothers abandoned one other, uncles abandoned nephews, sisters abandoned brothers, wives abandoned their husbands, and, unbelievably, parents even abandoned their own children....

With the sick now abandoned by neighbours and family and unable to find good servants, an unheard-of situation arose: a woman, however attractive she might be, did not scruple to have a man-servant, young or old, and show him every part of her body as she would have done with a woman, if the needs of her illness required it. This practice may have contributed to those who survived having looser morals afterward....

Most of the poor and middle classes stayed in their own homes and neighbourhoods, either because they hoped they would be safe there or because they could afford nothing else. They fell sick by the thousands every day, and having neither servants nor anyone else to care for them, they almost always died. Many died in the street, day or night, while those who died in their homes were noticed by their neighbours only when the smell of their decomposing bodies brought them to public attention.

There were corpses all over the city, and all were treated in much the same manner by their neighbours, who were moved as much by fear that the corrupted bodies would infect them as by pity toward the deceased.... Nor were these dead honoured with tears, flames or companions. Things had sunk to the level that human bodies were disposed of much as we would now dispose of a dead goat....

These ill winds blowing through our city did not spare the surrounding region. The towns suffered like smaller versions of the city, while throughout the villages and fields the poor, miserable peasants and their families, who lacked the care of doctors or the aid of servants, died more like beasts than humans: day and night, on the roads and in the fields. And like the city dwellers they became loose in their behaviour and stopped taking care of their possessions and occupations, and once they began to anticipate their own deaths, they stopped caring about making plans for the future of their beasts and their lands and instead concentrated on consuming whatever they had. Thus the cattle, donkeys, sheep, goats, pigs, chickens and even dogs were driven out into the fields where the wheat stood abandoned, unharvested and even uncut. The animals roamed where they pleased, though many, like rational beings, returned home each night after having eaten well during the day, without being encouraged to do so by a shepherd.

On all sides is sorrow; everywhere is fear
FRANCESCO PETRARCH, letters, Parma, Italy, 1348
The Florentine poet Francesco Petrarch (1304–1374) was in Parma during the Black Death years, and although he himself survived, he was touched by its tragedy. He lost his beloved muse Laura de Noves to the plague in 1348, and also discovered that his brother, a monk, was the sole survivor of his entire monastery. His writings of 1348 on the suffering are consequently highly emotional.

Letter to his brother
My brother! My brother! My brother! A new beginning to a letter, though one used by Cicero fourteen hundred years ago. Alas! my beloved brother, what shall I say? How shall I begin? Whither shall I turn? On all sides is sorrow; everywhere is fear. I would, my brother, that I had never been born, or, at least, had died before these times. How will posterity believe that there has been a time when without the lightnings of heaven or the fires of earth, without wars or other visible slaughter, not this or that part of the earth, but well-nigh the whole globe, has remained without inhabitants. When has any such thing been even heard or seen; in what annals has it ever been read that houses were left vacant, cities deserted, the country neglected, the fields too small for the dead and a fearful and universal solitude over the whole earth?...

Oh happy people of the future, who have not known these miseries and perchance will class our testimony with the fables. We have, indeed, deserved these [punishments] and even greater; but our forefathers also have deserved them, and may our posterity not also merit the same...

Letter to himself

O what has come over me? Where are the violent fates pushing me back to? I see passing by, in headlong flight, time which makes the world a fleeting place. Around me are dying throngs of both young and old, and nowhere is there a refuge. No haven beckons in any part of the globe, nor can any hope of salvation be seen. Wherever I turn my frightened eyes, their gaze is troubled by continual funerals: the churches groan encumbered with biers, and, without last respects, the corpses of the noble and the commoner lie in confusion alongside each other. The last hour of life comes to mind, and, obliged to recollect my misfortunes, I recall the flocks of dear ones who have departed, and the conversations of friends, the sweet faces which suddenly vanished, and the hallowed ground now insufficient for repeated burials.

This is what the people of Italy bemoan, weakened by so many deaths; this is what France laments, exhausted and stripped of inhabitants; the same goes for other peoples, under whatever skies they reside. Either it is the wrath of God, for certainly I would think that our misdeeds deserve it, or it is just the harsh assault of the stars in their perpetually changing conjunctions. This plague-bearing year threatens a tearful slaughter, and the highly charged air encourages death. From his diseased pole in heaven, cruel Jupiter rains diseases and grievous mortality upon the earth. The merciless Fates rush to sever the threads of life all at once, if they can: seeing so many ashen faces of the wretched people, and so many seeking gloomy Tartarus, I fear that they have been granted what they wish for....

It is just as when, unnoticed, a deadly fire has taken hold of ancient timbers and greedy flame licks resin-rich floorboards, the household, aroused by the commotion, suddenly gets out of bed, and the father rushes up to the top of the roof, gazing about him, and grasping his trembling son seeks to save him first from the dangerous fire, and works out in his mind how to escape with this burden through the opposing flames. Often in fear, clasping to myself my helpless soul, I too wonder whether there is an escape from the conflagration and try to extinguish the bodily flames with the water of tears. But the world holds me back. Headstrong desire draws me and I am bound ever more tightly by deadly knots. Dense shadows have covered me with fear. For whosoever thinks they can recall death and look upon the moment of their passing with fearless face is either mistaken or mad, or, if he is fully aware, then he is very courageous.

How to keep safe

TOMMASO DEL GARBO, *Consiglio Contro a Pistolenza* (*c.* 1350)
The Florentine poet Tommaso del Garbo (1305–1370) offered practical advice for avoiding infection.

Notaries, confessors, relations and doctors who visit plague victims should, on entering their houses, open the windows so that the air is refreshed, and wash their hands with vinegar and rose water and also their faces, especially around their mouth and nostrils. It is a good idea, before entering the room, to place cloves in your mouth and eat two slices of bread soaked in the best wine and then drink the rest of the wine. When leaving the room, douse yourself and your pulses with a sponge soaked in vinegar. Take care not to stay too close to the patient.

Prices fall, wages rise

HENRY KNIGHTON, *Chronicon* (*c.* 1350)
Henry Knighton (d. 1396) was a monk from Leicester, who wrote a history of England from 1066 to his own day. As well as describing the death and suffering caused by the Black Death in 1348, he was interested in the political and economic impact as well, and mentions abandoned villages: scores of these have been identified.

The dreadful pestilence penetrated the coast of England by Southampton and came to Bristol, and there almost the whole population of the town perished, as if it had been seized by sudden death; for few kept their beds more than two or three days, or even half a day. Then this cruel death spread everywhere around, following the course of the sun. And there died at Leicester in the small parish of St Leonard more than 380 persons, in the parish of Holy Cross, 400; in the parish of St Margaret's, Leicester,

700; and so in every parish, a great multitude. Then the bishop of London sent word throughout his diocese empowering each and every priest to hear confessions and to give absolution to all persons, except only in case of debt. In this case, the debtor was to pay the debt, if he was able, while he lived, or others were to fulfil his obligations from his property after his death. Likewise the Pope granted full remission of all sins to anyone receiving absolution when in danger of death, and granted that this power should last until Easter next following, and that everyone might choose whatever confessor he pleased.

In the same year sheep died everywhere in the kingdom, so that in one place in a single pasture more than 5,000 sheep died; and they putrefied so that neither bird nor beast would touch them. Everything was low in price because of the fear of death, for very few people took any care of riches or property of any kind. A man could have a horse that had been worth 40 shillings for half a mark [6s 8d], a fat ox for 4s, a cow for 12 pence, a heifer for 6d, a fat wether [castrated ram] for 4d, a sheep for 3d, a lamb for 2d, a large pig for 5d; a stone of wool was worth 9d. Sheep and cattle ran at large through the fields and among the crops, and there was none to drive them off or herd them; for lack of care they perished in ditches and hedges in incalculable numbers throughout all districts, and none knew what to do....

In the following autumn a reaper was not to be had for a lower wage than 8d, with his meals; a mower for not less than 10d, with meals. Wherefore many crops wasted in the fields for lack of harvesters. But in the year of the pestilence, as has been said above, there was so great an abundance of every type of grain that almost no one cared for it.

The Scots, hearing of the dreadful plague among the English, suspected that it had come about through the vengeance of God, and when they swore, would say 'be the foul deth of Engelond'. Believing that the wrath of God had befallen the English, they assembled in Selkirk forest with the intention of invading the kingdom, when the fierce mortality overtook them, and in a short time about 5,000 perished....

Meanwhile the king sent proclamations that reapers and other labourers should not take more than they had been accustomed to take. But the labourers were so lifted up and obstinate that they would not listen to the king's command, but if anyone wished to have them he had to give them what they wanted, and either lose his fruit and crops, or satisfy the greedy demands of the workmen. And when the king heard that they had not observed his command, and had given greater wages to the labourers, he levied heavy fines upon abbots, priors, knights, greater and lesser, and other great folk and small folk of the realm. And afterwards the king had many labourers arrested, and sent them to prison; many withdrew themselves and went into the forests and woods; and those who were taken were heavily fined. Their ringleaders were made to swear that they would not take daily wages beyond the ancient custom, and then were freed from prison. And in like manner was done with the other craftsmen in the boroughs and villages.

Public flagellation

ROBERT OF AVESBURY, *De Gestis Mirabilibus Regis Edwardi Tertii* (1350s)
A clerk to the archbishop of Canterbury at Lambeth Palace, Robert of Avesbury (d. 1359) wrote a history of the reign of Edward III in which he described the spectacle of public flagellation to avert the wrath of God.

In that same year of 1349, about Michaelmas, over six hundred men came to London from Flanders, mostly of Zeeland and Holland origin. Sometimes at St Paul's and sometimes at other points in the city they made two daily public appearances stripped bare other than cloths from the thighs to the ankles. Each wore a cap marked with a red cross in front and behind.

Each had in his right hand a scourge with three tails. Each tail had a knot and through the middle of it there were sometimes sharp nails fixed. They marched naked in a file one behind the other and whipped themselves with these scourges on their naked and bleeding bodies.

Four of them would chant in their native tongue and another four would chant in response like a litany. Thrice they would all cast themselves on the ground in this sort of procession, stretching out their hands like the arms of a cross. The singing would go on and, the one who was in the rear of those thus prostrate acting first, each of them in turn would step over the others and give one stroke with his scourge to the man lying under him.

This went on from the first to the last until each of them had observed the ritual to the full tale of those on the ground. Then each put on his customary garments and, still wearing their caps and carrying their whips in their hands, they retired to their lodgings. It is said that every night they performed the same penance.

A multi-faith service against the plague

IBN BATTUTA, *Travels in Asia and Africa* (1325–54)
The great North African traveller Ibn Battuta (1304–1369) visited Damascus in Syria in 1348, where he observed a remarkable multi-faith ceremony to avert the plague.

One of the celebrated sanctuaries at Damascus is the Mosque of the Footprints (al-Aqdam), which lies two miles south of the city, alongside the main highway which leads to the Hijaz, Jerusalem and Egypt. It is a large mosque, very blessed, richly endowed and highly venerated by the Damascenes. The footprints from which it derives its name are impressed upon a rock there, and are said to be the mark of Moses' foot. In this mosque there is a small chamber containing a stone with the following inscription 'A certain pious man saw in his sleep the Chosen one [Muhammad] who said to him, "here is the grave of Moses".'

I saw a remarkable instance of the veneration in which the Damascenes hold this mosque during the great pestilence on my return journey through Damascus in July 1348. The viceroy ordered all the people to fast for three days and that no one should cook anything in the market during the daytime (for most of the people there only eat food prepared in the market). So the people fasted for three days, the last of which was a Thursday, then they assembled in the Great Mosque, amirs, sharifs, qadis, theologians and all the other classes of people, until the place was filled to overflowing, and there they spent the Thursday night in prayers and litanies. After the dawn prayer next morning they all went out together on foot holding Korans in their hands, and the amirs barefooted. The procession was joined by the entire population of the town; the Jews came with their Book of the Law and the Christians with their Gospel, all of them with their women and children. The whole concourse, weeping and supplicating and seeking the favour of God through His Books and His Prophets, made their way to the Mosque of the Footprints, and there they remained until near midday. They then returned to the city and held the Friday service, and God lightened their affliction; for the number of deaths in a single day at Damascus did not attain 2,000, while in Cairo it reached the figure of 24,000 a day.

The entire inhabited world was changed

IBN KHALDUN, *Prolegomenon* (1377)

Ibn Khaldun (1332–1406), the Berber scholar from Tunisia, lost both parents to the Black Death. In his best-known work, the Prolegomenon *(1377), a vast history that covers many fields of human knowledge, he considered the impact and meaning of the Black Death, in both Christendom and the Islamic world.*

In the middle of the eighth [AD 14th] century, civilization both in the East and the West was visited by a destructive plague which devastated nations and caused populations to vanish. It swallowed up many of the good things of civilization and wiped them out. It overtook the dynasties at the time of their senility, when they had reached the limit of their duration. It lessened their power and curtailed their influence. It weakened their authority. Their situation approached the point of annihilation and dissolution. Civilization decreased with the decrease of mankind. Cities and buildings were laid waste, roads and way signs were obliterated, settlements and mansions became empty, dynasties and tribes grew weak. The entire inhabited world was changed.

The East, it seems, was similarly visited, though in accordance with and in proportion to the East's more affluent civilization. It was as if the voice of existence in the world had called out for oblivion and restriction, and the world had responded to its call. God inherits the earth and whomever is upon it.

St Roch, patron saint of plague victims and dogs

JACOBUS DE VORAGINE, *Golden Legend, Book V* (15th century)

Roch (Rocco, or Rocke) was a young 14th-century nobleman from Montpellier in southern France who gave away all his possessions and travelled to Italy where he tended the sick and performed miracles. Whether this was during the Black Death or before is uncertain, but by the early 15th century a cult had arisen around him in Italy, and it became common for people to ask him to intercede on their behalf at a time of plague.

This account of his life comes from the Golden Legend, *a comprehensive late medieval collection of lives of the saints.*

He came to a town called Acquapendente, where the pestilence was raging. When Roch heard of this, he went to the hospital and prayed of Vincent, master of the hospital, that he might serve the sick, night and day. Vincent was concerned that Roch himself should suffer the pestilence. But after he came there, he blessed the sick in the name of Christ, and when he touched them they were instantly healed. All that were sick, all those infected by the fire of pestilence, he soothed; he saved the whole hospital from that sickness...

He then went through the town and entered each house that was struck by pestilence, and with the sign of the cross and mind of the passion of Jesus Christ he delivered them all from the pestilence. Whoever Roch touched, the pestilence left him. And when the town of Acquapendente was free from the contagion, Roch went to Cesena which is a great city of Italy and was equally troubled by the pestilence, and in a short time delivered it too...

Then he came to Rome, where every house was infected by the pestilence, and found a cardinal of the title of Angleria, which is a province of Lombardy. And as Roch stood before him, a marvellous comfort and hope suddenly entered the cardinal. He understood the young man to be beloved of God, for his cheer, his manners and his gentleness showed it; so he asked Roch to deliver him from the pestilence. Then Roch made the sign of the cross on the cardinal's forehead with his finger. And straightaway a cross was seen impressed in his forehead, and the cardinal was preserved from the pestilence...

The cardinal asked Roch to remove the token of the cross from him, for fear that the people should consider it a new miracle. But Roch told the cardinal that he should carry the sign of the cross of our Redeemer in his forehead perpetually, and worship it reverently, as a sign that he was delivered from the hard pestilence....

And from there [he] went to Piacenza, where there was great pestilence.... And one day, when he had been long in the hospital of Piacenza, and had helped all the sick men, about midnight he heard in his sleep an angel saying: 'Awake and know that thou art smitten with the pestilence, study now how thou mayst be cured.' Then he felt himself taken with the pestilence under both his arms, and he gave thanks to our Lord for it. The pain was so bad that the men in the hospital were unable to sleep or rest, so Roch got up and went to the farthest place of the hospital, where he lay down to await the break of day. In the morning the people saw him, and complained to the master of the hospital for allowing the pilgrim to lie outside the hospital, but he replied: 'The pilgrim was struck down by the pestilence, and went out without our knowing.'

Then the angry citizens drove Roch from the city. In great pain...he went into a wood, still praising God, and there he built a shelter of boughs and leaves, all the while giving thanks to our Lord....

Some noblemen lived near the wood, one of whom, named Gotard, kept a great household and many hounds for hunting. One of these would boldly take bread from his master's table. And when Roch was hungry, the dog brought him bread from the lord's table bread. Gotard noticed the dog was taking so much bread, so he set a delicate loaf on the table, which the hound took away to Roch. But Gotard followed him and came to Roch's shelter, and saw the hound giving him the bread. Gotard reverently called out to the holy man but Roch said: 'Friend, leave me in peace, for the most violent pestilence holds me.' So Gotard returned home; but he said to himself, 'This poor man in the wood is surely a man of God, since the dog takes him bread. As a Christian, I should do the same.' So Gotard went back to Roch and said: 'Holy pilgrim, I wish to do for you anything that you need, and I shall never leave you.'

Lock down the women

TAQI AL-DIN AL-MAQRIZI, account of the plague in Cairo, Egypt, 1438
The Cairo-born Mamluk scholar Taqi al-Din al-Maqrizi (1364–1442) wrote more than two hundred works of history. He described the tensions in his city when the plague returned in 1438.

And the people asked about their sins, if the plague was their punishment from Allah. And the group said to him, indeed women's presence in the public spaces has spread among the people marked by the plague, and also among the women who adorn themselves and walk in the streets day and night. Some suggested that it would benefit the people to prevent women from walking to the market. Others argued for prohibiting only those women that are unveiled from being in the streets, but not the elderly and those with no family.

The sultan wished to prevent all women from going into the streets, thinking that this would lift the plague. The next day it was announced in Cairo, Egypt and the surrounding areas that all women were prohibited from walking in the streets and absolutely not allowed in the markets. Those who left their homes were threatened with death...and the governor of Cairo and others began to walk in the streets and strike any women that they found. As a result things lost their value, and some people had to make the rounds to the front doors to ask women to buy things. Sales of clothing and perfume fell and the markets closed.

Tensions increased towards those in charge of this injustice and the severity of the oppression, and the feelings in people – their phantoms, illusions, fear for their children and their servants and a quick death from the plague.... The tribulation intensified for the *dhimmi* [non-Muslim] in terms of Jews and Christians. The *wali* [governor] in charge ordered them to make lists from the dead among them and he lay in wait for them and insulted them, and he forced them to carry their documents of ownership in their hands and the frightfulness increased.

One boy died of the plague and his mother wanted to wash him, wrap him and take him in his coffin for burial in the desert. She was prevented from going out in the funeral procession because of the sultan's proclamation. She was wretched and threw herself from the highest floor to the ground so that she died. Another woman went from her home for an important and urgent matter, but the *wali* in charge chained her and shouted to the people to take her and beat her. Nothing happened but they arrested her; her mind left her and she fell unconscious from fear. She was carried to her home, broken and her mind was messed up; she became sick for that period....

Then the sultan ordered that all prisoners be exonerated of their crimes, and the prisoners left as a group and settled with their families. The prisons closed in Egypt and Cairo, and thievery and corruption spread throughout the land.

A Christian response to the plague

MARTIN LUTHER, letter to the Reverend Doctor Johann Hess, pastor
   at Breslau, 1527

In 1527 the German religious reformer Martin Luther (1483–1546) was
caught up in a plague epidemic when in Wittenberg. He remained in the
town with his family, and ministered to both the bodies and souls of
the sick and dying. When asked whether it was permissible to flee from
the epidemic where possible, he wrote an open letter, not condemning
those who had the opportunity to escape to safety without endangering
others, yet stressing the importance of acting at all times in accordance
with the teaching of Christ.

Grace and peace from God our Father and our Lord Jesus Christ. Your letter, sent to me at Wittenberg, was received some time ago. You ask whether it is proper for a Christian to run from a deadly plague....

Some believe firmly that one should not. Rather, since death is God's punishment that he sends for our sins, we must submit to God and with a true and firm faith patiently await this punishment. They look upon running away as an outright wrong and shows a lack of belief in God. Others take the position that one may properly flee, particularly if one holds no public office.

I cannot censure the former. They uphold a good cause, namely, a strong faith in God, and deserve commendation because they desire every Christian to hold to a strong, firm faith. It takes more than a milk faith to await a death before which most of the saints themselves have been in dread. Who would not acclaim these earnest people to whom death is a little thing? They willingly accept God's chastisement, yet without tempting God.

Those engaged in spiritual ministry such as preachers and pastors must remain steadfast before the peril of death.... Public officials – mayors, judges and the like – are under obligation to remain; to abandon a community that one has been called to govern, and to leave it without official or government, exposed to all kinds of danger, is a great sin. It is the kind of disaster the Devil would like to instigate wherever there is no law and order....

So too, persons who stand in a relationship of service or duty toward one another. A servant should not leave his master nor a maid her mistress except with the knowledge and permission of master or mistress. Again, a master should not desert his servant or a lady her maid unless provision for their care has been made.... Fathers and mothers are bound by God's law to serve and help their children, and children their parents. Likewise, public servants such as city physicians, city clerks and constables should not flee unless they furnish capable substitutes.

Yes, we are bound to each other so that no one may forsake another in his distress but is obliged to assist and help his neighbour as he himself would like to be helped.... Anyone who forsakes his neighbour and leaves him to his misfortune, becomes a murderer in the sight of God....

Now if a deadly epidemic strikes, we should stay where we are, make our preparations and take courage from the fact that we are bound together so that we cannot desert one another. We can be sure that God's punishment has come, not only to chastise us for our sins but also to test our faith and love – our faith in that we may see and experience how we should act toward God; our love in that we may recognize how we should act toward our neighbour. These epidemics, like any plague, are spread among the people by evil spirits who poison the air or exhale a pestilential breath which puts a deadly poison into the flesh. Nevertheless, this is God's decree and punishment to which we must patiently submit and serve our neighbour, risking our lives in this manner.

When anyone is overcome by repugnance in the presence of a sick person, he should take courage from the assurance that it is the Devil who stirs fear and loathing in his heart.... The Devil would shit us out of this life as he tries to make us despair of God, become unwilling and unprepared to die, and, under the stormy sky of fear and anxiety, forget Christ, our light and life, and desert our neighbour in his troubles. We would sin thereby against God and man; that would be the Devil's glory and delight....

This I know, that if it were Christ or his mother who were laid low by illness, everybody would be solicitous and would gladly become a servant. No one would flee but would come running. And yet people don't hear what Christ says, 'As you did to one of the least, you did it to me.' The command to love your neighbour is equal to the commandment to love God, and what you do, or fail to do, for your neighbour means doing the same to God.... If you won't serve your neighbour you can be sure that, if Christ lay there, you would let him lie there too....

Some are rash enough to tempt God and disregard everything that might counteract death and the plague. They disdain medicines; they do not avoid places and persons infected by the plague, but make sport of it to prove how independent they are. They say that this is God's punishment; if he wants to protect them he can do so without medicines or our carefulness. Yet this is not trusting God but tempting him. God has created medicines and provided us with intelligence to guard and take good care of the body so that we can live in good health.

No, my dear friends, that is no good. Use medicine; take potions; fumigate house, yard and street; shun persons and places wherever your neighbour does not need your presence or has recovered; act like a man who wants to help put out the burning city. What else is the epidemic but a fire which, instead of consuming wood and straw, devours life and body? You should think this way: 'Very well, by God's decree the enemy has sent us poison and deadly offal. Therefore I shall ask God mercifully to protect us. Then I shall fumigate, help purify the air, administer medicine and take it myself. I shall avoid places and persons where my presence is not needed. If God wishes to take me, he will surely find me and I will have done what he has expected of me and will be responsible for neither my own death nor the death of others. If my neighbour needs me, however, I shall go to him freely.'

Some keep the disease secret and believe that by contaminating others they can somehow rid themselves of the plague. So they enter streets and homes, trying to saddle children or servants with the disease and thus save themselves. This is the work of the Devil. I have been told of people who are so very vicious that they circulate among people and enter homes because they regret the plague has not reached that far and wish to carry it in, as though it were a prank like putting lice into fur garments or flies into someone's living room. I do not know whether to believe this; if it is true, perhaps we Germans are really devils and not human beings. It is true there are some extremely coarse and wicked people. The Devil is never idle. If any such persons are discovered, the judge should turn them over to Master Jack, the hangman, as outright and deliberate murderers. What else are such people but assassins in our town?

SWEATING SICKNESS

Of all the epidemics in this book, sweating sickness is perhaps the most mysterious. It first struck, in England, in the summer of 1485, and returned in 1507–8, 1517, 1528 and finally in 1551, during which outbreak nine hundred people died in a single week in Shrewsbury. It was seen in the Baltic region and in eastern Europe, yet was unknown elsewhere in western Europe (except in Calais) or in Scotland, and within England itself it appeared to mainly affect previously healthy, native-born men between fifteen and forty-five, and especially those who frequented alehouses or were well-to-do (it was sometimes called 'Stop-gallant'). Foreigners in London, for the most part, apparently felt safe. It was therefore known as *Sudor anglicus* (the English Sweat).

It was a devastating disease, one that brought death within hours of the first symptoms appearing, and it is thought that it had a mortality rate of 30–50 per cent. For those who survived the first twenty-four hours, the prognosis was good, although those who recovered were not immune from reinfection. Modern medical historians have put forward various suggestions for the cause, including typhus, anthrax and hantavirus, but none is universally accepted.

The sweating sickness may have helped to bring Henry Tudor to the throne. It was believed to have first appeared in a mercenary army sent by the French king Charles VIII to support Henry Tudor against Richard III. Henry's victory at Bosworth in 1485 was assisted by the fact that Richard's powerful ally, Thomas Stanley, Earl of Derby, refused to fight, using the sickness as his excuse.

Several well-known figures later suffered from it, including Thomas Wolsey and Anne Boleyn, both of whom survived the sickness.

A mysterious disease with similar symptoms was seen in the Low Countries in the 1710s; it became known as the Picardy sweat.

A new kind of sickness

EDWARD HALL, *Hall's Chronicle* (1548)

London lawyer and chronicler Edward Hall (1496–1547) compiled a chronicle of the history of England, in which he described the sweating sickness in graphic terms.

In this year [1485] a new kind of sickness came suddenly through the whole region even after the first entering of the king into this isle. It was so sore, so painful and so sharp that the like was never heard of to any man's remembrance before that time. For suddenly a deadly and burning sweat invaded their bodies and vexed their blood and with a most ardent heat infested the stomach and the head grievously. By the tormenting and vexation of which sickness men were so sore handled and so painfully panged, that if they were lain in their bed, being not able to suffer the importunate heat, they cast away the sheets and all the clothes lying on the bed. If they were in their apparel and vestures, they would put away all their garments even to their shirts. Others were so dry that they drank cold water to quench their importunate heat and insatiable thirst. Others that could or at least would abide the heat and stench (for indeed the sweat had a great and strong savour) caused clothes to be laid upon them as much as they could bear, to drive out the sweat if it might be.

All in manner as soon as the sweat took them or in a shorter space after yielded up the ghost. So that, of all them that sickened there was not one among a hundred that escaped. In so much that beside the great number which deceased within the City of London, two mayors successively died of the same disease within eight days, and six aldermen. And when any person had fully and completely sweat for twenty-four hours (for so long did the strength of this plague hold them) he should then be clearly delivered of his disease. Yet not so clean rid of it but that he might shortly relapse and fall again into the same evil pit, yes again and twice again as many a one indeed did which after the third time died of the same.

At length by study of physicians and experience of the people driven thereunto by dreadful necessity there was a remedy invented. For they that survived, considered the extremity of the pain in them that diseased, devised by things mere contrariant to resist and withstand the furious rage of that burning furnace by lukewarm drink, temperate heat and measurable clothes. For such persons as relapsed again into the flame after the first deliverance, observed diligently and marked such things as did them ease and comfort at their first vexation, and using the same as a medicine and remedy of their pain, adding ever somewhat thereto something that was comfortable and wholesome....

So that after the great loss of so many men, they learned a present and a speedy remedy for the same disease and malady, which is this: if a man in the daytime were plagued with the sweat, then he should straight lie down with all his clothes and garments, and lie still the whole twenty-four hours. If in the night he were taken, then he should not rise out of his bed for twenty-four hours and so cast the clothes that he might in no wise provoke the sweat, but so lie temperately that the water might distil out softly of its own accord, and to abstain from all meat if he might so long sustain and suffer hunger and to take no more drink neither hot nor cold than will moderately allay and quench his thirst appetite. One point diligently above all other is to be observed and attended, that he never put his hand or foot out of the bed to refresh or cool himself, then which to do is no less pain than short death.

Figures of the planets and stinking of the earth

THOMAS LE FORESTIER, *Treatise on the Venyms Fever of Pestilens* (1485)
Thomas le Forestier, a doctor from Normandy who served under both Richard III and Henry VII, observed and treated the 1485 outbreak in England. He recorded his observations of the epidemic in two treatises and suggested an explanation as to the ultimate source of the epidemic.

Unexpert men write and put letters upon gates and church doors as fools promising to help the people of their sickness without conning...for the errors of some false leeches.

The exterior is calm in this fever, the interior excited...the heat in the pestilent fever many times does not appear excessive to the doctor, nor the heat of the sweat itself particularly high.... But it is on account of the ill-natured, fetid, corrupt, putrid and loathsome vapours close to the region of the heart and of the lungs whereby the panting of the breath magnifies and increases and restricts of itself....

The far causes be the figures of the planets...when the celestial figures are doing or receiving the dispositions of the earth then there is great moistness in the air and stinking vapours. The nigh causes be the stinking of the earth, dead beasts or sticking waters for these be great causes of putrefaction and these corrupt the air, and so our bodies are infected of that corrupt air, of which thing [stinking water and fouled air] let any man that loves God and his neighbour amend.

A surprise of nature

FRANCIS BACON, *The History of King Henry VII* (1622)

The scientist, lawyer and Lord Chancellor Francis Bacon (1561–1626) wrote a history of Henry VII's reign, in which he described the onset of the sweating sickness in England.

About this time in autumn, towards the end of September [1485], there began and reigned in the city, and other parts of the kingdom, a disease then new: which, of the accidents, and manner thereof, they called the sweating sickness. This disease had a swift course, both in the sick body, and in the time and period of the lasting thereof: for they that were taken with it, upon four and twenty hours escaping, were thought almost assured. And, as to the time of the malice and reign of the disease, e're it ceased; it began about the one and twentieth of September, and cleared up before the end of October, insomuch that it was no hindrance to the King's coronation, which was the last of October: nor (which was more) to the holding of the Parliament, which began but seven days after. It was a pestilent fever, but (as it seems) not seated in the veins or humours, for that there followed no carbuncle, no purple or livid spots, or the like, the mass of the body not being tainted: only a malign vapour flew to the heart, and seized the vital spirits; which stirred nature to send it forth by an extreme sweat....

It was conceived not to be an epidemic disease, but to proceed from a malignity in the constitution of the air, gathered by the pre-dispositions of the seasons: and the speedy cessation thereof declared as much.

Reports from the English court

SEBASTIAN GIUSTINIANO and FRANCESCO CHIEREGATO, reports to
Italy, 6 August 1517

*Sebastian Giustiniano, the Venetian ambassador to the English court,
wrote about the development of the sweating sickness in this dispatch
to the Signory of Venice on 6 August 1517. On the same day, Francesco
Chieregato, the Pope's representative in London, gave an account of
how the sick were to be treated to Bortolomeo, Chief Secretary of the
Marquis of Mantua.*

Sebastian Giustiniano to the Signory

This disease makes very quick progress, proving fatal in twenty-four hours
at the furthest and many are carried off in four or five hours. The patients
experience nothing but a profuse sweat which dissolves the frame, and
when over the twenty-four hours the danger is passed. Few strangers are
dead but an immense number of natives.

Francesco Chieregato to Bortolomeo

During the fit it is fatal to take any cold beverage, or to allow any air to
penetrate the garments or bed clothes in which the patient commenced
perspiring. It is necessary to have rather more covering than usual, though
even in this great caution is needed, as some have been suffocated by a
more than requisite amount of covering. The bedchamber should have a
moderate fire, so as not to heat the room, but to keep it at a tepid temperature; the arms should be crossed on the patient's breast, and great care
be taken lest the least air reach the armpits. To neglect these precautions
ensures immediate death.

Safer on the battlefield than in the city

THOMAS MORE, letter to Desiderius Erasmus, 19 August 1517

The scholar and Henry VIII's lord chancellor Thomas More (1478–1535) witnessed the sweating sickness from close up. On 19 August 1517, he wrote to his friend and fellow-scholar Erasmus (who had himself suffered from the disease during an earlier visit to London) about the current outbreak, which had killed their Italian friend and the king's Latin secretary Andrea Ammonio.

If ever we were in trouble before, our distress and danger are at their greatest now, with many deaths on all sides and almost everyone in Oxford, Cambridge and London taking to their beds within a few days and the loss of many of my best and most honourable friends; among them (which I am sorry to think will bring you sorrow too) our dear Andrea Ammonio, who is a very great loss to learning and to all right-thinking men. He saw himself as very well protected against the contagion by his modest manner of life, thinking it due to this that, though he rarely met anyone whose whole household had not suffered, the evil has so far attacked none of his own people. Of this he boasted to me himself and many other men beside, not very many hours before he himself was carried off. For this sweating sickness is fatal only on the first day.

I and my wife and children are still untouched, and the rest of my household have entirely recovered. But of this I can assure you: one is safer on the battlefield than in the city. It has now begun, I hear, to rage in Calais at the moment when I am obliged to go there on a mission; as though it were not enough to have lived in the midst of contagion, but I must actually go in search of it. But what can one do? What one's lot brings must be endured. I have prepared my mind to face any outcome. Mind you at least keep well.

The king went a dozen miles off

JEAN DU BELLAY, letter to the Marshal of France, 18 June 1528

During an outbreak of the sweating sickness in 1528, Anne Boleyn, and many of her household, were sufferers. Jean du Bellay (1498–1560), the French ambassador to the English court, wrote of the scare caused by the way in which it swept through the household members, including the lady herself, at that time fervently wooed by Henry VIII.

One of the *filles de chambre* of Mlle Boleyn was attacked on Tuesday by the sweating sickness. The king left in great haste, and went a dozen miles off. This disease is the easiest in the world to die of. You have a slight pain in the head and at the heart; all at once you begin to sweat. There is no need for a physician: for if you uncover yourself the least in the world, or cover yourself a little too much, you are taken off without languishing. It is true that if you merely put your hand out of bed during the first 24 hours...you become stiff as a poker.

By her father's most fervent prayers miraculously recovered

WILLIAM ROPER, *Life of Sir Thomas More* (1626)

Thomas More's daughter Margaret was also struck down by the sickness during the 1528 outbreak. The event was graphically described by her husband and More's amanuensis, the lawyer William Roper (1496–1578), in this account of the disease at the heart of the More household.

To whom for his notable virtue and godliness God showed, as it seemed, a manifest miraculous token of his special favour towards him. At such time as my wife (as many other that year were) was sick of the sweating sickness; who lying in so great extremity of that disease as by no invention or devices that physicians in such cases, commonly use (of whom she had divers both expert, wise and well learned, then continually attendant about her), could she be kept from sleep, so that both the physicians and all other there present despaired of her recovery and gave her over.

Her father (as he that most entirely tendered her), being in no small heaviness for her, by prayer at God's hand sought to get her remedy. Whereupon going up, after his usual manner, into his aforesaid new building there in his chapel on his knees with tears most devoutly besought Almighty God that it would like his goodness, unto whom nothing was impossible, if it were his blessed will, at his mediation, to vouchsafe graciously to hear his humble petition. Where incontinent came into his mind that a glister [enema] should be the only way to help her. Which when he told the physicians, they by and by confessed that if there were any hope of health that that was the very best help indeed; much marvelling of themselves that they had not before remembered it. Then was it immediately administered to her sleeping, which she could by no means have been brought unto waking.

And albeit, after she was thereby thoroughly awaked, God's marks (an evident undoubted token of death) plainly appeared upon her, yet she, contrary to all their expectations, was, as it was thought, by her father's most fervent prayers miraculously recovered, and at length again to perfect health restored: whom, if it had pleased God, at that time to have taken to his mercy, her father said he would never have meddled with worldly matters more.

A new sweat

HENRY MACHYN, *The Diary of Henry Machyn, 1550–1563*

London clothier Machyn (1496–1563) wrote a chronicle of the years 1550–63 and described the last great outbreak of the sweating sickness. His trade was to supply cloth for funerals, and his chronicle took great note of all the deaths of each of the years he covered.

The seventh day of July [1551] began a new sweat in London...the 10th day of July the King's grace removed from Westminster unto Hampton Court, for there died certain beside the court, and caused the King's grace to be gone so soon, for there died in London many merchants and great rich men and women, and young men and old, of the new sweat...the 16th day of July died of the sweat the two young dukes of Suffolk of the sweat, both in one bed in Cambridgeshire...and there died from the seventh day of July unto the nineteenth died of the sweat in London of all diseases 872, and no more in all.

The ephemeral disease

JOHN CAIUS, *A Boke, or Counseill against the Disease Commonly Called the Sweate or the Sweating Sickness* (1552)

English doctor and scholar John Caius (1510–1573), who is also known as the refounder, in 1557, of Gonville and Caius College, Cambridge, wrote the 16th-century's most definitive account of the sweating sickness in A Boke, or Counseill against the Disease Commonly Called the Sweate or the Sweating Sickness.

This disease is almost peculiar unto us Englishmen, and not common to all men.... Therefore compelled I am to use this our English tongue as best to be understood to whom it most follows, most behoves to have speedy remedy, and often least nigh to places of succour and comfort at learned men's hands.

But it immediately killed some in opening their windows, some in playing with children in their street doors, some in one hour, many in two it destroyed, and at the longest, to them that merrily dined, it gave a sorrowful supper. As it found them so it took them, some in sleep some in wake, some in mirth some in care, some fasting & some full, some busy and some idle, and in one house sometime three sometime five, sometime more. If the half in every town escaped, it was thought great favour.

This disease (because it most did stand in sweating from the beginning until the ending) was called here, the Sweating Sickness: and because it first began in England, it was named in other countries, the English sweat. But if the name were now to be given, and at my liberty to make the same: I would of the manner and space of the disease make the name *Ephemera*, which is to say, a fever of one natural day. A fever, for the fervour or burning, dries & sweating feverlike. Of one natural day, for that it lasts but the time of twenty-four hours....

This disease is not a sweat only (as it is thought and called) but a fever, as I said, in the spirits by putrefaction venomous, with a fight, travail and labour of nature against the infection received in the spirits, whereupon by chance follows a sweat, or issues a humour compelled by nature.... That this is true, the self sweats do shew. For as in outer businesses, bodies that do labour, by travail of the same are forced to sweat, so in inner diseases, the bodies travailed and laboured by them, are moved to the like. In which labours, if nature be strong and able to thrust out the poison by sweat, the person escapes: if not, it dies. That it is a fever, thus I have partly declared, and more will straight by the notes of the disease, under one shewing, that it consists in the spirits.

First by the pain in the back, or shoulder, pain in the extreme parts, as arm or leg, with a flushing, or wind, as it seems to certain of the patients, flying in the same. Secondly by the grief in the liver and the nigh stomach. Thirdly by the pain in the head and madness of the same. Fourthly by the passion of the heart. For the flushing or wind coming in the outer and extreme parts, is nothing else but the spirits of those same gathered together, at the first entering of the evil air, against the infection, and flying the same from place to place, for their own safeguard.

Custom-shrunk by the sweat

WILLIAM SHAKESPEARE, *Measure for Measure* (1603/4)

More than half a century after the last outbreak, the sweating sickness was still sufficiently memorable for William Shakespeare (1564–1616) to mention it in Measure for Measure *(Act 1, Scene 2).*

MISTRESS OVERDONE: Thus, what with the war, what with the sweat, what with the gallows and what with poverty, I am custom-shrunk.

The truculent disease

GEORGE THOMSON, *The Lord Bacon's Relation to the Sweating-Sickness Examined* (1670)

Physician, medical writer and pamphleteer George Thomson (1619–1676) rejected the traditional Galenic approach to medicine and argued against medical bloodletting, purging and the doctrine of curing by 'contraries'. He discussed treatments for the sweating sickness in a pamphlet of 1670.

I cannot but make an animadversion upon that truculent disease which formerly raged in England, to the destruction of some thousands. It had its original undoubtedly from a degenerate latex [humoral fluid] turned into a malignant ichor [discharge], which caused a tabefaction [wasting] or colliquation of the blood and nutritive juice, which issuing forth in a copious measure symptomatically, without any Euphoria or alleviation, quickly consumed the stock of life. The attempt made at first to cure this malady by stopping the sweat by astringents and cooling things, proved not only frustraneous [ineffectual], but also very mortal, for the malignity being thereby more concentrated, wanting a Momentaneous vent through the universal membrane, it forthwith preyed upon the Archaeus [vital force], extinguishing the lamp of Life in such sort as a mephitis [stench], or subterraneous damp doth obfuscate, and at length put out the flame of a candle. Now the proper adequate remedies that took effect in this feral evil, were Eustomachies [elixirs], as likewise counterpoisons, that did immediately resist the venom by obliterating the idea thereof, by corroborating the enormon [vital spirit], exterminating the intoxicated ichor and ill-condition'd latex, through the habit of the body.

A 17th-century physician wearing the customary protective costume to prevent against catching the plague. Artist unknown, *c*. 1910.

PART III
PANDEMICS OF THE AGE OF EMPIRE

In the millennium before AD 1500, populations in each region of the world had adjusted to, and acquired a degree of immunity to, a range of endemic diseases, for example malaria and yellow fever in Africa, cholera in India, influenza in East Asia, and smallpox and measles in Europe. But when, from the late 15th century, European explorers, traders and soldiers relentlessly pushed out across the globe, they took with them diseases to which the peoples they encountered had no immunity, and brought back with them diseases that could devastate Europeans.

As a result, the age of empire that began with Columbus in 1492 and Vasco da Gama's visit to India six years later, also initiated an age of imperial pandemics that continued into the 19th century. The Spaniards inadvertently but disastrously took smallpox and measles with them to the Americas; on their return journeys they may have brought virulent syphilis to Europe. Influenza – which had been little known outside China – now moved eastwards along ancient trade routes, reaching Africa and Europe in about 1510, after which it was taken to the New World. The local authorities, whether in the Old or New World, made little attempt to stem these epidemics or relieve the distress they caused.

Meanwhile, more familiar diseases such as plague continued to blight Europe, recurring in localized outbreaks that could be severe: for example, in London (1563), Malta (1592), Italy (1629–31) and particularly in Naples (1656), London (1665) and Marseilles (1720). By the mid-17th century, however, western European states had begun to develop more effective mechanisms of national and civic government, and these began to make efforts to stem the infection and to manage the economic impact. At the same time, new medical knowledge and skills began to deliver more effective means of treating sufferers, even where the means of transmission remained unknown.

SYPHILIS

The syphilis pandemic struck Europe in a virulent form in the mid-1490s, and continued, somewhat more mildly for many decades, eventually becoming endemic within most societies across the world.

The pox, as it was known, was not Europe's first sexually transmitted disease – gonorrhoea had been known since antiquity – but its impact was more shocking and visible, especially in its tertiary stages, and was frequently terminal. The treatments prescribed were themselves often as painful as the disease itself; from 1500, the main treatment was mercury, which was supposed to cause the patient to salivate and thus expel the sickness, a treatment that had been recommended by Arabic physicians for leprosy and other diseases for some centuries. In 1496 the physician Gaspar Torella prescribed it for the attack of the pox suffered by Italian soldier Cesare Borgia, and twenty years later the influential Italian doctor Gabriele Fallopio recommended smearing a mercury-based ointment on the male genitals after intercourse as a prophylactic against infection.

Almost as soon as the pox first appeared, a belief arose that the disease – or distemper as it was often called – was endemic in the New World and had been brought back by Christopher Columbus on his first voyage in 1492. Whether this was its true origin is still debated: there is no clear evidence that any of his crew were infected, and some modern scholars believe the disease may already have been endemic in Europe and Asia, but in a much milder form. In the 16th century the wood of a New World tree, guaiacum, was believed to be the most effective treatment, and many considered that this pointed to a New World origin for the disease.

Since it quickly affected all levels of society, and because both the symptoms and the attempted cures were so debilitating, it became a topic of interest to philosophers and poets as much as to medical people.

Many commentators ascribed the onset of the pandemic to planetary influence, but a sexually transmitted pandemic with New World associations was also an easy target both for Christian moralists and to those who regarded the Native Americans as savages in a state of nature (some saw them as 'ignorant' and 'dirty' folk who infected Christians, others as innocents corrupted by the 'civilized' explorers). However, unlike earlier pandemics such as plague or leprosy, the authorities (perhaps accepting it as a consequence of male lust) took little action to prevent its spread other than periodically trying to close down brothels; some thinkers, such as Desiderius Erasmus, protested the injustices and dangers that such inaction brought about.

The virulence of syphilis declined, as did the incidence, from about 1700, so that it was an increasingly manageable disease: a large number of well-known cultural and political figures have been identified as sufferers. Caused by the spirochaete bacterium *Treponema pallidum*, it was only in the 20th century that effective treatments were developed: first the drug Arsphenamine, later known as Salvarsan, developed by Paul Ehrlich in 1907, and then the development of penicillin in the 1940s.

A celestial influenza

MARCELLO CUMANO, 1495

A physician serving with the Venetian army, Marcello Cumano was present at the battle of Fornovo near Parma in July 1495, at which an army led by Charles VIII of France, who was pursuing his claim to the throne of Naples, defeated the Holy League alliance of the Papal States, Milan and Venice. It has been claimed that several crew members who had been to the New World with Columbus were serving in Charles's army. Cumano described the alarming new disease that he observed; another physician, Niccolo Squillaci, commenting on the same event concluded, 'I exhort you to provide some new remedy to remove this plague from the Italian people. Nothing could be more serious than this curse, this barbarian poison.'

I can bear witness that in the year 1495, while I was in the camp of Novara with the troops of the Venetian and Milanese lords, I saw that many cavalrymen and foot soldiers were affected by a celestial influenza that became an outburst of humours, with many pustules on their faces and all over their bodies. These usually appeared on the outer surface of the foreskin on the glans, causing the patient to itch. Sometimes the first sign was a single pustule like a small blister, not painful but itchy. But when they scratched an ulcer formed as if it were a woodworm, and after a few days the sufferer was driven to distraction by the pains experienced in the arms, legs and feet, and by an eruption of enormous pustules which lasted for a year or more.

The French disease, or perhaps the Neapolitan
FRANCESCO GUICCIARDINI, *History of Italy*, Volume I (1530s)
The great Florentine historian of the Italian Renaissance era, Francesco Guicciardini (1483–1540) described the onset of the epidemic. He was one of the first to note the irony of the popular name given to the disease. While 'Morbus gallicus', or French disease, was in common use in early 16th-century Italy and Germany, the French called it the Italian disease, the Dutch the Spanish disease, and the Turks the Christian disease.

Among all other calamities which overwhelmed Italy by this invasion of the French, or were at least attributed to it, a new distemper broke out, by them called the Neapolitan, but by the Italians the French disease, because it showed itself first among the French while they were at Naples, and on their return was spread all over Italy.

This distemper, either quite new or never known before in our hemisphere, unless in its remotest parts, has made for a number of years such havoc that it deserves to be mentioned as a fatal calamity. It first discovered itself either with ugly boils, which often became incurable wounds, or with acute pains in all joints and nerves throughout the body. The inexperienced physicians applied not only improper, but often contrary medicines, which irritated the distemper and deprived of life a multitude of both sexes and of all ages.

Many became deformed, useless and subject to perpetual pains, and the best part of those who seemed to be cured relapsed into the same misery. But as some years are now elapsed, either because the celestial influence which produced it in so virulent a manner is mitigated, or that by length of time proper remedies have been found out, it has lost much of its malignity....

However, the French ought in justice to be cleared from this ignominious imputation, for it afterwards plainly appeared that the distemper was brought to Naples from Spain: nor was it the product of that country: it was conveyed thither from those islands which, about this time, through the means of Christopher Columbus, a Genoese, began to be known in our hemisphere. But Nature has been indulgent to the inhabitants of those islands in providing an easy remedy, for by drinking the juice of a particular medicinal wood which grows among them, they are entirely cured.

The disease of the Indies

GONZALO FERNÁNDEZ DE OVIEDO, *The Natural History of the Indies* (1526)

Gonzalo Fernández de Oviedo (1478–1557) was a Spanish nobleman who worked in the New World in the 1510s and wrote a history of the Indies, published in 1526 and addressed to the Emperor Charles V.

Many times in Italy I laughed, hearing the Italians speak of the French disease, and the French call it the disease of Naples, but in truth it would have been named better if it were called the disease of the Indies.

Your Majesty may take it as certain that this malady comes from the Indies where it is very common among the Indians, but not so dangerous in those lands as in our own.... The first time this sickness was seen in Spain was after Admiral Don Christopher Columbus had discovered the Indies and returned from those lands. Some Christians among those who went with him and took part in that discovery, and many more who made the second trip, brought back this scourge and from them it was passed on to others.

A dreadful, stinking, pimply and disgusting sickness

JOSEPH GRÜNPECK VON BÜRCKHAUSEN, *Neat Treatise on the French Evil* (1496)

German astrologer and moralist Joseph Grünpeck von Bürckhausen (1473–1532) served as private secretary to the Holy Roman Emperor Maximilian II. He caught syphilis in 1501 ('The disease loosed its first arrow into my priapic glans, which on account of the wound became so swollen that both hands could scarcely encircle it') *but recovered two years later. He had already written about the disease in a tract of 1496 entitled* Neat Treatise on the French Evil.

As I think upon the great misery, sorrow, fear and need which we feel daily, with which the Almighty Eternal God punishes us every hour and every moment, I cannot hold back my tears. I find in the old histories and stories great plagues and punishments which were laid upon the human race on account of their sins – great pestilences, shedding of blood and famines; but they are indeed not to be compared with that which fills the present time in which we are now living. There has arisen a previously unheard-of, unseen, unknown to all mortals, a dreadful, stinking, pimply and disgusting sickness with which people are being severely stricken the like of which has never before appeared on earth....

Speaking of natural remedies, there are these. The first is flight, that everyone should flee from those people that have this sickness, for it goes from one person to another. Also they should avoid their clothes and in fact all things which they have used. Also, everyone should keep away from large gatherings, in case one among those present might be poisoned. One should flee from the following things: a public bath, in which many people come; much eating and drinking; and if one should find oneself being depressed, he must be jolly and not think about the sickness because even imagination may bring it on. Fourth, everyone should always make good smell in his room with myrrh or white incense; fifth, food should be good with vinegar; sixth, keep away from women because this sickness is easily aroused by that. Seventh, avoid beer.

Horrible to behold
ULRICH VON HUTTEN, *De Morbo Gallico* (1519)
The German humanist scholar and religious reformer Ulrich von Hutten (1488–1523) wrote a major study of the pox, De Morbo Gallico, *in 1519. He had suffered from the disease for ten years by this time and died of it a few years later; his graphic descriptions of the treatments on offer are written with painful personal experience.*

The divines imputed this disease to the wrath of God, sent from Heaven as a scourge for our wickedness, and took upon them thus to preach openly, as if they had been admitted of council with God, and came to understand thereby that men never lived worse than we or as if in the Golden Age of Augustus and Tiberius when Christ was here on Earth.... As well may they prattle that of late in our times, because men are grown better in their lives, therefore is the remedy of *guaiacum* found out as a cure for this sickness. So well do these things accord, which these pretenders to the oracles of God do thus deliver to us.

Now also began the enquiry of the physicians, who searched not so much for proper remedy as for the cause – for they cared not even to behold it, much less at the first to touch the infected. For truly when it first began, it was horrible to behold.... They had boils that flood out like acorns, from whence issued such filthy stinking matter, that whosoever came within the scent, believed himself infected. The colour of these was of a dark green, and the very aspect as shocking as the pain itself, which yet was as if the sick had lain upon a fire.

Not long after its beginning, it made a progress into Germany, where it has wandered more largely than in any other place – which I ascribe to our greater intemperance than that of other nations.

It is thought this disease arises by infection from carnal contact, as in copulating with a diseased person, since it appears that young children, old men and others not given to fornication or bodily lust, are very rarely diseased.

The more a man is addicted to these pleasures, the sooner he catches it, and as they manage themselves after, either temperately or otherwise, so it the sooner leaves them, holds them a long time or utterly consumes them. Thus is it more easy to the Italians and Spaniards as well as others, living soberly, but through our surfeiting and intemperance it doth longer hold, and more grievously vex us.

The physicians have not yet certainly discovered the secret cause of this disease, although they have long and diligently enquired after the same. In this all agree, that through some unwholesome blasts of the air which happened about that time, the lakes, fountains and even the waters of the sea were corrupted, and the Earth...poisoned thereby. The pastures were infected, and venomous steams filled the whole air, which living creatures took in with their breath for this distemper at first was found among the cattle as well as among men.

The astrologers, deriving the cause from the stars, said that it proceeded from a conjunction of Saturn and Mars which happened not long before, and of two eclipses of the Sun....

We see diverse opinions very confidently held forth. The physicians of Germany, for the space of two years, were employed in such disputations, yet when I was a child they undertook to heal me.... I remember they forbad me to eat peas for in some places there were found certain worms therein which had wings, of which hog's flesh was also thought to be infected.

First there is a sharp ache in a man's joints, and yet nothing to be seen; but afterwards a flux of humours falls down, occasioning a swelling which, beginning to harden about a part, a most vehement pain arises.... I myself had such a knob or hard swelling above my left heel on the inside, which, after it was indurated for the space of seven years, could by no application be softened but still continued like a bone till by the help of *guaiacum* it gradually vanished.

In women the disease rests in their secret places, wherein are little pretty sores full of venomous poison, being very dangerous for such as unknowingly meddle with them; the which sickness, when contracted from these infected women, is so much the more grievous by how much they are more inwardly corrupted and polluted therewith....

After this there will appear small holes and sores, turning cankerous and fistulous, which the more putrid they grow the more they will eat into the bones and when they have been long corrupted the sick grows lean, his flesh wasting away. By this many fall into consumptions, having their inward parts corrupted.

While the physicians were thus confounded, the surgeons wretchedly lent a helping hand to the same error, and began to burn the sores with hot irons. But for as much as there seemed no end of this cruelty, they endeavoured now to avoid the same with their ointments, but all in vain, unless they added quicksilver thereunto. To this purpose they used the powders of myrrh, mastich, ceruse, bayberries, allum, bole armoniac, cinnabar, vermilion, coral, burnt salt, rust of iron, refine of turpentine, and all manner of the best oils as of bay, roses, turpentine, juniper, the oil of spike, also hogs-lard, neatsfoot oil, may butter, goats' and deers' suet, virgin honey, red worms dried to powder, or boiled up with oil, camphire, euphorbium, castor.

With these, they anointed the sick man's joints, his arms, thighs, his neck and back, with other parts of his body. Some taking these anointings once a day, some twice, others four times; others the patient being shut up in a stove with continual and fervent heat, some twenty, some thirty whole days. Some lying in bed within the stove were thus anointed, and covered with many clothes, being compelled to sweat. Part at the second anointing began to faint, yet was the ointment of such strength that whatever distemper was in the upper parts it drew it into the stomach, and thence to the brain and so the disease was voided by the nose and mouth, and put the patient to so great pain, that their teeth fell out, and their throats, their lungs, with the roofs of their mouths, were full of sores. Their jaws did swell, their teeth loosened and a stinking matter continually was voided from these places. What part soever it touched, the same was strait corrupted thereby, so that not only their lips, but the inside of their cheeks, were grievously pained, and made the place where they were, stink most abominably; which sort of cure was indeed so terrible, that many chose rather to die than to be eased thus of their sickness.

Howbeit, scarce one sick person in a hundred could be cured in this way, but quickly after relapsed. Whereby may be inferred what I suffered, who underwent the same in this fashion for eleven times, with great peril and jeopardy of life, struggling with the disease nine years together, taking whatever was thought proper to withstand the disease – such as baths with herbs, drinks and corrosives, of which arnic, ink, calcantum, verdegris and aquafortis, which occasioned such bitter pains that those might be thought very desirous of life who had not rather die than thus to prolong it.

For these cures were exceedingly painful and the more so, being set about by ignorant men, who knew nothing of their operation – for not only the surgeons, but every bold fellow played the physician in this business, using to all manner of sick people the same ointment, either as he had seen used by others, or as he had undergone it himself. And so they undertook to cure all with one medicine; or as the proverb says, 'The same shoe for every foot.' If anything happened wrong for want of good advice, they knew not what to do or say – and these men tormentors were suffered thus to practise on all persons as they were minded, while the physicians were as men struck dumb, not knowing what course to take; and thus without rule or order, with torment of heat and plenty of sweat, all were set upon after one fashion, without regard of time, habit or complexion.

The Unequal Marriage

DESIDERIUS ERASMUS, *Colloquies* (1529)

The Rotterdam humanist scholar Desiderius Erasmus (1466–1536) wrote many informal dialogues or Colloquies *on a range of personal and social issues. One, entitled 'The Unequal Marriage', saw two friends discussing the disastrous public health and moral impact of marrying young women to pox-ridden older men, and suggested this was a social issue that should be taken as seriously as the plague.*

GABRIEL: I have been at the wedding of a young gentleman with a lady of sixteen, who has every accomplishments you could wish for, beauty, good humour, family and fortune: a wife fit for Jupiter himself....

PETRONIUS: So why are you so melancholy? Do you envy the happy bridegroom?

GABRIEL: No, not that.

PETRONIUS: Then what was the matter? Was not Hymen [God of marriage] at the wedding?

GABRIEL: They called loudly for him with all the music, but to no purpose.

PETRONIUS: So was there no lucky godship at all to celebrate the wedding?

GABRIEL: No, only the goddess the Greeks call Psora [itch].

PETRONIUS: Why, this sounds like a scabby wedding indeed.

GABRIEL: Yes, a cankered and poxy one....

PETRONIUS: The groom has been for a long time famous in this town for two things: lying and the mange.

GABRIEL: He suffers from very proud distemper, one that would win all the prizes in a contest with leprosy, elephantiasis, tetters [a skin disease like eczema], gout or ringworm.

PETRONIUS: So we are told by the followers of Aesculapius.

GABRIEL: You would have thought the bride a goddess, had you seen her. Everything about her was graceful. Then came the bridegroom – with his distorted nose, dragging one leg after him, his hands itching, his breath stinking, his eyes heavy, his head bound up and his nose and ears running.

PETRONIUS: What were her parents thinking, to marry their daughter to a living mummy?

GABRIEL: To my kind it would have been kinder for them to have stripped her naked, and exposed her to bears, lions or crocodiles. For at least these beasts might have spared her for her exquisite beauty, or else put her speedily out of her pain. Imagine what kind of pleasure she must take in the kisses, embraces and nocturnal dalliances of this man.

PETRONIUS: Can this girl dare to embrace a carcass like this in the night-time?

GABRIEL: Perhaps the parents knew nothing of the bridegroom's distemper.

PETRONIUS: He must have something to recommend him to the parents.

GABRIEL: Only the glorious title of a knight.

PETRONIUS: A fine sort of a knight he is, that can scarcely sit in a saddle for the pox.

PETRONIUS: Well, what jointure does this bully settle upon his bride?

GABRIEL: Why a very great one: a thundering pox....

PETRONIUS: In the meantime, what advice can you give the poor girl?

GABRIEL: All I can suggest is, unless she likes being miserable, to clap her hands before her mouth whenever her husband tries to kiss her; and to put on armour when she goes to bed....

PETRONIUS: It is a wonder to me, that princes whose business it is to take care of the commonwealth should find no remedy for this evil. This egregious pestilence has infected a great part of the earth; yet they lie snoring and pay no attention, as if it were a matter not worth their notice.

GABRIEL: You can only have a marriage between living persons; but in this case, a woman has married a dead man.

PETRONIUS: I suppose you would permit poxy folks to marry poxy.

GABRIEL: If I could act for the public good, I'd let them marry but I'd burn them soon after.

PETRONIUS: Would it not be kinder to just geld them, or separate them and padlock the women up?

GABRIEL: Gentler perhaps, but my way is safer. For even castrated men have an itching desire upon them; and the infection can be conveyed by a kiss, by discourse, by touch, or by drinking with an infected party. And this distemper brings with it a certain malicious disposition of doing mischief, so that someone who has it enjoys propagating it to as many others as he can....

GABRIEL: But even if some people may get this distemper through no fault of their own; ...it can be lawful to put the innocent to death, if it be very much for the public good.... Do we Christians not go to war, even though the greatest share of the calamities falls on those who least deserve them?... Whenever the plague appears in Italy, infected houses are shut up, and the nurses that look after the sick are forbidden to appear in public. And though some call this inhumanity, it is actually the greatest humanity; for by this prudence, the calamity is stopped, by the burials of just a few persons....

GABRIEL: Some think it a very inhospitable thing, for the Italians – when there is just the barest rumour of a pestilence – to drive travellers from their very gates in an evening, and force them to lie all night in the open air. But I account it an act of piety to take care of the public good at the inconvenience of a few. Some people think themselves very courageous if they dare to venture to visit one that is sick of the plague, without any reason at all to do it; but what greater folly can there be, than by this courage to bring the distemper home to their wives and children, and all their family. And, how much more dangerous is the pox than the plague. The plague frequently passes by those that are nearest, and seldom affects the old; and as to those that it does affect, it either dispatches them quickly, or restores them to their health much sounder than they were before. But as for the pox, what is that but a lingering death?

The song of Syphilus

GIROLAMO FRACASTORO, *Syphilis, or A Poetical History of the French Disease* (1530)

The Venetian physician, poet and natural scientist Girolamo Fracastoro, or Fracastorius (c. 1478–1553) was the first major proponent of the germ theory of disease. He also wrote the epic poem Syphilis, or A Poetical History of the French Disease, *which was translated into English couplets in the late 17th century by poet Nahum Tate. It tells the story of a young man, Syphilus, who cursed Apollo for sending a drought and was punished with the disease – which is described in graphic detail. The poem gave its name to the disease.*

A shepherd once (distrust not ancient fame)
Possessed these downs, and Syphilus his name.
He first wore buboes dreadful to the sight.
First felt strange pains, and sleepless passed the night.
From him the malady received its name.
The neighbouring shepherds catched the spreading flame....

Through what adventures this unknown disease
So lately did astonished Europe seize,
Through Asian coasts and Libyan cities ran,
And from what seeds the malady began,
Our song shall tell: To Naples first it came
From France, and justly took from France his name,
Companion of the war—
The methods next of cure we shall express,
The wondrous wit of mortals in distress:
But when their skill too faint resistance made,
We'll shew the gods descending to their aid....

This new distemper from some newer cause;
Nor reason can allow that this disease,
Came first by commerce from beyond the seas;
Since instances in divers lands are shown,
To whom all Indian traffic is unknown:
Nor could th' infection from the western clime
Seize distant nations at the self same time;
And in remoter parts begin its reign,
As fierce and early as it did in Spain.
What slaughter in our Italy was made
Where Tiber's tribute to the oceans paid;
Where Po does through a hundred cities glide,
And pours as many streams into the tide.
All at one season, all without relief,
Received and languished with the common grief.
Nor can th' infection first be charged on Spain,
That fought new worlds beyond the western main.

Since from Pyrene's foot, to Italy,
It shed its bane on France, while Spain was free.
As soon the fertile Rhine its fury found,
And regions with eternal winter bound:
Nor yet did southern climes its vengeance shun,
But felt a flame more scorching than the Sun.
The palms of Ida now neglected stood,
And Egypt languished while her Nile o'erflowed;
From whence 'tis plain this pest must be assigned
To some more powerful cause and hard to find....

Yet with disturbance to the wretch diseased,
Who with unwonted heaviness is seized,
With drooping spirits, his affairs pursues,
And all his limbs their offices refuse,
The cheerful glories of his eyes decay,
And from his cheeks the roses fade away,
A leaden hue o'er all his face is spread,
And greater weights depress his drooping head;
Till by degrees the secret parts shall show,
By open proofs the undermining foe;
Who now his dreadful ensigns shall display,
Devour, and harass in the sight of day.
Again, when cheerful light has left the skies,
And night's ungrateful shades and vapours rise;
When every kind relief's retired within,
'Tis then the execrable pains begin;
Arms, shoulders, legs, with restless aches vexed,
And with convulsions every nerve perplexed;
For when through all our veins th' infection's spread,
And by what e'er should feed the body fed;
When Nature strives the vitals to defend,
And all destructive humours outward send:
These being viscous, gross and loath to start,
In its dull march shall torture every part;
Whence to the bloodless nerves dire pains ensue,

At once contracted, and extended too;
The thinner parts will yet not stick so fast,
But to the surface of the skin are cast,
Which in foul botches o'er the body spread,
Profane the bosom, and deform the head:
Here puscles in the form of acorns swelled,
In form alone, for these with stench are filled,
Whose ripeness is corruption, that in time,
Disdain confinement, and discharge the slime;
Yet oft the foe would turn his forces back,
The brawn and inmost muscles to attack,
And pierce so deep, that the bare bones have been
Betwixt the dreadful fleshy breaches seen;
When on the vocal parts his rage was spent,
Imperfect sounds, for tuneful speech was sent....

At first they knew, nor courage had to try,
But learnt by slow experience to appease,
To check, and last to vanquish the disease.
Yet after all our study we must own
Some secrets were by revelation known:
For though the stars in dark cabals combined,
And for our ruin with the furies joined,
Yet were we not to last destruction left,
Nor of the gods' protection quite bereft....

This path does to that sacred stream convey,
In which thy only hope remains: She said,
And under golden roofs her patient led,
Hard by, the lakes of liquid silver flowed,
Which to the wondering youth the goddess showed;
Thrice washed in these (said she) thy pains shall end,
And all the stench into the stream descend.
Thrice with her virgin hands the goddess threw
On all his suffering limbs the healing dew:
He, at the falling filth admiring stood,

And scarce believed for joy, the virtue of the flood.
When therefore you return to open day,
With sacrifice Diana's rage allay,
And homage to the fountain's goddess pay.
Thus spake the nymph, and through the realms of night,
Restored the grateful youth to open light.
This strange invention soon obtained belief,
And flying fame divulged the sure relief.
But first experiments did only join,
And for a vehicle use lard of swine:
Larch-gum and turpentine were added next,
That wrought more safe and less the patient vexed;
Horse-grease and bears with them they did compound,
Bdellium and gum of Cedar useful found;
Then myrrh, and frankincense were used by some,
With living sulphur and Arabian gum;
But if black hellebore be added too,
With rainbow flowers your method I allow;
Benzoin and galbanum I next require,
Lint-Ooil, and sulphur's e'er it feels the fire.
With these ingredients mixed, you must not fear
Your suffering limbs and body to besmear,
Nor let the foulness of the course displease,
Obscene indeed, but less than your disease:
Yet when you do anoint, take special care
That both your head and tender breast you spare,
This done, wrapped close and swathed, repair to bed,
And there let such thick coverings be o'er-spread,
Till streams of sweat from every pore you force:
For twice five days you must repeat this course;
Severe indeed but you your fate must bear,
And signs of coming health will straight appear.
The mass of humours now dissolved within,
To purge themselves by spittle shall begin,
Till you with wonder at your feet shall see,
A tide of filth, and bless the remedy.

For ulcers that shall then the mouth offend,
Boil flowers that privet and pomegranates send.
Now, only now, I would forbid the use
Of generous wine that noble soils produce;
All sorts without distinction you must fly,
The sparkling bowl with all its charms deny.
Rise, now victorious, health is now at hand,
One labour more is all I shall command,
Easy and pleasant; you must last prepare
Your bath, with rosemary and lavender,
Vervain and yarrow too must both be there;
'Mongst these your sleeping body you must lay,
To cheer you, and to wash all dregs away.

The standard treatment

THOMAS SYDENHAM, 'The History and Treatment of the Venereal
Disease' (*c.* 1673)

The great English physician Thomas Sydenham (1624–1689; see also
page 191) refused to moralize about his patients, but in 1673 clearly set
out an approach that formed the basis of standard treatment for the
next two hundred years. He, like many others of the time, believed that
gonorrhoea was an early form of syphilis.

When the blood is tainted by the long continuance of a gonorrhoea, or
the unadvised use of astringents, the true pox appears, which is attended
with buboes in the groin; pains in the head, and limbs between the joints,
which chiefly come in the night, after the patient is warm in bed; yellow
scabs also, and scurf in different parts of the body, which resemble an
honey-comb, and the more they spread, the less pain the patient feels;
exostoses [bony growths] in the cranium, legs and arms; inflammation
and caries of the bones; phagedenic ulcers in various parts of the body,
which generally seize the throat first, and eat by degrees through the
palate, to the cartilage or bridge of the nose, which they soon consume,
so that the nose, for want of its support, falls flat; the ulcers, caries and
pains increasing every day, the limbs rot away piecemeal, and the mangled
carcase, being at length grown hateful to the living, is buried in the earth.

Take of hog's lard, two ounces; quicksilver, an ounce; mix them together according to the rules of art, for a liniment, to be divided into three equal parts, with one of which the patient is to anoint his arms, thighs and legs, with his own hand, for three nights running.

If the salivation rises not in three days after the last unction, eight grains of turbith mineral may be given in a little conserve of red roses, or in weak habits a scruple of sweet mercury. If the salivation abates before the symptoms are quite gone off, it must be increased by exhibiting now and then a dose of sweet mercury occasionally.

The salivation should be so regulated, that the patient may spit about two quarts in twenty-four hours. If it rises too high, and is accompanied with great inflammation, and other symptoms of a like kind, it must be lowered to a proper degree by purgatives.

As soon as the symptoms are gone off, the patient's linen should be changed for what has been worn since it was washed. If a looseness succeeds, as it generally does soon after the salivation rises, it must be stopped by administering laudanum, increasing and repeating the dose, till it hath produced the desired effect.

If the mouth be ulcerated, it must be gargarized [gargled] or washed with rose-water, milk and water, or the following gargarism [gargling liquid]. Take of the roots of marshmallows, and pearl barley, of each an ounce; quince feeds, half an ounce; boil them together in enough spring-water to a quart, for a gargarism, to be frequently used.

The same regimen and diet are to be ordered in a salivation as are used in a course of purging, only the patient may live upon posset-drink, water-gruel, barley-gruel and warm small-beer, for a few days in the beginning of the course.

The course being duly finished, though the symptoms should seem gone off, and the distemper consequently cured, yet, in order to prevent a relapse, the patient should take a scruple of sweet mercury, once a week, for a month, or six weeks, though he appears to be perfectly well, and goes abroad.

NEW WORLD SMALLPOX

The arrival of the Spaniards in the New World, bringing with them diseases to which the indigenous population had no immunity, almost immediately proved disastrous. Worst was smallpox, which had been known in Eurasia at least since the time of the ancient Egyptians. Here there were sometimes devastating outbreaks, such as the Antonine plague of the 2nd century AD (see page 25) and that experienced by Japan in 735–37, which may have killed a third of the population. The expansion of the Huns across central Asia in the 5th century, the Arab expansion in the 7th, and the Crusades in the 11th–14th centuries all helped to spread the disease, until by 1500 it was present in most parts of the Old World except Russia. By then it was often a disease of childhood, and those Europeans who survived it had immunity against further infection.

When the small band of Spanish conquistadors led by Hernán Cortes invaded Mexico in 1519, they brought smallpox with them, and their final conquest of the apparently far more powerful Aztec Empire in 1521 was aided by the fact that the Aztecs were already suffering the devastating impact of the disease. Over the succeeding century, smallpox continued to scythe through the Mexican population, together with other Old World diseases such as measles, and these – together with famine, overwork and war – reduced the native population to just 10 per cent of its pre-Columbian size.

The story was similar in Peru, although here smallpox had already arrived from Spanish outposts Panama and Columbia and was already decimating the Inca population even before Francisco Pizarro and his small band of followers arrived in the empire's Peruvian heartlands in 1532. Again, the disease had directly benefited the invaders, by killing the Inca emperor Huayna Capac and his eldest son in 1524. The tensions between the two remaining sons Atahuallpa and Huascar created a power vacuum that the Spaniards were able to exploit to devastating effect in 1532–33.

From Mexico, the disease spread northwards into the Mississippi region. Further outbreaks of smallpox occurred in New England in the early 17th century, where it had been accidentally introduced by colonists.

How to distinguish smallpox and measles

Abu Bakr Muhammad ibn Zakariya Al-Razi, *Treatise on Smallpox and Measles* (9th century AD)

The Iranian physician Abu Bakr Muhammad ibn Zakariya Al-Razi (c. 854–925), known as Rhazes in the West, worked in Baghdad. He was the first major thinker to challenge the influential approach of the Greek physician Galen that saw disease as an imbalance between the four bodily humours. He wrote more than two hundred treatises on different diseases; his Treatise on Smallpox and Measles *provides probably the best early description of smallpox, which he regarded as an almost universal illness of childhood. Translated into Latin in the late 15th century, it proved influential for another two hundred years.*

The eruption of the smallpox is preceded by a continued fever, pain in the back, itching in the nose and terrors in the sleep. These are the more peculiar symptoms of its approach, especially a pain in the back with fever; then also a pricking which the patient feels all over his body; a fullness of the face, which at times comes and goes; an inflamed colour, and vehement redness in both cheeks; a redness of both the eyes, heaviness of the whole body; great uneasiness, the symptoms of which are stretching and yawning; a pain in the throat and chest, with slight difficulty in breathing and cough; a dryness of the breath, thick spittle and hoarseness of the voice; pain and heaviness of the head; inquietude, nausea and anxiety (with this difference that the inquietude, nausea and anxiety are more frequent in the measles than in the smallpox; while on the other hand, the pain in the back is more peculiar to the smallpox than to the measles); heat of the whole body; an inflamed colon and shining redness, especially an intense redness of the gums.

When, therefore, you see these symptoms, or some of the worst of them (such as pain of the back and the terrors of sleep, with the continued fever) then you may be assured that the eruption of one or the other of these diseases in the patient is nigh at hand; except that there is not in the measles so much pain of the back as in smallpox; nor in the smallpox so much anxiety and nausea as in measles, unless the smallpox be of a bad sort; and this shows that the measles came from a very bilious blood.

Agonizing sores from head to foot

BERNARDINO DE SAHAGÚN, *General History of the Things of New Spain,*
or *Florentine Codex* (1576)

The Franciscan friar Bernardino de Sahagún (1499–1590) was one of the
first Catholic missionaries in Mexico. He recorded Aztec history, culture
and beliefs in the native language Nahuatl, including a description of
the Spanish conquest from the Aztec point of view. This was translated
and published as the General History of the Things of New Spain, *or*
Florentine Codex. *The work, therefore, is effectively an Aztec account*
of the arrival of smallpox among them.

While the Spaniards were in Tlaxcala, a great plague broke out here in
Tenochtitlan. It began to spread...and lasted for seventy days, striking
everywhere in the city and killing a vast number of our people.

Sores erupted on our faces, our breasts, our bellies; we were covered
with agonizing sores from head to foot. The illness was so dreadful that
no one could walk or move. The sick were so utterly helpless that they
could only lie on their beds like corpses, unable to move their limbs or
even their heads. They could not lie face down or roll from one side to
the other. If they did move their bodies, they screamed with pain. A great
many died from this plague, and many others died of hunger. They could
not get up to search for food, and everyone else was too sick to care for
them, so they starved to death in their beds.

Some people went down with a milder form of the disease; they suffered less than the others and made a good recovery. But they could not
escape entirely. Their looks were ravaged, for wherever a sore broke out,
it gouged an ugly pockmark in the skin. And a few of the survivors were
left completely blind.

The first cases were reported in Cuatlan. By the time the danger was
recognized, the plague was so well established that nothing could halt it,
and eventually it spread all the way to Chalco. Then its virulence diminished
considerably, though there were isolated cases for many months after. The
first victims were stricken during the fiesta of Teotlecco, and the faces of
our warriors were not clean and free of sores until the fiesta of Panquezal-
iztli. By then, the brave warriors of the Mexicans were able to recover from
the pestilence. And when this had happened, then the Spaniards came.

Native Mexican annals of the year 1520

The dramatic events of the 1520s were also recorded in annals prepared in the native Nahua language, and later translated and preserved by the Spaniards. The native language had no existing word for smallpox, but the translators well enough understood which disease the annals referred to.

Nahuatl annal Upon the death of Montezuma, those of Mexico made Cuitlavazi from Estapalapa, brother of Montezuma, their leader. He was lord for eighty days: smallpox was given to all the Indians and many died, before the Castilians returned to conquer the city.

The Annals of Tlatelolco Then a plague broke out of coughing, fever and pox. When the plague lessened somewhat, the Spaniards came back.

The Annals of Cuauhtitlan Then Yohualtonatiuh was inaugurated. It was in his time that the Spaniards arrived. Both Citlalcoatl and Yohualtonatiuh died of the smallpox.

They died in heaps, like bedbugs

TORIBIO DE BENAVENTE MOTOLINÍA, *History of the Indians of the New Spain* (1541)

The Franciscan missionary Toribio de Benavente Motolinía (1482–1568) arrived in Mexico in 1524. He worked with the indigenous peoples and adopted as his name the first word he learned in the Nahuatl language, motolinía, *meaning 'poor' or 'afflicted'. He is said to have baptized almost half a million, and became sympathetic to the sufferings caused by the arrival of the Spaniards, although he rejected the wholesale condemnation of Spanish behaviour in Mexico that was made by the Dominican Bartolomé de Las Casas. His* History of the Indians of the New World *compared the sufferings of the Mexican people with the biblical plagues of Egypt.*

God struck and chastened with ten terrible plagues this land and all who dwelt in it, both natives and foreigners.

The first was a plague of smallpox, and it began in this manner. When Hernando Cortés was captain and governor, at the time that Captain

Pánfilo de Narváez landed in this country, there was in one of his ships a negro stricken with smallpox, a disease which had never been seen here. At this time New Spain was extremely full of people, and when the smallpox began to attack the Indians it became so great a pestilence among them throughout the land that in most provinces more than half the population died; in others the proportion was little less. For as the Indians did not know the remedy for the disease and were very much in the habit of bathing frequently, whether well or ill, and continued to do so even when suffering from smallpox, they died in heaps, like bedbugs. Many others died of starvation, because, as they were all taken sick at once, they could not care for each other, nor was there anyone to give them bread or anything else. In many places it happened that everyone in a house died, and, as it was impossible to bury the great number of dead, they pulled down the houses over them in order to check the stench that rose from the dead bodies so that their homes became their tombs. This disease was called by the Indians 'the great leprosy' because the victims were so covered with pustules that they looked like lepers. Even today one can see obvious evidences of it in some individuals who escaped death, for they were left covered with pockmarks.

Eleven years later there came a Spaniard who had measles, and from him the disease was communicated to the Indians; if great care had not been taken to prevent their bathing, and to use other remedies, this would have been as terrible a plague and pestilence as the former. Even with all these precautions many died. They called this the year of the 'little leprosy'.

The second plague was the great number of those who died in the conquest of New Spain, especially around Mexico....

The third plague was a very great famine which came immediately after the taking of the city of Mexico. As they were unable to plant because of the great wars, some of them defending the land and helping the Mexicans and others fighting on the side of the Spaniards, and as what was planted by one side was cut down and laid waste by the other, they had nothing to eat....

The fourth plague was that of the *calpixques* or overseers, and the negroes. As soon as the land was divided, the conquerors put into their allotments and into the towns granted to them servants or negroes to collect the tributes and to look after their various affairs.... In the first years these overseers were absolute in their maltreatment of the Indians, over-loading them, sending them far from their land and giving them many other tasks, that many Indians died because of them and at their hands, which is the worst feature of the situation.

The fifth plague was the great taxes and tributes that the Indians paid....

The sixth plague was the gold mines, for in addition to the taxes and tributes paid by the towns which had been granted to the Spaniards, the latter began to seek for mines, and it would be impossible to count the number of Indians who have, up to the present day, died in these mines....

The seventh plague was the building of the great city of Mexico, which, in the first years, employed more people than the building of Jerusalem.... Many Indians died there....

The eighth plague was the slaves whom the Spaniards made in order to put them to work in the mines. So great was their haste, in some years, to make slaves that from all parts of Mexico they brought in great herds of them, like flocks of sheep, in order to brand them....

The ninth plague was the service of the mines, to which the heavily laden Indians travelled sixty leagues [about 300 km/200 miles] or more to carry provisions.... For half a league around these mines and along a great part of the road one could scarcely avoid walking over dead bodies or bones, and the flocks of birds and crows that came to feed upon the corpses were so numerous that they darkened the sun....

The tenth plague was the divisions and factions which existed among the Spaniards in Mexico; this was the one that most endangered the country....

Well considered, there are differences between these plagues and those of Egypt. First, in only the last of those of Egypt were there deaths of people; but here, in each of these there have been many deaths. Second, in each one of the houses there remained someone to mourn the dead, and here many houses were left abandoned, because all their occupants died. Third, in Egypt, all the plagues lasted only a few days, and here, some a very long time. Those, by the commandment of God: most of these by the cruelty and depravity of men, although God permitted it.

So it was that we became orphans

THE ANNALS OF THE CAKCHIQUELS, 16th century

The Mayans of present-day Guatemala kept a chronicle through the 16th century that records the arrival of both smallpox and the Spaniards in their region, and a second outbreak in the 1560s.

During the twenty-fifth year [1520] the plague began, oh, my sons! First they became ill of a cough, they suffered from nosebleeds and illness of the bladder. It was truly terrible, the number of dead there in that period. The prince *Vakaki Ahmak* died then. Little by little heavy shadows and black night enveloped our fathers and grandfathers and us also, oh, my sons! when the plague raged.

On the day 1 Ah [3 October 1520] ended one cycle and five years after the revolution, while the plague spread.

During this year when the epidemic broke out, our father and grandfather died, *Diego Juan.*

On the day 5 Ah [12 March 1521] our grandfathers started a war against *Panatacat [a town on the Pacific coast of Guatemala]*, when the plague began to spread. It was in truth terrible, the number of dead among the people. The people could not in any way control the sickness.

Forty days after the epidemic began, our father and grandfather died; on the day 12 Camey [14 April 1521] the king Hunyg, your great-grandfather, died.

Two days later also died our father, the Ahpop Achí Balam, your grandfather, oh, my sons! Our grandfathers and fathers died together.

Great was the stench of the dead. After our fathers and grandfathers succumbed, half of the people fled to the fields. The dogs and vultures devoured the bodies. The mortality was terrible. Your grandfathers died, and with them died the son of the king and his brothers and kinsmen. So it was that we became orphans, oh, my sons! So we became when we were young. All of us were thus. We were born to die!...

On the day 1 Akbal [8 April 1560] Governor Pedro Ramirez transferred tenure to the governor don Diego Pérez. In the sixth month after the arrival of the Lord President in Pangán, the plague which had lashed the people long ago began again. Little by little it arrived here. In truth a fearful death fell on our heads by the will of our powerful God. Many families [succumbed] to the plague. Now the people were overcome by intense cold and fever, blood came out of their noses, then came a cough growing worse and worse, the neck was twisted, and small and large sores broke out on them. The disease attacked everyone here. On the day of Circumcision [1 January 1560], a Monday, while I was writing, I was attacked by the epidemic....

One month and five days after Christmas my mother died, and a little later death took my father. We buried my mother and six days later we buried my father. At the same time, on the day 11 Akbal, doña Catalina, the wife of don Jorge, died.

Seven days after Christmas the epidemic broke out. Truly it was impossible to count the number of men, women and children who died this year. My mother, my father, my younger brother and my sister, all died. Everyone suffered nosebleeds....

Sickness and death were still rampant at the end of the sixty-third year after the revolution [1562]....

The sixty-fifth year after the revolution was completed [16 July 1564]. Many people died of smallpox, which was then prevalent.

The death of the Inca

PEDRO DE CIEZA DE LEÓN, *The Second Part of the Chronicle of Peru* (1550s)
The Second Part of the Chronicle of Peru was written by Pedro de Cieza de León (1520–1554) who travelled to Peru in the later 1530s and in 1548 became the official chronicler of the Spanish conquest. In this extract he describes the impact of smallpox on the Inca Empire in 1524, seven years before the arrival of Spanish conquistador Francisco Pizarro. The untimely death of the powerful Emperor Huayna Capac led to a civil war that Pizarro was able to exploit ruthlessly.

Huayna Capac was in Quito [in present-day Ecuador] with a great company of people. He was very powerful, his dominion extending from the river of Ancasmayu [north of Quito] to the river of Maule [south of Santiago, in present-day Chile], a distance of more than 1,200 leagues [6,000 km/4,000 miles]. He was so rich, that they relate that he had caused to be brought to Quito over 500 loads of gold, more than 1,000 of silver, many precious stones and much fine cloth. He was feared by all his subjects, because he was a stern dispenser of justice.

In the midst of his power, they say that a great pestilence broke out, which was so contagious, that over 200,000 souls died throughout the provinces, for it prevailed in all parts. The Inca caught the disease, and all that was said to free him from death was of no avail, because the great God was not served by his recovery. When he felt that the pestilence had touched him, he ordered great sacrifices to be offered up for his health throughout the land, and at all the *huacas* [sacred sites] and temples of the Sun. As he became worse, he called his captains and relations and addressed them on several subjects. Among other things, they relate that he foretold that the people who had been seen in the ship, would return with great power and would conquer the country.

This was probably a fable, and if he said so, it must have been through the mouth of a devil, for who could know that the Spaniards went to arrange their return as conquerors? Others say that, considering the extensive territory of the Quillacingas and Popayan, and that the empire was very extensive for one person to rule, he ordained that from Quito to the north, the dominion should be under his son Atahuallpa, whom he loved dearly, because he had always accompanied him in his wars. He desired that the rest of the empire should be ruled by Huascar, the sole heir of the whole. Other Indians say that he did not divide the kingdom, but that he said to those who were present, that they well knew how he had wished that his son Huascar, by his sister Chimpu Ocllo, should be lord after his own time, at which all the people of Cuzco were well contented. He had other sons of great valour, among whom were Nanque Yupanqui, Tupac Inca, Huanca Auqui, Tupac Hualpa, Titu, Huaman Hualpa, Manco Inca, Huascar, Cusi Hualpa, Paullu Tupac Yupanqui, Conono, Atahuallpa. He did not desire to give them anything of the great possessions he left, but that they should receive all from their brother, as he had inherited all from his father. For he trusted much that his son would keep his promise, and that he would fulfil all that his heart desired, although he was still a boy. He ordered his chiefs to love him and treat him as their sovereign, and that, until he was of full age to govern, Colla Tupac, his uncle, should be his guardian. When he had said this, he died.

God sent punishment to Peru

GUAMAN POMA, *The First New Chronicle and Good Government* (*c.* 1615)
*A Quechua aristocrat, native to Peru, Guaman Poma (*c. 1535*–*c. 1616*)*
served as a translator and an advocate for the rights of the indigenous
population, criticizing Spanish colonial rule. His extensive volume The
First New Chronicle and Good Government *was partly written in*
Spanish, partly in Quechua, and emphasizes how the suffering of the
Andean people had endured to his own day.

God sent pestilence in the time of the Incas and at present also. God sent
punishment. In the time of the Inca it rained fire on the town of Cacha
in the Collao. It rained sand. The volcano Putina erupted and covered
the city of Arequipa and the whole region.

The illness of measles and smallpox caused great harm during the
time of the Inca Huayna Capac. A great many people died, including
the Inca himself. They say that he went into a cave in a stone for fear
of this disease and he died inside there.

Many people die from earthquakes. In the time of the Inca Pachacuti
[r. 1438–71] it did not rain for ten years. This reminds one of the seven years
of hunger in Egypt. They say that at this time stones burst into bits, crops
froze, hail fell on the crops, pestilence of worms destroyed the crops in
the fields and moths got into the house. There was also a pestilence of
mice that destroy [*sic*] from the highland to the plains; pestilence of birds,
screeching parrots, black birds, deer, skunks and foxes.

A sorer disease cannot befall them

WILLIAM BRADFORD, *Of Plymouth Plantation* (1630–51)
Yorkshireman William Bradford (1590–1657) travelled from England to
the New World on the Mayflower *in 1620. He served as governor of the*
new Plymouth Colony from 1621, and for much of the rest of his life. He
recorded his experiences in his journal, now known as Of Plymouth
Plantation, *in which he described the impact of a smallpox epidemic*
that struck the Algonquin people up much of New England to the St Law-
rence in 1633–34. Some of the colonists, such as the clergyman Increase
Mather, saw the epidemic as a gift from God: the colonists, who survived

the epidemic without difficulty, were able to extend their reach with far less opposition from the indigenous peoples.

I am now to relate some strange and remarkable passages. There was a company of people lived in the country, up above in the river of Connecticut, a great way from their trading house there, and were enemies to those Indians which lived about them, and of whom they stood in some fear (being a stout people). About a thousand of them had enclosed them selves in a fort, which they had strongly palisaded about. Three or four Dutch men went up in the beginning of winter to live with them, to get their trade and prevent them for bringing it to the English.... But their enterprise failed, for it pleased God to visit these Indians with a great sickness, and such a mortality that, of a thousand, above nine hundred and a half of them died, and many of them did rot above ground for want of burial, and the Dutch men almost starved before they could get away, for ice and snow....

This spring, also, those Indians that lived about their trading house there fell sick of the smallpox, and died most miserably; for a sorer disease cannot befall them; they fear it more than the plague; for usually they that have this disease have them in abundance, and for want of bedding and linen and other helps, they fall into a lamentable condition, as they lie on their hard mats, the pox breaking and mattering, and running one into another, their skin cleaving (by reason thereof) to the mats they lie on; when they turn them, a whole side will flay off at once (as it were) and they will be all of a gore blood, most fearful to behold; and then being very sore, what with cold and other distempers, they die like rotten sheep. The condition of this people was so lamentable, and they fell down so generally of this disease, as they were (in the end) not able to help one another; no, not to make a fire, nor to fetch a little water to drink, nor any to bury the dead; but would strive as long as they could, and when they could procure no other means to make fire, they would burn the wooden trays and dishes they ate their meat in, and their very bows and arrows; and some would crawl out on all fours to get a little water, and sometimes die by the way and not be able to get in again.

But those of the English house (though at first they were afraid of the infection), yet seeing their woeful and sad condition, and hearing their pitiful cries and lamentations, they had compassion of them, and daily fetched them wood and water, and made them fires, got them victuals while they lived, and buried them when they died. For very few of them escaped, notwithstanding they did what they could for them, to the hazard of themselves. The chief Sachem himself now died, and almost all his friends and kindred.

But by the marvellous goodness and providence of God not one of the English was so much as sick, or in the least measure tainted with this disease, though they daily did these offices for them for many weeks together. And this mercy which they shewed them was kindly taken, and thankfully acknowledged of all the Indians that knew or heard of the same; and their masters here did much commend and reward them for the same.

COCOLIZTLI EPIDEMIC

Mexico, newly under Spanish control and subject to the devastating impact of Old World diseases such as measles and smallpox (see page 105), suffered a demographic disaster in the early 16th century, and there was further devastation in store for which Europeans can apparently not be blamed.

In 1545–48, and again in 1576–78, Mexico (then known as New Spain) suffered two epidemics of a mysterious disease known in the native Nahuatl language as Cocoliztli, or 'pest'. The first wave is thought to have killed 5–15 million people; if the higher figure is correct, it would be the equivalent of 80 per cent of the extant population. The second wave killed another 2–2.5 million, or half the remaining population. If so, it was one of the most devasting epidemics in human history in both absolute and relative terms. As a result of this epidemic, as well as smallpox, measles, war and slavery, by the end of the century Mexico had lost a staggering 90 per cent of its pre-contact population.

The symptoms described by Spanish doctors were not consistent with any known Old World disease, and the fact the disease mainly affected the highlands also suggests it did not derive from European contact. Instead, a virus – perhaps an arenavirus – carried by rodents has been suggested, but none has been identified.

New Spain was left almost empty

JUAN DE TORQUEMADA, *Monarquia Indiana* (1615)

The Franciscan friar Juan de Torquemada (c. 1562–1624) went to the New World as a child, and worked there as a missionary and administrator before returning to Spain for the final years of his life. He compiled his massive Monarquia Indiana *on the history and culture of the peoples of central Mexico, much of it based on oral evidence he had collected, including this account of the 1576–78 outbreak of cocoliztli.*

In the year 1576 a great mortality and pestilence that lasted for more than a year overcame the Indians. It was so big that it ruined and destroyed almost the entire land. The place we know as New Spain was left almost empty. It was a thing of great bewilderment to see the people die. Many were dead and others almost dead, and nobody had the health or strength to help the diseased or bury the dead. In the cities and large towns, big ditches were dug, and from morning to sunset the priests did nothing else but carry the dead bodies and throw them into the ditches without any of the solemnity usually reserved for the dead, because the time did not allow otherwise. At night they covered the ditches with dirt.... It lasted for one and a half years, and with great excess in the number of deaths. After the murderous epidemic, the viceroy Martin Enriquez wanted to know the number of missing people in New Spain. After searching in towns and neighbourhoods it was found that the number of deaths was more than two million.

The disease described

FRANCISCO HERNÁNDEZ, *The Mexican Treasury* (c. 1570)

The physician-in-chief of New Spain, Francisco Hernández (1514–1587) became personal physician to Philip II in 1567, and three years later travelled to the New World for seven years, studying medicinal plants. While there he observed native medical practices, as well as the 1576 cocoliztli epidemic at first hand, and performed autopsies on some of the dead.

The fevers were contagious, burning and continuous, all of them pestilential, in most part lethal. The tongue was dry and black. Enormous thirst. Urine of the colours sea-green, vegetal-green and black, sometimes passing from the greenish colour to the pale. Pulse was frequent, fast, small and weak – sometimes even null. The eyes and the whole body were yellow. This stage was followed by delirium and seizures. Then, hard and painful nodules appeared behind one or both ears along with heartache, chest pain, abdominal pain, tremor, great anxiety and dysentery [diarrhoea]. The blood that flowed when cutting a vein had a green colour or was very pale and dry.... In some cases gangrene...invaded their lips, genital regions and other regions of the body with putrefact members. Blood flowed from the ears and in many cases blood truly gushed from the nose. Of those with recurring disease, almost none was saved. Many were saved if the flux of blood through the nose was stopped in time; the rest died. Those attacked by dysentery were usually saved if they complied with the medication. The abscesses behind the ears were not lethal. If somehow their size was reduced either by spontaneous maturation or given exit by perforation with cauteries, the liquid part of the blood flowed or the pus was eliminated; and with it the cause of the disease was also eliminated, as was the case of those with abundant and pale urine. At autopsy, the liver was greatly enlarged. The heart was black, first draining a yellowish liquid and then black blood. The spleen and lungs were black and semi-putrefacted...the abdomen dry. The rest of the body, anywhere it was cut, was extremely pale. This epidemic attacked mainly young people and seldom the elder ones. Even if old people were affected they were able to overcome the disease and save their lives. The epidemic started in June 1576 and is not over in December, when I am writing these lines. Of all New Spain, the disease invaded highlands in a perimeter of 400 miles, and had a lesser effect on the lowlands. The disease attacked primarily regions populated by Indians, then the habitations of Indians and Africans, then the mixed populations of Indians and Spaniards, later still, the Africans, and now finally it attacks the Spanish settlements. The weather was dry and tranquil, even though there were earthquakes, the air was impure and cloudy, but the clouds did not resolve into rains, but converted themselves into a virtual incubator of putrefaction and corruption.... Vital energy was consumed quickly.

THE GREAT PLAGUE

The 17th century saw the continuation of the 'second plague' pandemic that had begun with the Black Death (see page 56), with major outbreaks through the century across western Europe, notably in Italy in the 1620s–1650s and England in the mid-1660s. The final great outbreak was in Marseilles in 1720. The Great Plague in London is probably the best known, not least because writers such as Samuel Pepys and Daniel Defoe have left vivid and moving descriptions of the strangeness and sadness of the times.

A time of transition from traditional medical practice towards a more scientific method saw increased debate about the cause of the disease and its means of transmission; there was also an attempt to drive out the more barbaric forms of treatment, and to expose the worst of the many quack remedies on offer. The more rational-minded similarly railed against the more absurd theories lapped up by the credulous public. Nevertheless, public health provisions such as accurate and detailed recording of outbreaks, and restricting the movement of people, were more effective and set a template for future pandemics.

Combating the plague in Naples

An Account of the Plague at Naples, 2 June 1656

In 1655–56, perhaps 150,000 people – about half the population of the city of Naples – died of the plague. The city authorities did their best to identify the outbreak at the start, with the help of a committee of experts, but the protective measures suggested – mostly to protect people from the miasma or 'bad air' that was thought to carry the plague – were inadequate to prevent its spread. The crowded poorer districts were strictly quarantined, but the epidemic spread through southern Italy and more than a million people may have died in the Kingdom of Naples as a whole. This outbreak, following on from others in northern Italy in 1629–31, contributed to the long decline of Italy as a locus of cultural, economic and political power.

In the opening at that time of two dead bodies, one of a man, the other of a woman, on the first of June in the year 1655, by order from his Excellence and the most illustrious magistrates deputed by this most faithful city, about the sickness then rife, it was observed by the most expert anatomists Marco Aurelio Severino and Felice Martorella that all the bowels were infected with black spots, that is to say, the heart, lungs, liver, stomach and the intestines. Besides, that the bladder of gall was plainly found to be full of black, viscid and very thick choler, which pertinaciously stuck to its membrane; but above all, the vessels of the heart were full of a grumous and black blood.

This being related by the same Signor Felice, it was decreed, that, together with the Signori Domenico Coccia, Onosrio Riccia, Carolo Pignataro, Francesco Casaro, Giovanni Giacomo Carbonello, Carolo Joveue, Andrea di Mauro and Salvator Borrello, they should determine and order what ought to be done, as well for the preservation as for the cure of this sickness. Wherefore these being met, they ordered for preventives (as to remedies most easy, and at hand) that it was greatly helpful. First, to make in the houses fires with fumes of rosemary, bay-berries, juniper, frankincense and the like. Secondly, treacle-water, treacle, mithridate, pills of rufus, against the plague. The composition of dry figs, rue, walnut and salt, which was King Mithridates' preservative, and found in his desk or cabinet written with his own hand. The magistral bezoar vinegar, made with brimstone, rue, garlic, cloves, saffron and walnuts: the use of which is to dip in a piece or slice of bread, and take it fasting.

City of London, Concerning the Infection of the Plague

LORD MAYOR AND COURT OF ALDERMEN, London, 1665

When plague broke out in London early in 1665, the Privy Council quickly imposed restrictive measures to seal up infected houses; and the mayor instituted a comprehensive system of social distancing, isolation of the infected and hygiene within the city. Similar orders for towns and cities across England followed by royal command. Bills of mortality by parish were kept and published, allowing citizens to follow the progress of the plague in detail.

Examiners to be appointed in every Parish

First, it is thought requisite, and so ordered, that in every parish there be one, two or more persons of good sort and credit chosen and appointed by the alderman, his deputy and common council of every ward, by the name of examiners, to continue in that office the space of two months at least....

That these examiners be sworn by the aldermen to inquire and learn from time to time what houses in every parish be visited, and what persons be sick, and of what diseases, as near as they can inform themselves; and upon doubt in that case, to command restraint of access until it appear what the disease shall prove. And if they find any person sick of the infection, to give order to the constable that the house be shut up; and if the constable shall be found remiss or negligent, to give present notice thereof to the alderman of the ward.

Watchmen

That to every infected house there be appointed two watchmen, one for every day, and the other for the night; and that these watchmen have a special care that no person go in or out of such infected houses whereof they have the charge, upon pain of severe punishment. And the said watchmen to do such further offices as the sick house shall need and require; and if the watchman be sent upon any business, to lock up the house and take the key with him; and the watchman by day to attend until ten of the clock at night, and the watchman by night until six in the morning.

Searchers

That there be a special care to appoint women searchers in every parish, such as are of honest reputation, and of the best sort as can be got in this kind; and these to be sworn to make due search and true report to the utmost of their knowledge whether the persons whose bodies they are appointed to search do die of the infection, or of what other diseases, as near as they can....

That no searcher during this time of visitation be permitted to use any public work or employment, or keep any shop or stall, or be employed as a laundress, or in any other common employment whatsoever.

Chirurgeons [surgeons]

For better assistance of the searchers, forasmuch as there hath been heretofore great abuse in misreporting the disease...it is therefore ordered that there be chosen and appointed able and discreet chirurgeons...and the said chirurgeons...to join with the searchers for the view of the body, to the end there may be a true report made of the disease. The said chirurgeons shall visit and search suchlike persons as shall either send for them or be named and directed unto them by the examiners of every parish, and inform themselves of the disease of the said parties.

Every of the said chirurgeons shall have twelve-pence a body searched by them, to be paid out of the goods of the party searched, if he be able, or otherwise by the parish.

Nurse-keepers

If any nurse-keeper shall remove herself out of any infected house before twenty-eight days after the decease of any person dying of the infection, the house to which the said nurse-keeper doth so remove herself shall be shut up until the said twenty-eight days be expired.

Notice to be given of the Sickness

The master of every house, as soon as anyone in his house complains, either of blotch or purple, or swelling in any part of his body, or falls otherwise dangerously sick, without apparent cause of some other disease, shall give knowledge thereof to the examiner of health within two hours after the said sign shall appear.

Sequestration of the Sick

As soon as any man shall be found by this examiner, chirurgeon or searcher to be sick of the plague, he shall the same night be sequestered in the same house; and in case he be so sequestered, then though he afterwards die not, the house wherein he sickened should be shut up for a month, after the use of the due preservatives taken by the rest.

Airing the Stuff

For sequestration of the goods and stuff of the infection, their bedding and apparel and hangings of chambers must be well aired with fire and such perfumes as are requisite within the infected house before they be taken again to use.

Shutting up of the House

If any person shall have visited any man known to be infected of the plague, or entered willingly into any known infected house, being not allowed, the house where he inhabits shall be shut up for certain days by the examiner's direction.

None to be removed out of infected Houses, but, &C.

Item, that none be removed out of the house where he falls sick of the infection into any other house in the city, except it be to the pest-house or a tent, or unto some such house which the owner of the said visited households in his own hands and occupies by his own servants; and so as security be given to the parish whither such remove is made, that the attendance and charge about the said visited persons shall be observed and charged in all the particularities before expressed, without any cost of that parish...and this remove to be done by night....

Burial of the Dead

That the burial of the dead by this visitation be at most convenient hours, always either before sun-rising or after sun-setting, with the privity of the churchwardens or constable, and not otherwise; and that no neighbours nor friends be suffered to accompany the corpse to church, or to enter the house visited, upon pain of having his house shut up or be imprisoned.

And that no corpse dying of infection shall be buried, or remain in any church in time of common prayer, sermon or lecture. And that no children be suffered at time of burial of any corpse in any church, churchyard or burying-place to come near the corpse, coffin or grave. And that all the graves shall be at least six feet deep.

No infected Stuff to be uttered

That no clothes, stuff, bedding or garments be suffered to be carried or conveyed out of any infected houses, and that the criers and carriers abroad of bedding or old apparel to be sold or pawned be utterly prohibited and restrained, and no brokers of bedding or old apparel be permitted to make any outward show, or hang forth on their stalls, shop-boards or windows, towards any street, lane, common way or passage, any old bedding or apparel to be sold, upon pain of imprisonment....

No person to be conveyed out of any infected House

If any person visited do fortune...to come or be conveyed from a place infected to any other place, the parish from whence such party hath come, shall at their charge cause the said party so visited and escaped to be carried and brought back again by night, and the parties in this case offending to be punished at the direction of the alderman of the ward, and the house of the receiver of such visited person to be shut up for twenty days.

Every visited House to be marked

That every house visited be marked with a red cross of a foot long in the middle of the door, evident to be seen, and with these usual printed words, that is to say, 'Lord, have mercy upon us', to be set close over the same cross, there to continue until lawful opening of the same house.

Every visited House to be watched

That the constables see every house shut up, and to be attended with watchmen, which may keep them in, and minister necessaries unto them at their own charges, if they be able, or at the common charge, if they are unable; the shutting up to be for the space of four weeks after all be whole....

Inmates

That where several inmates are in one and the same house, and any person in that house happens to be infected, no other person or family of such house shall be suffered to remove him or themselves without a certificate from the examiners of health of that parish; or in default thereof, the house whither he or they so remove shall be shut up as in case of visitation.

Hackney-coaches

That care be taken of hackney-coachmen, that they may not (as some of them have been observed to do after carrying of infected persons to the pest-house and other places) be admitted to common use till their coaches be well aired, and have stood unemployed by the space of five or six days after such service.

The streets to be kept clean

First, it is thought necessary, and so ordered, that every householder do cause the street to be daily prepared before his door, and so to keep it clean swept all the week long.

That rakers take it from out the Houses

That the sweeping and filth of houses be daily carried away by the rakers, and that the raker shall give notice of his coming by the blowing of a horn.

Laystalls [dung-heaps] to be made far off from the city

That the laystalls be removed as far as may be out of the city and common passages, and that no nightman or other be suffered to empty a vault into any garden near about the city.

Care to be had of unwholesome fish or flesh, and of musty corn

That special care be taken that no stinking fish, or unwholesome flesh, or musty corn, or other corrupt fruits of what sort soever, be suffered to be sold about the city, or any part of the same. That the brewers and tippling-houses be looked unto for musty and unwholesome casks. That no hogs, dogs or cats, or tame pigeons, or conies [rabbits], be suffered to be kept within any part of the city, or any swine to be or stray in the streets or lanes, but that such swine be impounded and the owner punished, and that the dogs be killed by the dog-killers appointed for that purpose.

Beggars

...that constables, and others whom this matter may any way concern, take special care that no wandering beggars be suffered in the streets of this city in any fashion or manner whatsoever, upon the penalty provided by the law, to be duly and severely executed upon them.

Plays

That all plays, bear-baitings, games, singing of ballads, buckler-play [fighting] or suchlike causes of assemblies of people be utterly prohibited, and the parties offending severely punished by every alderman in his ward.

Feasting prohibited

That all public feasting, and particularly by the companies of this city, and dinners at taverns, alehouses and other places of common entertainment, be forborne till further order and allowance; and that the money thereby spared be preserved and employed for the benefit and relief of the poor visited with the infection.

Tippling-houses

That disorderly tippling in taverns, alehouses, coffee-houses and cellars be severely looked unto, as the common sin of this time and greatest occasion of dispersing the plague. And that no company or person be suffered to remain or come into any tavern, alehouse or coffee-house to drink after nine of the clock in the evening....

SIR JOHN LAWRENCE, Lord Mayor.

SIR GEORGE WATERMAN

SIR CHARLES DOE, Sheriffs.

Panic and fake news

WILLIAM BOGHURST, *Loimographia* (1666)

William Boghurst (1631–1685), an apothecary from St-Giles-in-the-Fields, London, wrote Loimographia, *a study of the plague outbreak. In it he was as critical of the standard treatments such as sweating, as he was of the popular irrationality concerning the origins of the epidemic. He also criticized what he saw as excessive caution over touching possibly infected objects, and also the policy of quarantining infected houses, which he believed to be ineffective in stopping the spread.*

Solomon says a wise man foresees the evil and hides himself, but in this point how many wise men had we in our country, or were in the world two years ago? Yea, those curious observers who pretend to be most exquisite in the foresight of future contingencies of good or evil, and therefore in their yearly prediction fill the world with noises of wars, plagues, destruction and overthrows of kingdoms, monarchies, that to this said nothing at all, yet they will name the stars to be in all the fault....

I think it may be said of the plague, as is said of the wind, that it bloweth where it listeth, and we hear the sound thereof, but know not whence it cometh nor whether it goeth, but what things have occurred to men's weak observations I shall briefly set down, and so proceed.

Signs foreshowing a Plague coming are such as these, viz:

1. Times and seasons, altering from their common state.
2. Many changes of weather in a short time.
3. Comets, gleams of fire and fiery impressions in the air.
4. Increase of vermin, as frogs, toads, mice, flies, ants etc.
5. Death of cattle, as horses, sheep, hogs etc.
6. Famine; also war.
7. Children in sport fancying and aping out funerals.
8. South and west winds blowing long while together.
9. The smallpox or spotted fever growing very rife.
10. Extraordinary flowing and ebbing of springs and rivers.
11. Much cloudy weather without rain.
12. A very dry spring, such a one as we had six months together.
13. The nights very cold, and the days very hot, also a cold summer.
14. Birds, with foul and wild beasts leaving their accustomed places; few swallows were seen in the years 1664 and 65.
15. Women miscarrying upon every slight occasion.
16. Fruit corrupted or altered from its common taste or colour and goodness.
17. Ill conditions of the stars, if you will believe the astrologers.
18. The spotted fever growing rife; the measles and other epidemical diseases.
19. Generally any unusual change in the elements or creatures, whereby it seems nature to be out of course.
20. Change of the waters, frogs, lice, flies, murrain of cattle, boils and blains, extraordinary hail, and strange kinds of locusts preceded the Plague of Death of the first-born in Egypt....

I shall digress a little concerning the vanity and cruelty of people's unreasonable fear in all places, cities, towns, villages, single houses. Surely it is the great mistake which they have in them about the nature of the disease, which makes them egregiously fearful and consequently so uncharitable, superstitious and cruel. They have been wormed in the ears with so many lying stories and horrible relations, and having heard some hideous terms and frightening aphorisms as terrible Plague, noisome pestilence, burning pestilence and that common speech so often used in pulpits: 'Fly from sin as from a plague', and many such like expressions, which make many people believe the plague is like a basilisk or salamander, which kill all they see or touch. And therefore I would undeceive people as far as their vain fear will let me, which commonly is so great and sinful that it stops and shuts up all counsel, reason, charity, truth, etc., and makes people fall upon such vain and ridiculous courses.

What care was taken about letters: some would sift them in a sieve, some wash them first in water and then dry them at the fire, some air them at the top of a house, or a hedge, or a pole, two or three days before they opened them. Some would lay them between two cold stones two or three days, some set them before the fire like a toast, some would not receive them but on a long pole. A countryman delivered one thus to my wife at the shop door, because he would not venture too near her.

Concerning money, some would take none, becoming *mentis inops* [pitiable], growing modest (so that one would take them for saints, nothing idolizing the God of this world); but as soon as the supposed infection is over, shew themselves partial and returning to the old mire. Some would needs take it in water and wash it.

But for clothes, they were so gravelled that they would not once come near them if they came from London, especially linen and woollen. The same with cats, dogs, hogs, etc., and generally any thing that came near or out of London; which made them keep watch and ward so strictly, as if they would have kept the winds out of the town, forcing some to lie and die in ditches, and under hedges and trees, and there lie unburied for a prey to dogs and fowls of the air....

Some have stopped the keyholes of their doors, and avoided the occasions of action and communication with all people & creatures, yet have not their fears been more vain then the antidotes – foolish, superstitious, troublesome, weak and ridiculous – which some people have used and others appointed....

Mr Garencieres says the plague is the easiest disease in the world to cure, and so said Mr Stoakes the apothecary – though he dared not venture on it, but he is dead since. But whoever thinks, like Mr Garencieres, to cure 19 of 20 only with sweating or by taking of Venice treacle will miss their mark I believe....

Sweating was the most general course taken, yet were not other ways left unattempted by rude and ignorant people, as purging, vomiting, bleeding. For the physicians almost all going out of town left the poor people for a prey to these devouring blunt fellows, blind Bayards, who were very bold to turn doctors. These were all such timber-headed fellows that, notwithstanding their confident fearless familiarity, they could make no accurate observations at all which the physicians could easily have done had they the same courage, and the new upstart empirics made sad work both with people's bodies and purses, selling their idle medicines at an extraordinary dear rate.

One sold purging pills at half a crown a pill, and an ointment at 5d. an ounce, these also sold pomanders very dear and plasters 5 shillings a piece. One gave Mathews his pill to sweat, made with hellebore, opium, etc., which choked people. A wheelwright and a shoemaker used these. I happened into the company of one of them, who bragged much of a water he had. I asked him which way the water would effect the cure, and he told me by purging, vomiting and bleeding all at a time....

Diary of the Great Plague

SAMUEL PEPYS, London, 1665

The English naval administrator and celebrated diarist Samuel Pepys (1633–1703) remained in London in 1665 and at his desk throughout the epidemic. He recorded his own fears, his attempts to preserve himself, his family and his goods from the danger, his fascination with the detailed weekly death toll, and his response to the loss of so many friends and others who were close to him.

30 April Great fears of the sickness here in the City, it being said that two or three houses are already shut up. God preserve us all!

24 May Up, and by four o'clock in the morning, and with W. Hewer, there till 12 without intermission putting some papers in order. Thence to the coffee-house, where I have not been a great while, where all the news is of the Dutch being gone out, and of the plague growing upon us.

10 June In the evening home to supper; and there, to my great trouble, hear that the plague is come into the City (though it hath these three or four weeks since its beginning been wholly out of the City); but where should it begin but in my good friend and neighbour's, Dr Burnett, in Fenchurch Street: which in both points troubles me mightily. To the office to finish my letters and then home to bed, being troubled at the sickness, and my head filled also with other business enough, and particularly how to put my things and estate in order, in case it should please God to call me away, which God dispose of to his glory!

27 July At home met the weekly Bill, where above 1,000 increased in the Bill, and of them, in all about 1,700 of the plague.

28 July Set out with my Lady all alone with her with six horses to Dagenhams; going by water to the Ferry. And a pleasant going, and good discourse; and when there, very merry, and the young couple now well acquainted. But, Lord! to see in what fear all the people here do live would make one mad, they are afeared of us that come to them, insomuch that I am troubled at it, and wish myself away. But some cause they have; for the chaplain, with whom but a week or two ago we were here mighty high disputing, is since fallen into a fever and dead.

10 August In great trouble to see the Bill this week rise so high, to above 4,000 in all, and of them above 3,000 of the plague. And an odd story of Alderman Bence's stumbling at night over a dead corpse in the street, and going home and telling his wife, she at the fright, being with child, fell sick and died of the plague....

Thence to the office and, after writing letters, home, to draw over anew my will, which I had bound myself by oath to dispatch by tomorrow night; the town growing so unhealthy, that a man cannot depend upon living two days to an end. So having done something of it, I to bed.

11 August Back again and at my papers, and putting up my books into chests, and settling my house and all things in the best and speediest order I can, lest it should please God to take me away, or force me to leave my house.

12 August The people die so, that now it seems they are fain to carry the dead to be buried by daylight, the nights not sufficing to do it in. And my Lord Mayor commands people to be within at nine at night all, as they say, that the sick may have liberty to go abroad for air.

31 August Thus this month ends with great sadness upon the public, through the greatness of the plague everywhere through the kingdom almost. Every day sadder and sadder news of its increase. In the City died this week 7,496 and of them 6,102 of the plague. But it is feared that the true number of the dead, this week is near 10,000; partly from the poor that cannot be taken notice of, through the greatness of the number, and partly from the Quakers and others that will not have any bell ring for them.

3 September Up; and put on my coloured silk suit very fine, and my new periwig, bought a good while since, but durst not wear, because the plague was in Westminster when I bought it; and it is a wonder what will be the fashion after the plague is done, as to periwigs, for nobody will dare to buy any hair, for fear of the infection, that it had been cut off of the heads of people dead of the plague....

Church being done, my Lord Bruncker, Sir J. Minnes, and I up to the vestry...in order to the doing something for the keeping of the plague from growing; but Lord! to consider the madness of the people of the town, who will (because they are forbid) come in crowds along with the dead corpses to see them buried; but we agreed on some orders for the prevention thereof. Among other stories, one was very passionate, methought, of a complaint brought against a man for taking a child from London from an infected house. Alderman Hooker told us it was the child of a citizen in Gracious Street, a saddler, who had buried all the rest of his children of the plague, and himself and wife now being shut up and in despair of escaping, did desire only to save the life of this little child; and so prevailed to have it received stark-naked into the arms of a friend, who brought it (having put it into new fresh clothes) to Greenwich; where upon hearing the story, we did agree it should be permitted to be received and kept in the town.

4 September ... It troubled me to pass by Coombe farm where about twenty-one people have died of the plague, and three or four days since I saw a dead corpse in a coffin lie in the Close unburied, and a watch is constantly kept there night and day to keep the people in, the plague making us cruel, as dogs, one to another.

6 September … Strange to see in broad daylight two or three burials upon the Bankside, one at the very heels of another: doubtless all of the plague; and yet at least forty or fifty people going along with every one of them.

7 September Up by five of the clock, mighty full of fear of an ague, but was obliged to go, and so by water, wrapping myself up warm, to the Tower, and there sent for the Weekly Bill, and find 8,252 dead in all, and of them 6,878 of the plague; which is a most dreadful number, and shows reason to fear that the plague hath got that hold that it will yet continue among us.

10 September Walked home; being forced thereto by one of my watermen falling sick yesterday, and it was God's great mercy I did not go by water with them yesterday, for he fell sick on Saturday night, and it is to be feared of the plague. So I sent him away to London with his fellow.

14 September I away back again to the Bear at the Bridge foot, and there called for a biscuit and a piece of cheese and gill of sack, being forced to walk over the Bridge, toward the 'Change, and the plague being all thereabouts…. And Lord! to see how I did endeavour all I could to talk with as few as I could, there being now no observation of shutting up of houses infected, that to be sure we do converse and meet with people that have the plague upon them…. So home, and put up several things to carry to Woolwich, and upon serious thoughts I am advised…to let my money and plate rest there, as being as safe as any place, nobody imagining that people would leave money in their houses now, when all their families are gone. So for the present that being my opinion, I did leave them there still….

When I come home I spent some thoughts upon the occurrences of this day, giving matter for as much content on one hand and melancholy on another, as any day in all my life. For the first; the finding of my money and plate, and all safe at London, and speeding in my business of money this day. The hearing of this good news to such excess, after so great a despair of my Lord's doing anything this year; adding to that, the decrease of 500 and more, which is the first decrease we have yet had in the sickness since it begun: and great hopes that the next week it will be greater. Then, on the other side, my finding that though the Bill in general is abated, yet the City within the walls is increased, and likely to continue so, and is close to our house there. My meeting dead corpses of the plague, carried to be buried close to me at noon-day through the City in Fenchurch Street. To see a person sick of the sores, carried close by me by Gracechurch in a hackney-coach. My finding the Angel tavern, at the lower end of Tower Hill, shut up, and more than that, the alehouse at the Tower Stairs, and more than that, the person was then dying of the plague when I was last there, a little while ago, and I overheard the mistress of the house sadly saying to her husband somebody was very ill, but did not think it was of the plague. To hear that poor Payne, my waiter, hath buried a child, and is dying himself. To hear that a labourer I sent but the other day to Dagenhams, to know how they did there, is dead of the plague; and that one of my own watermen, that carried me daily, fell sick as soon as he had landed me on Friday morning last, when I had been all night upon the water...and is now dead of the plague.... And, lastly, that both my servants, W. Hewer and Tom Edwards, have lost their fathers, both in St Sepulchre's parish, of the plague this week, do put me into great apprehensions of melancholy, and with good reason. But I put off the thoughts of sadness as much as I can, and the rather to keep my wife in good heart and family also.

20 September Lord! what a sad time it is to see no boats upon the river; and grass grows all up and down White Hall court, and nobody but poor wretches in the streets! And, which is worst of all, the Duke showed us the number of the plague this week, brought in the last night from the Lord Mayor; that it is increased about 600 more than the last, which is quite contrary to all our hopes and expectations, from the coldness of the late season.

The argument for contagion

NATHANIEL HODGES, *Loimologia* (1672)

Nathaniel Hodges (1629–1688) was an English physician who, unlike many of his colleagues, remained in London during the plague and attended a large number of plague patients and victims. Like Boghurst and other medical experts, he was extremely concerned about the spread of misinformation and downright dangerous treatments offered by untrained quacks. He believed in separating the sick from the healthy, and that drinking sack, a fortified white wine, was an effective preventative measure against infection – a practice that he personally used successfully throughout the epidemic.

Since that the nature of this pest in relation to its primary cause is most obscure, we cannot more surely arrive at the knowledge of it than by the discoveries it makes of itself in propagation. When therefore I do well ponder the wonderful energy of pestilential effluviums, which can instantaneously imprint indelible characters on bodies before sound and healthful...I am induced to think that its principles are chiefly saline...I need not produce examples to illustrate the inexpressible vigour of these ferments, it being well known that many have died without the least sense of contagion or apprehension of illness thereby.

I come to the manner of the pest's invasion, which is unanimously agreed on to be by contagion, viz,. when venenate expirations are transmitted from infectious bodies to others working a like change and alteration in them; whereupon I conclude, that no person is seized with the plague except he receives into his body these pestilential effluxes, which however they do more effectually infect by how much nearer the bodies are, yet it is not to be doubted but that at a very considerable distance where no person is sick, these most malignant corpuscles being carried in the motion of the air, may so preserve their venom, as to surprise such bodies amid their greatest securities; and I am apt to think that such effects are oft-times appropriated to imagination, the operations of which can easily ferment the juices of the body, and raise symptoms not unlike those of the pest.

Notwithstanding that infection is so apparent in the pest, yet some have lately in their discourses and pamphlets argued that it is not contagious. Such persons deserve rather the magistrates' censure than my refutation. The Order published by the Queen Elizabeth was in those days the most proper expedient to suppress that opinion, which is not otherwise now than by authority to be silenced. These ground their hypotheses upon the escape of some persons who converse with the infected; but this proof is not admissible as sufficient, because there are very many causes why such bodies are not equally obnoxious to contagion as others; for besides the particular providence of God, the security of such persons may be attributed to the shape of their pores not admitting pestilential atoms of a disproportioned figure, or vigour of the spirits to expel this enemy before he can fix in their bodies. Such persons might as rationally affirm that bullets will not wound and kill, because some, in the hottest battles amid showers of small shot, walk untouched by any of them; when these escape rather upon the account of the various happy postures they are in during the charge, than their fancy of being shot-free.

A Journal of the Plague Year

DANIEL DEFOE, 1722

The journalist and novelist Daniel Defoe (c. 1660–1731) was a child at the time of the Great Plague, but his Journal of the Plague Year *provides a vivid and detailed insight into the months of the epidemic. Whether it was purely a work of fiction, or whether Defoe based his work on documentary or oral evidence has long been debated. The title page claims it was 'written by a citizen who continued all the while in London' whose initials are given as 'H.F.'. It seems likely that this was Defoe's uncle, Henry Foe. The book covers many aspects of London at the time, including detailed anecdotes, as well as descriptions of city life under lockdown.*

The face of London was now indeed strangely altered.... Sorrow and sadness sat upon every face; and though some parts were not yet overwhelmed, yet all looked deeply concerned; and, as we saw it apparently coming on, so every one looked on himself and his family as in the utmost danger.... London might well be said to be all in tears; the mourners did not go about the streets indeed, for nobody put on black or made a formal dress of mourning for their nearest friends; but the voice of mourners was truly heard in the streets. The shrieks of women and children at the windows and doors of their houses, where their dearest relations were perhaps dying, or just dead, were so frequent to be heard as we passed the streets, that it was enough to pierce the stoutest heart in the world to hear them....

It was a most surprising thing to see those streets which were usually so thronged now grown desolate, and so few people to be seen in them, that if I had been a stranger and at a loss for my way, I might sometimes have gone the length of a whole street, and seen nobody to direct me except watchmen set at the doors of such houses as were shut up. One day...I went up Holborn, and there the street was full of people, but they walked in the middle of the great street, neither on one side or other, because, as I suppose, they would not mingle with anybody that came out of houses, or meet with smells and scent from houses that might be infected....

While the fears of the people were young, they were increased strangely by several odd accidents which, put altogether, it was really a wonder the whole body of the people did not rise as one man and abandon their dwellings.... They were so many, and so many wizards and cunning people propagating them, that I have often wondered there was any (women especially) left behind.

In the first place, a blazing star or comet appeared for several months before the plague, as there did the year after another, a little before the fire. The old women and the phlegmatic hypochondriac part of the other sex whom I could almost call old women too, remarked that those two comets passed directly over the city, and that so very near the houses that it was plain they imported something peculiar to the city alone; that the comet before the pestilence was of a faint, dull, languid colour, and its motion very heavy, solemn and slow; but that the comet before the fire was bright and sparkling, or, as others said, flaming, and its motion swift and furious; and that, accordingly, one foretold a heavy judgment, slow but severe, terrible and frightful, as was the plague; but the other foretold a stroke, sudden, swift and fiery as the conflagration....

These things had a more than ordinary influence upon the minds of the common people, and they had almost universal melancholy apprehensions of some dreadful calamity and judgment coming upon the city.... The apprehensions of the people were likewise strangely increased by the error of the times; in which, I think, the people...were more addicted to prophecies and astrological conjurations, dreams and old wives' tales than ever they were before or since.... Books frightened them terribly, such as *Lilly's Almanack*, *Gadbury's Astrological Predictions*, *Poor Robin's Almanack* and the like; also several pretended religious books, one entitled, *Come out of her, my People, lest you be Partaker of her Plagues*; and many such, all, or most part of which, foretold...the ruin of the city. Nay, some were so enthusiastically bold as to run about the streets with their oral predictions, pretending they were sent to preach to the city; and one in particular, who, like Jonah to Nineveh, cried in the streets, 'Yet forty days, and London shall be destroyed.'... Another ran about naked, except a pair of drawers about his waist, crying day and night... 'Oh, the great and the dreadful God!' and said no more, but repeated those words continually, with a voice and countenance full of horror, a swift pace; and nobody could ever find him to stop or rest, or take any sustenance, at least that ever I could hear of....

Some endeavours were used to suppress the printing of such books as terrified the people, and to frighten the dispersers of them, some of whom were taken up; but nothing was done in it, as I am informed, the government being unwilling to exasperate the people, who were, as I may say, all out of their wits already.

Neither can I acquit those ministers that in their sermons rather sank than lifted up the hearts of their hearers.... We had some good men, and that of all persuasions and opinions, whose discourses were full of terror, who spoke nothing but dismal things; and as they brought the people together with a kind of horror, sent them away in tears, prophesying nothing but evil tidings, terrifying the people with the apprehensions of being utterly destroyed, not guiding them, at least not enough, to cry to heaven for mercy....

These things agitated the minds of the common people for many months, while the first apprehensions were upon them, and while the plague was not yet broken out. But the more serious part of the inhabitants behaved after another manner. The government encouraged their devotion, and appointed public prayers and days of fasting and humiliation, to make public confession of sin and implore the mercy of God to avert the dreadful judgment which hung over their heads....

But even those wholesome reflections...had a quite contrary extreme in the common people, who...were now led by their fright to extremes of folly...they ran to conjurers and witches, and all sorts of deceivers, to know what should become of them (who fed their fears, and kept them always alarmed and awake on purpose to delude them and pick their pockets), so they were as mad upon their running after quacks and mountebanks, and every practising old woman, for medicines and remedies; storing themselves with such multitudes of pills, potions and preservatives, as they were called, that they not only spent their money but even poisoned themselves beforehand for fear of the poison of the infection; and prepared their bodies for the plague, instead of preserving them against it....

The posts of houses and corners of streets were plastered over with doctors' bills and papers of ignorant fellows, quacking and tampering in physic, and inviting the people to come to them for remedies, which was generally set off with such flourishes as these, viz.: 'Infallible preventive pills against the plague.' 'Never-failing preservatives against the infection.' 'Sovereign cordials against the corruption of the air.' 'Exact regulations for the conduct of the body in case of an infection.' 'Anti-pestilential pills.' 'Incomparable drink against the plague, never found out before.'...

And here I must observe again, that this necessity of going out of our houses to buy provisions was in a great measure the ruin of the whole city, for the people caught the distemper on these occasions one of another, and even the provisions themselves were often tainted....

However, the poor people could not lay up provisions, and they must go to market to buy, and others to send servants or their children; and as this was a necessity which renewed itself daily, it brought abundance of unsound people to the markets, and a great many that went thither sound brought death home with them.

People used all possible precaution. When anyone bought a joint of meat in the market they would not take it off the butcher's hand, but took it off the hooks themselves. On the other hand, the butcher would not touch the money, but have it put into a pot full of vinegar, which he kept for that purpose. The buyer carried always small money to make up any odd sum, that they might take no change. They carried bottles of scents and perfumes in their hands, and all the means that could be used were used, but then the poor could not do even these things, and they went at all hazards....

All that had friends or estates in the country retired with their families; one would have thought the very city itself was running out of the gates and that there would be nobody left behind; from that hour all trade, except such as related to immediate subsistence, was, as it were, at a full stop.

For example:

1. All master-workmen in manufactures, especially such as belonged to ornament and the less necessary parts of the people's dress, clothes and furniture for houses, such as riband-weavers and other weavers, gold and silver lacemakers, and gold and silver wire drawers, seamstresses, milliners, shoemakers, hatmakers and glovemakers; also upholsterers, joiners, cabinetmakers, looking-glass makers and innumerable trades which depend upon

such as these; I say, the master-workmen in such stopped their work, dismissed their journeymen and workmen, and all their dependents.

2. As merchandising was at a full stop, very few ships ventured to come up the river and none at all went out, so all the extraordinary officers of the customs, likewise the watermen, carmen, porters and all the poor whose labour depended upon the merchants, were at once dismissed and put out of business.

3. All the tradesmen usually employed in building or repairing of houses were at a full stop, for the people were far from wanting to build houses when so many thousand houses were at once stripped of their inhabitants; so that this one article turned all the ordinary workmen of that kind out of business, such as bricklayers, masons, carpenters, joiners, plasterers, painters, glaziers, smiths, plumbers and all the labourers depending on such.

4. As navigation was at a stop, our ships neither coming in or going out as before, so the seamen were all out of employment, and many of them in the last and lowest degree of distress; and with the seamen were all the several tradesmen and workmen belonging to and depending upon the building and fitting out of ships, such as ship-carpenters, caulkers, ropemakers, dry coopers, sailmakers, anchor-smiths and other smiths; block-makers, carvers, gunsmiths, ship-chandlers, ship-carvers and the like. The masters of those perhaps might live upon their substance, but the traders were universally at a stop, and consequently all their workmen discharged. Add to these that the river was in a manner without boats, and all or most part of the watermen, lightermen, boat-builders and lighter-builders in like manner idle and laid by.

5. All families retrenched their living as much as possible, as well those that fled as those that stayed, so that an innumerable multitude of footmen, serving-men, shopkeepers, journeymen, merchants' bookkeepers and such sort of people, and especially poor maid-servants, were turned off, and left friendless and helpless, without employment and without habitation, and this was really a dismal article.

The plague in Marseilles

ANON, letter written from Marseilles, 1721

Following the 1665 epidemic in London, many theories were developed on the causes of the plague, some linking it strongly with poverty, and others claiming that it could not be bred in Britain but had to be imported from warmer climates. The 1720 eruption of plague in Marseilles in southern France matched that of London in severity, killing perhaps 100,000 people. In the resulting panic, the British Parliament quickly passed the Quarantine Act to prevent the epidemic reaching these shores. This anonymous description of the Marseilles outbreak – with its reminder that the spread of the disease resulted from the arrival and incautious treatment of an infected ship from the Levant – was written on New Years' Day, 1721 and published in Bristol later that year. The Marseilles outbreak turned out to be the last major visitation of the plague in western Europe.

This mortal distemper, the plague, wherewith this city has been thus visited, was unhappily brought among us by a ship from *Sidon* (a noted town near *Tyre*, in *Asia*, as mentioned in the *New Testament*) which came into our road the 15th of June last. The porters first employed in opening her cargo were immediately seized with violent pains in the head, reaching to vomit, and a general faintness all over their limbs and bodies; and in six or eight hours' time buboes and *plague sores* began to rise, of which they died in three days. Those that succeeded them were taken and died in the same manner.

Upon this, all the noted physicians and chirurgeons were summoned together by the magistrates, to consult the nature of the distemper, who all agreed that it was really the *plague*. However, proper care was not immediately taken; for, instead of burning the said ship and goods (which ought to have been done) the goods only were removed to a desert island, called *Jarre,* two leagues off, where all those that went to air them died suddenly of the same distemper. Several officers belonging to the ship were admitted to come into the city, and the sailors brought abundance of goods on shore by stealth, by which means a considerable *mortality* soon began to spread in that part of the town where they lodged.

Notwithstanding all this, proper care and remedies to prevent its fatal consequences were still neglected till the beginning of *August*, by which time the number of the infected was too great for the hospitals to contain, and they began to die a thousand in a day. The infection now being spread into all parts of the city, runs from one family to another like *wildfire,* so that 20 lied often dead at once in a house. And the worst of all is, that they cannot be buried, but lie in the houses or streets many days, which are full of dead bodies and bedding. 27 carts appointed to carry them out, not being sufficient.

The magistrates have been assisted with 500 galley slaves to clear the streets of the dead; yet there are still above 3,000 dead bodies that lie about the streets unburied, which cause an intolerable stench. And 'tis computed, that (in all) about 80,000 are dead of the plague, two thirds of which are observed to be women, most of 'em with child, whose died of the infection after miscarriages or lying-in, purely for want of help.

In short, the calamity is so bad, that the poor can hardly get even water, because none will go near them. The rich and able are gone into the country with all manner of provisions, and there is not a church or shop left open. So that we, who were but four months ago in so flourishing a condition, are now overwhelmed with misery.

Doctors wear protective uniforms outside a hospital in Fuchiatien, China, during the 'third plague pandemic'.

PART IV
CITIES, SCIENCE AND PUBLIC HEALTH

The 19th century saw an alarming increase in the appearance of epidemics of diseases such as cholera, yellow fever, typhus and typhoid, all associated with insanitary conditions in the crowded towns and cities of the industrial age, with large armies and with the intercontinental movement of refugees and poor migrants from the Old World to the New.

For as long as the causative agent of these diseases – and some older ones such as plague – was unknown, they proved lethal, but as the century progressed the development of professional institutions and a global scientific community allowed major steps to be taken in identifying the pathogens responsible, and in establishing more effective treatment and preventive measures, whether in the form of widespread vaccination, improved sanitation and clean water, and other public health measures. Taking their lead from George Washington and Napoleon, both of whom had inoculated their armies against smallpox, military authorities – who saw the value in keeping their men healthy and strong – were increasingly in the forefront of this work. As a result, by the mid-20th century many of the diseases that had blighted the previous century were on the decline in the West, and efforts to combat them had moved to the Third World.

Similarly, the parasite that causes the common endemic disease malaria (the very name of which – 'bad air' – points to the miasmic theory of disease), was identified by a French army doctor in the 1880s, and the role of the mosquito in its transmission by a young British doctor in India, Ronald Ross, in 1897. This paved the way for campaigns to eradicate it using insecticides and draining swamps, but malaria still kills more than half a million people each year.

CHOLERA

During the 19th century, the growth of crowded, unsanitary cities, and the emergence of the mass movement of peoples across the globe – whether for imperialist reasons or as migrants seeking a new life – meant that cholera, which could spread quickly through a population and kill its victims in a matter of hours, became perhaps the most feared disease of all.

Long endemic to the Ganges region of India, cholera has seen seven distinct epidemics that have spread across the globe, the first (1817–24) beginning in Bengal and the last (1961–75) in Indonesia; the death rate could be as high as 50 per cent of those infected. The third pandemic (1852–60) killed up to a million people in Russia alone. Localized outbreaks continue to occur – for example, after the earthquake in Haiti in 2010 – and infect several million people each year, though the disease has been less deadly since the development of antibiotics and effective treatment regimes.

The appearance of cholera in Britain in the 1830s was a major contributor to the development of a public health service, with the establishment of, first, local boards and then a national Board of Health, which led the world in sanitary reform to provide clean water and safe sewage disposal for Britain's unhealthily crowded cities.

The question of how cholera spread, and whether it was contagious or spread through a miasma, remained a contentious one, even after the *Vibrio cholerae* bacterium was identified, separately, by Filippo Pacini in Italy (1854) and Robert Koch in Germany (1883). It is now known that cholera is transmitted in unsafe water and in poorly prepared food contaminated with faeces containing the bacterium.

It suddenly destroys the vigour of life

SANSKRIT TEXT, Tibet, early 9th century AD

This medical text, written in Sanskrit and believed to have been written in Tibet during the early 9th century AD, described the symptoms of cholera, which it called 'nja'.

When the strength of virtues and merits decreases on earth, there appear among the people, first among those living on the shores of big rivers,

various ailments which give no time for treatment, but prove fatal immediately after they appear. At times the *nja* carries away the fourth part of
the *Dschambudwip* [region of ancient Tibet]. It suddenly destroys the vigour
of life and changes the warmth of the body into cold, but sometimes this
changes back into heat. The various vessels secrete water so that the body
becomes empty. The disease is propagated by contact and infection. The
nja kills invariably. Its first signs are dizziness, a numb feeling in the head,
then most violent purging and vomiting.

Moryxy in India

GASPAR CORREA, *Legends of India* (1543)

*The first description of the disease by a European is found in the writings
of the Portuguese historian Gaspar Correa (c. 1492–1563), who lived for
much of his life in India. He wrote the history of the Portuguese explorer
Vasco da Gama in 1498, and studied Indian legends and folklore, in his*
Legends of India. *He named the disease 'moryxy'.*

So grievous were the throes, and so bad a sort that the very worst poison
seemed there to take effect, as proved by vomiting, with drought of water
accompanying it as if the stomach were parched up, and cramps that fixed
in the sinews of the joints and flat of the foot with pain so extreme that
the sufferer seemed at the point of death, the eyes dimmed to sense and
the nails of the hands and feet become black and arched.

No one felt himself safe for an hour

H. H. WILSON, *History of British India 1805–1835*, Volume II (1846)

*The English doctor and orientalist scholar H. H. Wilson (1786–1860)
worked in India until 1832 when he became professor of Sanskrit at
Oxford. He described the initial outbreak of cholera in 1817 in his* History
of British India.

The malady known by the name of spasmodic cholera, evacuations of acrid
bilious matter accompanied by spasmodic contractions of the abdominal
muscles and a prostration of strength terminating frequently in the total
exhaustion of the vital functions, had been known in India from the
remotest periods and had, at times, committed fearful ravages. Its effects,

however, were in general restricted to particular seasons and localities and were not so extensively diffused as to attract notice or excite alarm. In the middle of 1817, however, the disease assumed a new form and became a widely spread and fatal epidemic. It made its first appearance in the eastern districts of Bengal in May and June of that year, and after extending itself gradually along the north bank of the Ganges, it crossed the river and passing through Rewa, fell with particular virulence upon the centre division of the grand army in the first week of November.

After creeping insidiously for several days among the lower classes of the camp followers and engaging little observation, it at once burst forth with irresistible violence and by the 14th of the month had overspread every part of the camp. Although the casualties were most numerous among the followers of the camp and the native soldiery, the ravages of the disease were not confined to the natives but extended to Europeans of every rank. The appalling features of the malady were the suddenness of its accession and the rapidity with which death ensued. No one felt himself safe for an hour, and yet, as there was no appearance of infection, the officers generally were active in assisting the medical establishment in administering medicines and relief to the sick.

The whole camp put on the character of a hospital: a mournful silence succeeded to the animating notes of preparation which had hitherto resounded among the tents; in place of the brisk march of soldiers in the confidence of vigour and in the pride of discipline, were to be seen continuous and slowly moving trains of downcast mourners, carrying their comrades to the funeral pyre and expecting that their own turn would not be long delayed. Even this spectacle ceased; the mortality became so great that hands were insufficient to carry away the bodies and they were tossed into the neighbouring ravines or hastily committed to a superficial grave on the spots where the sick had expired. The survivors then took alarm and deserted the encampment in crowds; many bore with them the seeds of the malady and the fields and roads for many miles around were strewed with the dead.

Death and desertion were rapidly depopulating the camp, when, after a few days of unavailing struggle against the epidemic, it was determined to try the effects of a change of situation. The army accordingly retrograded in a south-easterly direction, crossed the Betwa and, encamping upon its lofty and dry banks at Erich, was relieved from the pestilence. The disease disappeared. During the week of its greatest malignity it was ascertained that seven hundred and sixty-four fighting men and eight thousand followers died.

Native remedies were of a frivolous or pernicious nature

JAMES JAMESON, *Report on the Epidemick Cholera Morbus* (1820)

In 1820, James Jameson, a British doctor working for the Bengal Medical Board, produced a report on the 1817–19 epidemic in Bengal in which he contrasted the Western medical orthodoxy, which prescribed bloodletting, enemas, castor oil, opium, brandy and plugging of the anus, with the traditional Indian treatment of the disease (salt, water and opium). Rehydration treatment for cholera using salt, sugar and water became common only in the 20th century.

In the early periods of the epidemic, the generality of the Native patients were brought in, either moribund, or in such a stale of exhaustion, as to render all attempts at bleeding useless. But, even at a later period, when the Natives, having become sensible of the great danger of delay, applied for assistance soon after the commencement of the attack, venesection [taking blood from a vein] was usually impracticable. Whether from the greater violence of the disorder in this quarter, or from the constitution of this class of persons being more readily depressed, than that of Europeans, the powers of life appeared to be in them almost immediately extinguished, and universal collapse soon took place. An entire stop seemed to be put to the circulation and the blood wholly forsook the superficial veins.... In such cases the strongest stimulants seemed necessary to revive the sinking powers; and all, accordingly, placed their main dependence on powerful and repeated doses of ether, brandy, oil of peppermint, camphor, with laudanum, calomel [mercury oxide, used as a purgative], blisters and other topical means. That these were often successful, it cannot be doubted; but still they so frequently failed, as to convince the most sensible observers that, bleeding among Europeans being alone excepted, but little confidence was to be placed on any mode of treatment hitherto discovered and that the disease often attacked with such awfully fatal violence, as to baffle all human skill.

Every enquiry into the practice followed by the Natives, in resisting this most formidable disease, has only tended to shew, that wherever they departed from the methods usually pursued by European practitioners, the remedies used by them were either of a frivolous, or of a pernicious nature. In the Muhammadan cities of Upper India, the Native physicians adhered to the rules laid down by the writers of the Arabian school; and after cleansing the *primae viae* [the digestive tract] of their noxious secretions, by means of salt and water, and mild diluents and then had recourse to opium. This practice was tried very successfully by the Native doctor with Colonel Skinner's Horse at Shapoor in Rajpootana in the autumn of 1818. Every man was as soon as taken ill, vomited with salt and water, and then had opiates; and although the Corps was largely affected, not a single death occurred. They were then given spices: cardamoms and the different sorts of pepper. Sometimes they used preparations of lime, decoctions of the bark of the Neem tree and other powerful astringents. Where, again, the judgment of the medical attendant was warped by some absurd theory of the malady originating in great internal heat, he placed his chief dependence on cold drinks, and killed his patient with deluges of rose water and lemonade. And, as if these were not sufficiently speedy in their operation, he often stripped the sufferer completely naked, and having rubbed his body over with dust of sandal wood, kept fanning him, until the little heat and life remaining, was extinguished. But, the great mass of the people expressed by their conduct how fully they were convinced of the inutility of all human aid to subdue the calamity; for no sooner did the disease appear, than they fled for assistance to their offended deities, and allowed the sufferer to expire amid their unavailing prayers and incantations. Latterly, however, when they saw their superstitions fail them, men even of the highest castes, throwing off all their religious prejudices, applied to the European practitioners, and learnt to place their faith in the only means which have been yet found in any measure adequate to resist the attack.

The eyes of many were shut by dogma

JAMES COPLAND, *Of Pestilential Cholera: Its Nature, Prevention, and Curative Treatment* (1832)

The Scottish physician and medical writer James Copland (1791–1870) was a proponent of 'contingent contagionism', an approach to infection that believed that a disease might be contagious under fetid atmospheric conditions but not in 'pure air'. He published his views on cholera – and the responsibilities of the authorities to take steps to prevent its spread – in 1832, at a time the second epidemic was reaching many British cities.

The eyes of many were shut by previously entertained dogmas on the subject of contagion, and several, even when they were arguing against its existence, were actually adducing important facts in support of what I have been cautiously led to believe in, namely that the disease manifested a tendency to propagate itself by means of a morbid effluvium exhaled from the bodies of the affected, similar to what is evinced by measles and fevers whose infectious properties have been well ascertained and generally admitted.

It appears extremely singular that, notwithstanding the evidence which has now been quoted, no means of preventing the propagation of the malady were resorted to during the number of years it has existed in the east. Surely the doubts even of the sceptical ought to have led to a careful enquiry; and most certainly the natives of the country, and the European population under the British dominion, had even a *right* to expect that those placed to watch over their health and to devise measures for its preservation would have attended to the unequivocal opinions expressed by a number of the best informed medical officers in the service.... At all events, the error – if error it could be called – should have been on the safe side, and the Medical Boards, superintending surgeons or others to whom the duty appertained, should have pointed out the importance of preventative measures....

That no precautions of any description were taken in India to prevent the extension of the disease may be stated without any reservation; and hence most probably the reason of its extension over so very large a portion of the whole globe.

Liverpool's cholera riots

Liverpool Chronicle, June 1832

Among the cities to be affected by cholera for the first time in 1831–32 were Newcastle, Liverpool and London. In Liverpool, several week of riots ensued, involving both those who feared the disease, and those who believed that the hospitalization of the poor was an excuse by the medical profession to acquire bodies for dissection (the 'Burke and Hare' scandal, in which two men in Edinburgh had murdered several victims for just this purpose, had broken just a few years previously). Eventually the Catholic Church, powerful in the city, was able to restore order and confidence in the medical authorities.

1 June Stones and brickbats were thrown at the premises of the Cholera Hospital, several windows were broken, even in the room where the woman, now in a dying state, was lying, and the medical gentleman who was attending her was obliged to seek safety in flight. Several individuals were pursued and attacked by the mob and some hurt. The park constables were apparently panic struck, and incapable of acting.

A poor woman who had been seen coming out of the Cholera Hospital yard in Lime Street was attacked by a crowd, who threw mud at her exclaiming that she was a 'Burker'. The mob followed her into Islington where she escaped from her ignorant and brutal pursuers by taking refuge in the yard of Mr Whitter, the joiner, the gates of which were instantly shut.

11 June We the pastors of the Catholic congregations in Liverpool, feel it incumbent on us to offer you a few words of advice on the subject of the melancholy disease which has made its appearance among us.... We have, for some time past, witnessed with regret the line of conduct which some of you have thought proper to adopt in respect of the disease just mentioned....

We understand that some of you disbelieve entirely the existence, in this town, of the disease but too well known by the name of the cholera, and that you suppose it to be the pure invention of interested persons; while others among you who are sensible of the disease imagine that the medical men wilfully concur in rendering it ravages more fatal for some horrible but unknown purpose. In both of these opinions you are greatly in error.

Kitty Wilkinson, the 'saint of the slums'

JAMES NEWLAND, 1856

As the 1831–32 cholera epidemic in Liverpool progressed, a more benign popular perception arose, built around the saintly figure of Kitty Wilkinson, a housewife who helped the poorest by doing their laundry despite the dangers. James Newland, a Liverpool borough engineer, wrote in 1856:

In 1832 when the cholera ravaged the town, the necessity of cleanliness as a means of arresting or abating the plague became apparent; but poor families huddled, healthy and sick together, often in a single apartment, and that an underground cellar, had not the means for personal cleanliness and still less for washing their clothes and bedding, and thus nothing could be done by them to prevent the spreading of the infection. It was left to one of their own class and station, Mrs Catherine Wilkinson of Frederick Street, Liverpool, to provide a remedy. She, the wife of a labourer, living in one of the worst and most crowded slums of the town, allowed her poorer neighbours, destitute of the means of heating water, to wash their clothes in the back kitchen of her humble abode, and to dry them in the covered passage and backyard belonging to it.

Aided by the District Provident Society, and some benevolent women, this courageous self-denying woman contrived to provide the washing of, on an average, 85 families per week. Poor people contributed one penny per week towards the running expenses....

Here then was the germ of public wash-houses, institutions called into existence as a means of palliating a great evil.

The Broad Street pump

JOHN SNOW, *On the Mode of Communication of Cholera* (1855)

London's 1855 cholera outbreak was the worst that the city experienced, claiming over three thousand lives, but it provided the opportunity for a groundbreaking work of epidemiological research by doctor John Snow (1813–1858). His detailed study of a major outbreak of cholera close to his home in Soho allowed him to identify a particular water pump as the source of the infection; after having the pump handle removed, the outbreak ended. Snow was a proponent of the germ theory of disease, and his microscopic analysis of the water revealed the presence of various impurities, some of them organic. (The bacterium Vibrio chol-erae, *responsible for the disease, had been isolated the previous year by Filippo Pacini in Italy; however, Snow was not aware of this.) It was later discovered that the well that Snow had identified had been con-taminated by a nearby cesspit.*

The 1855 cholera outbreak, followed three years later by the 'Great Stink' – the result of untreated sewage in the river Thames in hot weather – led to the construction of London's comprehensive sewerage system by Joseph Bazalgette, which ended the threat of cholera in the city.

The most terrible outbreak of cholera which ever occurred in this kingdom, is probably that which took place in Broad Street, Golden Square, and the adjoining streets, a few weeks ago. Within two hundred and fifty yards of the spot where Cambridge Street joins Broad Street, there were upwards of five hundred fatal attacks of cholera in ten days. The mortality in this limited area probably equals any that was ever caused in this country, even by the plague; and it was much more sudden, as the greater number of cases terminated in a few hours. The mortality would undoubtedly have been much greater had it not been for the flight of the population. Persons in furnished lodgings left first, then other lodgers went away, leaving their furniture to be sent for when they could meet with a place to put it in....

There were a few cases of cholera in the neighbourhood of Broad Street, Golden Square, in the latter part of August; and the so-called outbreak, which commenced in the night between the 31st August and the 1st September, was, as in all similar instances, only a violent increase of the malady. As soon as I became acquainted with the situation and extent of this irruption of cholera, I suspected some contamination of the water of the much-frequented street-pump in Broad Street, near the end of Cambridge Street, but on examining the water, on the evening of the 3rd September, I found so little impurity in it of an organic nature, that I hesitated to come to a conclusion. Further inquiry, however, showed me that there was no other circumstance or agent common to the circum-scribed locality in which this sudden increase of cholera occurred, and not extending beyond it, except the water of the above-mentioned pump. I found, moreover, that the water varied, during the next two days, in the amount of organic impurity, visible to the naked eye, on close inspection, in the form of small white, flocculent particles; and I concluded that, at the commencement of the outbreak, it might possibly have been still more impure.

I requested permission, therefore, to take a list, at the General Register Office, of the deaths from cholera, registered during the week ending 2nd September, in the sub-districts of Golden Square, Berwick Street and St Ann's, Soho. Eighty-nine deaths from cholera were registered, during the week....

On proceeding to the spot, I found that nearly all the deaths had taken place within a short distance of the pump. There were only ten deaths in houses situated decidedly nearer to another street pump. In five of these cases the families of the deceased persons informed me that they always sent to the pump in Broad Street, as they preferred the water to that of the pump which was nearer. In three other cases, the deceased were children who went to school near the pump in Broad Street. Two of them were known to drink the water; and the parents of the third think it probable that it did so....

With regard to the deaths occurring in the locality belonging to the pump, there were sixty-one instances in which I was informed that the deceased persons used to drink the pump-water from Broad Street, either constantly or occasionally. In six instances I could get no information, owing to the death or departure of everyone connected with the deceased individuals; and in six cases I was informed that the deceased persons did not drink the pump-water before their illness.

The result of the inquiry then was, that there had been no particular outbreak or increase of cholera, in this part of London, except among the persons who were in the habit of drinking the water of the above-mentioned pump-well.

I had an interview with the Board of Guardians of St James's parish, on the evening of Thursday, 7th September, and represented the above circumstances to them. In consequence of what I said, the handle of the pump was removed on the following day....

The water [from the well] was used for mixing with spirits in all the public houses around. It was used likewise at dining-rooms and coffee-shops. The keeper of a coffee-shop...which was frequented by mechanics, and where the pump-water was supplied at dinner time, informed me that she was already aware of nine of her customers who were dead. The pump-water was also sold in various little shops, with a teaspoonful of effervescing powder in it, under the name of sherbet; and it may have been distributed in various other ways. The pump was frequented much more than is usual, even for a London pump in a populous neighbourhood....

The limited district in which this outbreak of cholera occurred, contains a great variety in the quality of the streets and houses; Poland Street and Great Pulteney Street consisting in a great measure of private houses occupied by one family, while Husband Street and Peter Street are occupied chiefly by the poor Irish. The remaining streets are intermediate in point of respectability. The mortality appears to have fallen pretty equally among all classes, in proportion to their numbers. Masters are not distinguished from journeymen in the registration returns of this district, but, judging from my own observation, I consider that out of rather more than six hundred deaths, there were about one hundred in the families of tradesmen and other resident householders. One hundred and five persons who had been removed from this district died in Middlesex, University College, and other hospitals, and two hundred and six persons were buried at the expense of St James's parish; the latter number includes many of those who died in the hospitals, and a great number who were far from being paupers, and would on any other occasion have been buried by their friends, who, at this time, were either not aware of the calamity or were themselves overwhelmed by it. The greatest portion of the persons who died were tailors and other operatives, who worked for the shops about Bond Street and Regent Street, and the wives and children of these operatives....

There is no doubt that the mortality was much diminished, as I said before, by the flight of the population, which commenced soon after the outbreak; but the attacks had so far diminished before the use of the water was stopped, that it is impossible to decide whether the well still contained the cholera poison in an active state, or whether, from some cause, the water had become free from it. The pump-well has been opened, and I was informed by Mr Farrell, the superintendent of the works, that there was no hole or crevice in the brickwork of the well, by which any impurity might enter; consequently in this respect the contamination of the water is not made out by the kind of physical evidence detailed in some of the instances previously related. I understand that the well is from twenty-eight to thirty feet in depth, and goes through the gravel to the surface of the clay beneath. The sewer, which passes within a few yards of the well, is twenty-two feet below the surface. The water at the time of the cholera contained impurities of an organic nature, in the form of minute whitish flocculi, visible on close inspection to the naked eye, as I before stated. Dr Hassall, who was good enough to examine some of this water with the microscope, informed me that these particles had no organized structure, and that he thought they probably resulted from decomposition of other matter. He found a great number of very minute oval animalcules in the water, which are of no importance, except as an additional proof that the water contained organic matter on which they lived. The water also contained a large quantity of chlorides, indicating, no doubt, the impure sources from which the spring is supplied....

We must conclude from this outbreak that the quantity of morbid matter which is sufficient to produce cholera is inconceivably small, and that the shallow pump-wells in a town cannot be looked on with too much suspicion, whatever their local reputation may be.

Many persons were inclined to attribute the severity of the malady in this locality to the very circumstance to which some people attribute the comparative immunity of the city of London from the same disease, viz., to the drains in the neighbourhood having been disturbed and put in order about half a year previously. Mr Bazalgette, however, pointed out, in a report to the commissioners, that the streets in which the new sewers had been made suffered less than the others; and a reference to the map will show that this is correct, for I recollect that the streets in which the sewers were repaired about February last, were Brewer Street, Little Pulteney Street and Dean Street, Soho.

The bacterium identified

ROBERT KOCH, *On the Bacteriological Diagnosis of Cholera, Water Filtration and Cholera* (1894)

The German physician and bacteriologist Robert Koch (1843–1910) had identified the agents responsible for anthrax and tuberculosis before studying cholera in Egypt and India in 1883. Unaware of the work of Filippo Pacini some thirty years earlier, he isolated Vibrio cholerae *in*

Calcutta. Despite his eminence in the field, he still faced hostility from
proponents of the miasmatic theory. This extract is taken from his study
of an outbreak in Hamburg and other German cities in 1892–93.

Soon after the cholera-bacteria and their relations to cholera became known, opposition arose in various quarters to the opinion that these bacteria were the exclusive concomitants of cholera, and might be turned to account in its diagnosis. I may remind the reader that people professed to have found the same bacteria in the mucus of the teeth of healthy persons, in the water of districts free of cholera, in cholera nostras, etc; but I may also remind him that these statements were very soon refuted. As moreover the regular occurrence of the cholera-bacteria in genuine Asiatic cholera was confirmed a thousand times over in several epidemics which developed in the following years in France, Italy, Spain and South America, and as all the experience of the present epidemic has taught the same, we may now, I think, regard it as an ascertained fact that the cholera-bacteria are the inseparable concomitants of Asiatic cholera, and that the demonstration of their presence is an infallible proof of the presence of this disease. So far as I know, this proposition is no longer disputed by anyone whose opinion deserves serious consideration. That in my eyes, and in the eyes of everyone who possesses an adequate knowledge of bacteriology and of the nature of infectious diseases, the proof of the specific character of the cholera-bacteria is at the same time a proof that they are the cause of cholera, need hardly, I think, be expressly stated at this time of day; and I do state it here once more only because, strange to say, there still are medical men who doubt the causative relation between cholera-bacteria and cholera, though they cannot give even the semblance of a proof of any other relation between these two inseparably connected things....

The proper field of bacteriological work is the beginning and the end of an epidemic, when all depends on the correct judging of each individual case, and the swiftest possible prevention of danger to the neighbourhood. In former times the beginning and end of a local epidemic could hardly ever be recognized with the necessary certainty; they were to a certain extent veiled, so that one could indeed trace the rude lines of the epidemic proper, but generally lost the thread towards the beginning and the end. Hence too it came that the first measures were taken too late, and, when the epidemic began to abate, the efforts to combat it were stopped much too early. A material change has taken place in these respects. In the highly complicated net which cholera forms in its ways and in its spread only isolated threads still remain hidden to us; all the rest, to the tiniest off-shoots, lies clear and distinct before our eyes. Now at last we can oppose the pestilence step by step, and combat it when it is small and weak, that is, when the prospect of success is greatest; and the course the present epidemic in Germany has hitherto taken has shown the high utility of this kind of cholera-prophylaxis, directed against individual cases, beyond a doubt.

Cholera to Come

Toronto Evening News, headlines, 1892
The fifth cholera epidemic (1881–96), claimed hundreds of thousands of lives in Russia, Spain and Germany. At a time when migration of the 'poor, huddled masses' from the Old World to the New was approaching its peak, some in the United States and Canada feared that the immigrants would disastrously bring the disease with them. This fear was directed above all at eastern European and Russian Jews. Toronto in Canada was typical in anticipating this threat with dread. Through the autumn of 1892, the Toronto Evening News *ran a long string of scare stories about the imminent danger, and about Canada's lack of preparedness. In the event, no epidemic materialized.*

IS THIS DREAD CHOLERA?
CHOLERA MAY COME
NEW YORK IS READY
CHOLERA TO COME NEXT YEAR
WATCH JEWISH IMMIGRANTS
CHOLERA IS IN ENGLAND
THE PLAGUE'S PATH
WAKE UP, TORONTO
GROSSE ISLAND CONDEMNED
BARRIER AT DETROIT
THOSE JEWS COMING TO CANADA
QUEBEC CLOSES ITS DOORS

KEEP AWAY FROM US
GUARDING THE FRONTIER
IS CHOLERA HERE?
A VOYAGE OF HORROR
FEAR IT'S CHOLERA
TORONTO IS READY TO CLEAN THE CESSPOOL

An eminently controllable disease

ALY TEWFIK SHOUSHA, *Cholera Epidemic in Egypt in 1947* (1947)

An official at the ministry of public health in Cairo, Aly Tewfik Shousha (1930–2002) expressed his concern at the international response to an outbreak of cholera in Alexandria in 1947. He argued for rational international protocols for responding to such outbreaks and was a founder member of the World Health Organization, which was established the following year.

In Alexandria, the very crowded old quarter, where a large number of poor and middle-class people resides, suffered much. The houses in this quarter, which contain the worst slums in the city, leave much to be desired. On the other hand, it is interesting to note that practically no cholera cases occurred in Ramleh, which is the best quarter in the city and mostly the residence of the rich and more enlightened. Its sanitation attains a very high level. The incidence of cholera was highest in farms and lowest in towns. This was due to higher standards of living and education, and better hygienic conditions, in towns as compared with villages and farms. Absence of administrative machinery in the case of small farms also played a part.

During the epidemic, restrictive measures far exceeding the provisions of the international sanitary conventions were taken. Certain countries, and not always those at risk, actually closed their frontiers to all passengers and goods coming from Egypt. One country, after a short interval, abruptly forbade admittance to passengers and even mail from Egypt. Another, after requiring sea and air traffic from Egypt to call at specified places, ended by suspending all such traffic. A third country prohibited the importation of all foodstuffs, not only from Egypt, but from eight countries 'threatened' with cholera. Other countries prohibited not only foodstuffs, but also Egyptian cotton, forgetting the fact that they had been importing for years jute from Bengal and rice from China and Indo-China, the main endemic and epidemic centres of cholera, without any evil consequence. It seems that what had happened was not an application of existing conventions, but a partial return to the 'quarantine of the jungle', as *The Lancet* called it. International control, as provided for in the conventions, ought not to be set at naught and disregarded on the principle of each country for itself.

The problem of primary importance in the epidemiology of cholera is the existence of areas in which cholera is permanently present. These endemic centres form a menace to adjoining areas, for which they constitute a continuous reservoir of infection. The areas in which cholera is endemic are few in number and limited to certain parts of India and China. The major true endemic centres are lower Bengal and the Yangtse Valley. Other probable endemic areas are a portion of central and southern Madras, Burma and the Philippines. Cholera is eminently a controllable disease. A high degree of success has been attained in preventing its spread from the endemic areas by the application of quarantine and other sanitary measures.... The application of a long-term policy of sanitary improvement in the known endemic areas...would in time result in a great reduction of risk, and might even succeed in eventually eliminating infection altogether. If such a policy were adopted by the World Health Organization, cholera might be eradicated in the same way as certain species of vectors have been eradicated from some countries.

YELLOW FEVER

Yellow fever, a viral disease transmitted by mosquitoes and named for the yellow skin that results from liver damage, is primarily found in tropical regions, and despite the development of an effective vaccine in the 1930s it is still responsible for up to 50,000 deaths a year, mainly in Africa, where the disease originated. It was taken to the Americas by enslaved Africans in the 17th century and was much feared by sailors. In North America, several epidemics occurred through the 18th and 19th centuries; most were short-lived, ending at the onset of colder weather. Outbreaks also occurred occasionally in Europe: in 1821 an outbreak in Barcelona led the French to send an army to close the border by setting up what became known as a '*cordon sanitaire*' (medical quarantine area).

By 1800 yellow fever had become endemic in tropical regions of Central America and it proved a serious threat to imperialist expansion in the region. Napoleon's armies in the Caribbean lost many men to the disease and this may have contributed to his abandonment of any ambitions in the region and his consequent decision to sell French lands in North America to the United States in 1803. Yellow fever also cost many lives in the initial work on the Panama Canal by a French company in the 1880s and 1890s. The US Army therefore made serious efforts to understand the disease and successfully identified mosquitoes as the vectors, a discovery that made possible the completion of the canal under US auspices after 1904. Large-scale vaccination programmes in the 1940s and 1960s reduced the threat of the disease in many areas.

Yellow fever follows revolution

SAMUEL BRECK, account of the epidemic in Philadelphia, 1793

In the summer and autumn of 1793, some 5,000 people died and another 20,000 (almost half the population) left the city of Philadelphia, the capital of the young United States. The epidemic, identified as yellow fever by physician and humanitarian Dr Benjamin Rush (1746–1813), was perhaps brought to the city by refugees from the revolution that had begun in Saint-Domingue (Haiti) two years earlier. Samuel Breck (1771–1862) was the son of a wealthy merchant and became a leading churchman in the city.

I had scarcely become settled in Philadelphia when in July 1793, the yellow fever broke out, and, spreading rapidly in August, obliged all the citizens who could remove to seek safety in the country. My father took his family to Bristol on the Delaware, and in the last of August I followed him…I was compelled to return to the city on the 8th September, and spend the 9th there. Everything looked gloomy, and forty-five deaths were reported for the 9th. And yet it was nothing then to what it became three or four weeks later, when from the first to the twelfth of October one thousand persons died. On the twelfth a smart frost came and checked its ravages.

The horrors of this memorable affliction were extensive and heart rending. Nor were they softened by professional skill. The disorder was in a great measure a stranger to our climate, and was awkwardly treated. Its rapid march, being from ten victims a day in August to one hundred a day in October, terrified the physicians, and led them into contradictory modes of treatment. They, as well as the guardians of the city, were taken by surprise. No hospitals or hospital stores were in readiness to alleviate the sufferings of the poor. For a long time nothing could be done other than to furnish coffins for the dead and men to bury them. At length a large house in the neighborhood was appropriately fitted up for the reception of patients, and a few pre-eminent philanthropists volunteered to superintend it. At the head of them was Stephen Girard, who has since become the richest man in America.

In private families the parents, the children, the domestics lingered and died, frequently without assistance. The wealthy soon fled; the fearless or indifferent remained from choice, the poor from necessity. The inhabitants were reduced thus to one half their number, yet the malignant action of the disease increased, so that those who were in health one day were buried the next. The burning fever occasioned paroxysms of rage which drove the patient naked from his bed to the street, and in some instances to the river, where he was drowned. Insanity was often the last stage of its horrors.

We sought not fee nor reward

RICHARD ALLEN and ABSALOM JONES, account of Philadelphia epidemic, 1794

Many people in Africa, exposed to yellow fever from childhood, had developed a degree of natural immunity to the disease, and some physicians wrongly believed this to be a racial characteristic. In 1793, Dr Benjamin Rush therefore urged the free black community in Philadelphia to volunteer to assist and nurse their white fellow citizens. The Free African Society, led by Richard Allen and Absalom Jones, agreed to help; around 250 of its members died.

Early in September, a solicitation appeared in the public papers, to the people of colour to come forward and assist the distressed, perishing and neglected sick; with a kind of assurance, that people of our colour were not liable to take the infection. Upon which we and a few others met and consulted how to act on so truly alarming and melancholy occasion. After some conversation, we found a freedom to go forth, confiding in Him who can preserve in the midst of a burning fiery furnace, sensible that it was our duty to do all the good we could to our suffering fellow mortals. We set out to see where we could be useful. The first we visited was a man in Emsley's alley, who was dying, and his wife lay dead at the time in the house, there were none to assist but two poor helpless children. We administered what relief we could, and applied to the overseers of the poor to have the woman buried. We visited upwards of twenty families that day – they were scenes of woe indeed! The Lord was plentiful to strengthen us, and removed all fear from us....

In order the better to regulate our conduct, we called on the mayor the next day, to consult with him on how to proceed, so as to be the most useful. The first object he recommended was a strict attention to the sick, and the procuring of nurses. This was attended to by Absalom Jones and William Gray; and, in order that the distressed might know where to apply, the mayor advised that upon application to them they would be supplied. Soon after, the mortality increased, the difficulty of getting a corpse taken away, was such, that few were willing to do it, when offered great rewards. The black people were looked to. We then offered our services in the public papers, by advertising that we would remove the dead and procure nurses. Our services were the production of real sensibility – we sought not fee nor reward, until the increase of the disorder rendered our labour so arduous that we were not adequate to the service we had assumed.

The panic spread like electricity
THOMAS DRYSDALE, letter to Benjamin Rush, 1794
A similar, though smaller, epidemic of yellow fever broke out in Baltimore the following year, notably affecting Fell's Point, an area frequented by sailors and labourers. One of them was Thomas Drysdale (d. 1798), a young doctor who had studied with Benjamin Rush (see page 160) and who wrote to him about the epidemic.

Before the close of September, a panic spread through the town and drove a great number of families to seek refuge in the country. As I rode on the morning of the thirtieth through the Point, I was struck with the melancholy change induced by a very few days. The streets were no longer crowded and noisy with business or festivity. The eye would scarcely meet a dozen persons in its longest street. In the rooms of the sick, I more particularly observed the stillness of the streets. But a little before, even when the reduced violence of disease would have permitted them to doze, every slumber was broken or banished by noise. Now the whole day resembled in silence the hours of night.

A happy change of weather at this time checked the rapid progress of the fever and rescued the town from sharing the general misfortune of the Point. The disease declined and by the middle of October the health committee closed the accounts of the dead. The citizens returned to their homes and business, and in a very short time a person passing through the Point itself would be reminded of its late situation only by observing in some alleys the bodies of a number of dead cats.

I have been, sir, as concise as possible in the preceding observations. To have a more enlarged view of our situation, while the mind was assailed on the one part by the actual representation of disease and mortality, and supported on the other by the wish and assurance that our fears beheld the occurrences through a magnifying glass, you must only submit yourself to the guidance of memory while she bids the misfortunes of your own city glide before your imagination. The retrospect will remind you of that principle of the human mind which subjects our senses to our wishes. The eye is unwilling to behold a scene that gives certainty to our apprehensions of misfortune, and we prefer lingering in a state of suspense to an absolute knowledge of our situation.... We can scarcely believe what we wish to be untrue....

Hence sir, it was long before our citizens could shake off their fancied security by believing the existence of danger. But when the charm was dissolved, the panic spread like electricity from mind to mind. Now, too late, it was remembered that the dictates of reason had been lulled to rest and truth had been heard but opposed, ridiculed and condemned. ADIEU!

Nursing the victims of yellow fever

JOHN P. DROMGOOLE, *Yellow Fever Heroes, Honors, and Horrors of 1878*
  (1879)

In 1878 the Mississippi valley suffered an outbreak of yellow fever, in which around 20,000 people died. John P. Dromgoole (c. 1826–1890), a Memphis doctor, published a book to collect the folk remedies and celebrate the city's nurses and other heroes and heroines of the outbreak.

There were women of pluck and unsurpassed devotion in Memphis who did everything for those they love. The faithless are of the other sex, of those whom the world, in one of its greatest misnomers, has dubbed 'the stronger sex'. While John Donovan forsakes his wife and leaves his children to die in strangers' hands; while a son goes to Arkansas Springs and leaves his mother and two brothers to be borne by other hands to the grave, in contrast shines out the faithfulness of woman as a devoted mother, as patient, attentive wife, as a life-risking daughter, sister, friend. By the bedside of the burning body, inhaling the poison of the sick-room, foul with that odour that tells the nature of the dreadful disease, performing services which none other will do, wearing a smile while the heart is breaking and lifting up her head when in the last agony; her person is befouled by that most repulsive and horrible of all substances, black vomit. She sits and watches and nurses and cares for her loved one till he lives again or passes beyond her aid. The penalty of her service of love is generally death.

Instances come to the writer's mind faster than he can record them, instances which are but a few of the many which have become like a part of heaven in so much of earth's hell:

A Citizens' Relief Committeeman walked into a humble cottage in the southern portion of the city. There he found two children ill, one weak and listless, but evidently convalescing, and the other tossing in burning fever. A little woman in black sat between the two and was in the act of kissing the brow of the little fevered one.

'Can't I send you a nurse, madam?' asked the visitor.

'No, sir' (the pale little woman smiled), 'I have brought one child through and I shall bring the other.'

'But you are worn out.'

'Oh no sir, a kind Italian woman nearby comes in and helps me sometimes.'

She would not yield; no other hand but hers could minister to her little ones.

A sick man's lady friend wrote, 'Please let me come.' And when his friends thought the die was cast, they consented to summoning her. Boldly she laid aside her hat, pushed back her hair and, forcing a smile to her lips, entered the room. Some of his male friends stood outside on the doorsteps to inquire, 'how the dear old boy is getting along'.

The keeper of a house of ill-fame on Gayoso Street dared the loss of her 'business', dared the desertion of her place by all but one of its inmates, to nurse faithfully to the end one who was to her a comparative stranger, but whom chance had brought plague-stricken to her door....

Only drunkards and the dissipated contract yellow fever

RALPH EMMETT AVERY, *America's Triumph at Panama* (1913)
The late 19th century saw a French company led by the engineer Ferdinand de Lesseps, who had built the Suez Canal, seek a similar triumph with a canal across the Panama Isthmus. Work, which began in 1884, was desperately slow and costly, not least because of the threat of yellow fever. In the early years of the 20th century the canal project was bought by the United States, which introduced comprehensive sanitation and drained the malarial swamps to complete the canal in 1914. This account of the failed French project comes from a 1913 book by American Ralph Emmett Avery.

The French attempt to construct a waterway across the Isthmus was fore-doomed to failure because the project fell into the hands of promoters and speculators. A contributory cause was the very high sick and death rate among the French employees on the Isthmus. This added greatly to the cost of administration and resulted in an unstable labour force.... The company had to pay high wages and offer special inducements to persuade men to take the chance of high wages and offer special inducements to persuade men to take the chance of one in five of surviving an attack of yellow fever which they were liable to contract. Had the work been in the charge of a rich and powerful government, public opinion would not have allowed the work to have been carried on at such an appalling cost of life. When the enterprise was started the method of transmission of malaria and yellow fever was unknown, and, even if the French had taken the sanitary precautions prevailing at that time, they could not have stamped out these two fevers which gave the Isthmus the reputation of being the most unhealthy place in the world for a white man....

There formerly stood on the western slope of Ancon Hill a building that commanded ready attention from passers-by on the road from Panama to La Boca, now Balboa. It was the prospective home of M. Jules Dingler, director-general of the first French company. Work on the mansion was begun shortly after he came to the Isthmus in February 1883, and the cost including the grounds is said to have been about $50,000. The experience of M. Dingler on the Isthmus constitutes, perhaps, one of the saddest incidents in French canal history. Stories of the fatal effect the climate of the Isthmus was said to have on foreigners reached France, but Dingler scoffed at these reports. 'I am going to show them,' he is credited with having said, 'that only drunkards and the dissipated contract yellow fever and die.' In this spirit he brought with him to the Isthmus, his wife, son and daughter. His son...shortly fell victim to yellow fever and died.... His wife also sickened and died from the same fell disease. Dingler later relinquished his post and went back to France a man broken in mind and body....

During the period of greatest activity there were probably 2,000 Frenchmen on the Isthmus, all non-immune to yellow fever. Life was a gamble and, with no suitable social diversion, they naturally resorted to the only forms of amusement available, the saloons, gambling rooms and houses of ill-repute. Colón and Panama became the Mecca of the parasites of society, the non-workers who live on vice, with the result that an efficient labour force could not be kept long under such conditions, and it was continually changing....

Hospital records show that during the construction period – 1881–89 – there were 5,618 deaths, 1,041 of which were from yellow fever.... The West Indian negroes were immune to yellow fever, and very few of them were admitted to the hospitals. The victims, therefore, were nearly all white persons, and mostly Frenchmen.

Brought to heel by the US Army

WILLIAM GORGAS, *Sanitation in Panama* (1915)

Yellow fever remained a real danger in the Caribbean and Central America well into the 20th century, and American expansion into that region provided an impetus for further study of the disease. The Spanish-American war of 1898 took the US Army to Cuba to support its fight for independence from Spain, but the disease took its toll of the army. The Army Medical Corps doctor, Major Walter Reed (1851–1902), assisted by Chief Sanitary Officer William Gorgas (1854–1920), undertook a major study of the disease in Havana, and demonstrated that it was caused not by dirt, as previously thought, but by mosquitoes. Gorgas, who described this work in Sanitation in Panama, *then developed programmes of eradication of mosquitoes by draining swamps and improving public water provision; his work enabled the completion of the Panama Canal, which had up until then been bedevilled by yellow fever.*

It is very difficult to convey to a reader any idea of the conditions which exist during an epidemic of yellow fever. All business is entirely paralyzed, the quarantines not allowing any communication between the affected districts and those not affected. In an epidemic of any extent this means hundreds of local quarantines. Some idea of the condition of affairs can be obtained by picturing what would occur in any community if all the income of that community should entirely cease for six months. And this was the condition of business all over the Mississippi valley every time yellow fever gained entrance....

It was known in the United States that yellow fever was always brought somewhere from the littoral of either the Gulf of Mexico, or the Caribbean Sea, and the city of Havana...was known to be the center of this endemic area.

Yellow fever in 1898 was looked upon as the example of a filth disease, *par excellence*, and it was thought that if Havana were put in a proper state of cleanliness, it might cease to be the great point of infection for the United States. It was known that yellow fever had existed in the city of Havana continuously for one hundred and fifty years. It is interesting to note that the endemic infection of Havana occurred in 1762, when Havana was besieged and captured by American troops. I say American troops, because the expedition was largely composed of men from the present United States, then colonies of Great Britain. It is also interesting to note that this infection was supposed to have been brought by a vessel from Vera Cruz....

When we went to Havana in 1898 we knew no more of the sanitation of yellow fever than we had known a century before. The army which went to Santiago suffered as severely from yellow fever and other tropical diseases as any military expedition into the tropics had suffered before that time, and its death rate, had it remained, would have been just as high as was that of the French army of similar size, which was exterminated in the island of Haiti just one hundred years before.

A very deep impression was made upon me by the condition of our army at the end of two months' campaigning in this tropical region. It was utterly used up and of no value whatever as a fighting machine. Fully four-fifths of the men were having fever. This small army of sixteen thousand men was as fine a body of soldiers when they landed at Siboney as could probably be gotten together, but after two months' campaigning in this tropical jungle, and after several weeks of fever from which no one was free, their stamina and morale were completely gone. After the surrender of the Spanish garrison there was a complete let-down on our side. Everybody wanted to go home. No one could see any need of staying in Cuba, and every individual was perfectly certain that he would die if he remained there a month longer. Officers and men became nervous and hysterical. I commanded the base hospital at Siboney, and it was my disagreeable duty to select from day to day those who would have to remain. Many times every day the poor fellows, officers and men, would break down and cry when told that they could not leave on the next ship....

Being immune to yellow fever, I made application to go with the troops that took possession of Havana. We arrived there in December 1898. The military authorities concluded that this was the opportunity which the United States had been awaiting for the past two hundred years. Thinking that yellow fever was a filth disease, they believed that if we could get Havana clean enough, we could free it from yellow fever. It was felt that if we could eliminate Havana as a focus of infection, the United States would cease to be subject to epidemics. This meant so much to the United

States, financially and otherwise, that the authorities determined to make all other efforts secondary to this sanitary effort.

The city was cleaned as well as it was possible to cleanse it. This remark applies as well to the private premises as to the public highways. Energetic and capable army officers were placed at the head of various municipal departments, and these departments were thoroughly organized and made as efficient as possible.... I believe that Havana was cleaner than any other city had ever been up to that time....

Dr Reed, to make his experiments of any value, had to get human beings who had neither suffered from yellow fever itself, nor had lived long enough in an endemic center to acquire immunity. Havana for a number of years had received a considerable Spanish immigration. At the time to which I refer, it amounted to about twenty thousand a year. These immigrants believed that they were going to have yellow fever, and though they knew that a considerable number of them must succumb during the process, they were anxious to have the disease and be done with it. There was a very general belief among the Spaniards in Havana that a person with what they called 'thin blood' as contra-distinguished from a robust, plethoric, full-blooded person, was much more likely to recover from yellow fever. They tried, therefore, with their newly arrived friends, relatives and dependents from Spain to bring about this condition of their blood. They kept them confined in a darkened room and fed them on a very limited diet, and certainly succeeded in rapidly reducing the strong, florid, robust Gallego to a very marked condition of anemia and debility. The Spaniard believed that he thus saved many lives. I was convinced that he thus killed a good many of his friends and dependents.

The newly arrived Spaniard, as soon as he had had yellow fever and could present a certificate of immunity, could command double the wages that he could get before he had the disease. So that when Dr Reed proposed to some of these men that they should go out to his camp, have a mild case of yellow fever, be well cared for and when recovered be given by him a certificate of immunity, he found no difficulty in getting volunteers, and when, in addition to that, he promised each man who had the disease a bonus of two hundred and fifty dollars, the service became exceedingly popular.

TYPHUS AND TYPHOID FEVER

For much of history, these two diseases – which have similar symptoms, notably a high fever accompanied by a rash of small red spots – were taken to be different forms of the same disease, named from the Greek word *typhos* ('smoke' or 'haze'), the term used by Hippocrates to describe the mental confusion caused by high fevers. They both flourished in crowded and insanitary conditions, and were found among the urban poor in 19th-century Europe and America. However, in the 1830s it became clear that they were quite different: typhus is caused by the *Rickettsia prowazekii* bacterium carried by lice, whereas typhoid fever is a Salmonella infection of the gut, transmitted in water contaminated by human faeces.

Both diseases caused serious epidemics in the 18th and 19th centuries; typhoid remains endemic in many poor countries and is still a threat in emergency situations where sanitation is disrupted.

Distinguishing typhus from typhoid
WILLIAM WOOD GERHARD, 'On the Typhus Fever' (1837)
The Philadelphian doctor William Wood Gerhard (1809–1872) studied in Paris where he made a particular study of communicable diseases. He was present at the typhus epidemic that broke out in his native city in 1836, and his careful study of its symptoms allowed him to demonstrate for the first time that it was a distinct disease from typhoid.

During a residence of two or three years at Paris, I had studied with great care the pathology and treatment of the disease usually termed, in the French hospitals, typhoid fever. There is another designation for it, more directly in accordance with modern medical nomenclature; it is dothinenteritis. This variety of fever...is almost the only fever which can be said to be endemic in Paris.... It is one of the most frequent and the most severe acute affections observed at Paris, and has been studied with extreme accuracy. The work of Dr Louis is a model in its kind; he has analyzed the symptoms and pathological phenomena of the fever so accurately and fully, as to surpass any other description of individual diseases.

It affords us, then, great advantages in the investigation of the history of fevers, to begin with the typhoid, as the best known of these affections. Assuming this disease as the basis of our investigations, much greater certainty can be given to our ulterior researches, if we compare the symptoms of any fever which is little known and imperfectly described, with those of the typhoid fever.

This inquiry was in accordance with a desire which I had long cherished of investigating the most common fevers in the middle states of America, where, from our geographical position, we witness the fevers observed at the northern, and occasionally those of the southern states. The commercial relations of Philadelphia are so frequent with the whole southern coast of the United States, and the passage to the north so rapid in the summer and autumnal months, that we receive into our hospitals a considerable number of patients taken ill on the coast of North Carolina, Virginia, and even Alabama and Louisiana. There are, therefore, few places where such a study could be pursued to more advantage than at Philadelphia.

Dothinenteritis is by no means a rare disease at Philadelphia, although less common than at Paris.... The patients were chiefly those who had resided but a short time at Philadelphia, and they were taken ill on shipboard, or under some other circumstances causing an abrupt change of food and habits of life. They were also young persons, but few having passed the age of twenty-five years. Both these conditions of age and change of habit are observed to be essential to the development of typhoid fever at Paris....

The typhus fever, which is so common throughout the British dominions, especially in Ireland, is not attended with ulceration or other lesion of the glands of Peyer [lymphoid follicles in the small intestine membrane].... The lesion of the glands of Peyer is well known to the British physicians, but an error frequently committed by them is that they regard this affection (dothinenteritis) as a mere complication of their ordinary typhus, or a modified form of it. I do not recollect anyone who has clearly stated that the two diseases are always distinct, before the publication of a note in the *Dublin Journal*, by Dr Lombard of Geneva (Sept. 1836).

TYPHUS

German epidemiologist August Hirsch claimed that, 'the history of typhus is the history of human misery'. It has long been associated with large bodies of people living together in poor conditions. The first recorded major outbreak in Europe occurred in 1489 in the forces of the Spanish monarchs fighting the Moors; it killed some 17,000 men. For several centuries thereafter, it was frequently spread in and by armies, notably during the Thirty Years' War (1618–48); during Napoleon's retreat from Moscow in 1812, when the disease killed more soldiers than enemy action had done; and among the rival armies of the American Civil War. In England, it was often known as gaol fever or ship fever. In the 20th century, major typhus epidemics occurred in Soviet territory in the 1920s, and in the appalling conditions of the German concentration camps. In the First World War all the main armies had made sustained efforts to control lice in their ranks and none suffered seriously from typhus.

> **The man's remains were placed in meal-sacks**
> ROBERT WHYTE, *The Ocean Plague* (1848)
> *In the 1830s a major outbreak of typhus in Ireland killed 100,000. A few years later, the famine of 1845–49 drove large numbers of starving Irish to emigrate, many to the Americas. The crowded insanitary conditions on the so-called 'coffin ships' that carried the emigrants resulted in a death toll of up to a third of the passengers, from a combination of starvation and typhus; major typhus epidemics also broke out in the cities in which they landed, notably Quebec, Montreal, Boston and New York. Robert Whyte, an Irish emigrant, described conditions on one of the coffin ships en route to Quebec, in his book* The Ocean Plague.

Friday, 9 July 46 deg. N. lat., 58 deg. W. lon. A few convalescents appeared upon deck. The appearance of the poor creatures was miserable in the extreme. We now had fifty sick, being nearly one half the whole number of passengers. Some entire families being prostrated, were dependent on the charity of their neighbours, many of whom were very kind; but others seemed to be possessed of no feeling.... The brother of the two men who died on the sixth instant, followed them today. He was seized with dismay from the time of their death, which no doubt hurried on the malady to its fatal termination. The old sails being all used up, his remains were placed in two meal-sacks, and a weight being fastened at foot, the body was placed upon one of the hatch battens, from which, when raised over the bulwark, it fell into the deep, and was no more seen. He left two little orphans, one of whom, a boy seven years of age, I noticed in the evening, wearing his deceased father's coat. Poor little fellow! he seemed quite unconscious of his loss, and proud of the accession to his scanty covering. The remainder of the man's clothes were sold by auction, by a friend of his who promised to take care of the children. There was great competition, and the 'Cant', as they called it, occasioned jibing and jesting, which was painful to listen to, surrounded as the actors were (some of whom had just risen from a bed of sickness) by famine, pestilence and death.

Saintly ministry and apostolic charity

'THE TYPHUS OF 1847', ANNALS OF THE GREY NUNS (1847)

On arrival in the Americas, emigrants were quarantined on Staten Island in New York or at Grosse-Isle in Quebec, where the authorities and religious organizations did their best to nurse the sick. Nevertheless, typhus spread on shore, both among the emigrants and the wider community, with 20,000 victims in Quebec, 6,000 in Montreal and several hundred in New York. This journal commemorated the efforts of the Grey Nuns, or Sisters of Charity of the Hôpital Général of Montreal, on behalf of the sick in Quebec in 1847.

Despite the diligent services of the Faculty of Medicine and the precautions implemented, a great number of emigrants died at Grosse-Isle and at the Hospital of the Marine. We had arranged to transport the convalescent who seemed to have not yet caught the contagion to Montreal.... Fifty-one priests were directed towards Grosse-Isle or towards the Hospital of the Marine to exercise their saintly ministry. Twenty-five caught the contagion;...five priests were victims of their apostolic charity.

Montreal prepared itself with anxiety to receive the emigrants.... An emigration committee was organized with the instruction to take immediate measures to properly receive Ireland's unfortunate children.... Since the first days of June, people shipped from overseas have been arriving at the city. Funeral convoys arrive day and night from which hundreds of men and women, pale, exhausted from misery and suffering, were disembarking from the warehouse and even from the end of the platform. A great number died during the voyage.... Poor emigrants! They arrive to this strange land after having suffered during the crossing.... And what do they find, most of them?... A tomb ready to receive them. What could Montreal offer these poor brothers in faith? Its citizens, especially in this day and age, were more compassionate than fortunate....

The Messieurs of Saint-Sulpice, parish pastors, were the first to run to the ships. M. John Richard spent the first night there, administering the confession to all those in danger of dying.... Mgr. Bourget, Bishop of Montreal arrived from his second voyage to Rome. Barely recovered from his fatigue, His Eminence occupied himself with ways to relieve the poor children of Ireland.... Towards mid-June, 6,000 Irish disembarked on our shores, 3,500 of which stopped at the sheds or ambulances. 2,000 disappeared in search of more favourable pastures; many died. There nevertheless still remains 250 in the shelters. On 25 June of this same year, the sick numbered 850 in the shelters; around twenty were dying each day. 2 July, the sick numbered 1,300, the number of those who died went from thirty to forty a day. Death...also victimized those in the city, as the contagion began to spread, and spiritual relief was becoming more and more urgent in several neighbourhoods....

The revered mother Forbes-McMullen, worthy superior of the Grey Nuns of Montreal, was tender, generous and compassionate towards the unfortunate.... The good mother...went right away to present herself to the emigration office accompanied by Sister Ste Croix, whose devotion would be remarkable during this disastrous period. They were welcomed with great courtesy and deference by the government steward, who gave all authorization necessary to the Grey Nuns to visit and take care of the pestilent, authorizing them to engage faithful men and women.... Seeing the embarrassment of the steward in finding sufficient personnel to tend to the needs of the sick and dying, he suggested asking the Sisters of Charity if they would provide aid....

The steward hastened to conduct them to a home almost in ruin by the river, under the name of the hospital.... Hundreds of people were laying there, most of them on bare planks, pell-mell, men, women and children.

The moribund and cadavers are crowded in the same shelter, while there are those that lie on the quays or on pieces of wood thrown here and there along the river. It was a spectacle that should have discouraged Mother McMullen and her generous companion. On the contrary, they felt their souls lifted to the heights of the mission that the heavens were preparing for them. The meeting they are in at this moment with the Seminary superior and the intrepid M. Morgan fills them with enlightenment. The latter has occupied himself with a poor sick individual that he covers in earth, suffocated by his own vomit; he puts them with such charity on a poor pallet, that they feel animated by a new ardour to come themselves, to save these unfortunate poor....

One day, a poor Irishman who had disembarked that day arrived at the Sheds and asked about his wife who had preceded him on his journey to Montreal. No one was able to give him news: he ran about the shelters worried and disconsolate without finding her; he finally arrived at the place where the cadavers of those who had died during the night were put; he examined them one by one: he stopped and threw himself on the ground while screaming in lament, dragging himself to one of the cadavers which he covered in kisses and tears. He had found the one who had been his companion and his consolation in life. His despair knew no bounds and he left at a slow pace, convinced that he was the only one left of his family. These scenes repeat themselves every day, when we proceed to the sepulchre of the dead; fathers, mothers, husbands, wives and children, surrounding those who are so dear to them, so opposed to their departure, letting outcries that provoke tears.

A disease of bad air

REPORT OF THE COMMITTEE ON PRACTICAL MEDICINE (1849)

The committee report on the New York typhus epidemic in 1849 makes clear the difficulty in preventing an epidemic before the 1880s when Louis Pasteur and Robert Koch proved that infectious diseases are spread by germs. While the committee evidently understood that the conditions on the coffin ships had enabled the spread of the disease, it was still believed that typhus was a disease spread through foul air (miasma) and particular climatic conditions.

Of all forms of infectious diseases, the one from which the greatest amount of mortality has occurred in most of the larger Atlantic cities of the New England and Middle states is typhus.

In the city of New York, the disease was epidemic in 1818, 1827–28, 1837 and 1846–47. The deaths in 1847 reached the frightful sum of 1,396, while in 1846 they numbered only 256. The reporter infers from these facts, and doubtless correctly, that the diffusion of typhus is favoured by certain periodical meteoratious [epidemic produced by atmospheric conditions] influences. But the immediate cause of the prevalence of typhus among us during the last year, however much aerial influences may have contributed to the diffusion of the *materies morbi* [immediate cause] and propagation of the disease, was more tangible than this. It consisted in the arrival in our harbour of over 100,000 emigrants from Great Britain and Europe in 1847. Many of these came, under circumstances of distress, mental and bodily, excellently calculated to engender the typhus *idio-miasm* [disease caused by human excretions], in a close steerage in over-crowded ships, on board of which the disease broke out and was raging on arrival. It is not remarkable then that the typhus spread in the hospitals which were provided for their reception among physicians, nurses and patients; nor that in the city many cases occurred in the apartments occupied by the lower classes of Germans and Irish who had sheltered their friends. The number of persons admitted into the Marine Hospital at Staten Island in 1847 was 6,932; of this number 5,277 were sick with fever, 1,662 died. 2,229 cases were registered typhus, of which 457 died and 3,020 as remittent and typhus remittent (many of them ship-fever cases), of which 205 died. The total number of deaths from typhus at the Quarantine Hospital and within the city of New York was scarcely less than 2,000.

Controlling typhus in liberated Naples

COLONEL CHARLES WHEELER, 'Control of Typhus in Italy 1943–1944 by use of DDT' (1946)

When liberating occupied areas in the Second World War, Allied forces sometimes had to deal with serious epidemics, including one of typhus in Naples in 1943. A mass delousing programme, regularly dusting the population with DDT, was instituted, as Colonel Charles Wheeler of the America Typhus Commission described in the American Journal of Public Health.

The development of three dusting powders lethal to lice (MYL and DDT in the United States, and AL-63 in England); the demonstration in the laboratory and in the field of the effectiveness of these powders in the control of lice; and the arresting of small typhus epidemics in native villages of Mexico, Algeria and Egypt through the use of these powders were proof that the use of louse powder in the developing typhus emergency in Italy was the control method of choice in the field....

The procedure adopted for the application of powder to the clothing of infested individuals was speedy, economical in the amount of powder used, and eliminated the necessity for the removal of the clothing from the body of the person to be dusted. Essentially the procedure consisted of forcefully blowing powder, by hand-dusters or power-dusters, between the layers of clothing worn by the individual and between the innermost layer of clothing and the skin of the body. This was accomplished by a uniform technique, inserting the nozzle of the duster up the sleeves, down the neck (both front and back), around the waist-line and into the crotch area of clothing. Hair and any cap or hat were dusted thoroughly. An infested person properly dusted is no longer a menace to others and will remain so for a period of at least two weeks, at the end of which time he should be redusted. Approximately 1 to ½oz of powder per person is sufficient to insure the thorough dusting of all clothing worn.

Actual dusting operations were instituted on 15 December 1943, by a dusting team previously trained by a member of the Health Commission of the Rockefeller Foundation. This team of workers dusted all outbound passengers boarding a train scheduled to leave Naples for Bari. The following day, 16 December, contact dusting teams were organized and sent out to addresses of reported cases of typhus emanating from homes or institutions. On the night of 27 December, the first dusting of persons living in air-raid shelters was undertaken. In addition to their regular dusting duties, each team was instructed to report any new cases or suspected cases of typhus. These teams discovered many new cases which previously had not been reported to nor isolated by civil health authorities. The importance of proper case finding and reporting was so apparent that a special case finding section...was organized. The case finding and dusting operations were severely handicapped for the lack of proper assistants and dependable transportation....

By 26 December 1943, the typhus control program, approved by the War Department, provided for six operational sections. Four of these sections were utilized from the outset, namely:

1. The case finding section
2. The contact delousing section
3. The mass delousing section
4. The immunization section.

These four sections were in operation a few days before the fifth section, the flying squadron, became active. Later in the month of January a refugee delousing section was established to complete the table of organization as planned.

TYPHOID FEVER

The disease, also called enteric fever, may have been the cause of the Athenian plague (see page 20) and is commonly seen in conditions of poor or disrupted sanitation. The widespread introduction of clean water and effective sewerage in most cities in the later 19th century removed much of the threat of the disease in the West. Until the development of an effective vaccine in the late 19th century, which was first used by the British Army in the Anglo-Boer War and later by the US Army in the First World War, typhoid fever had often proved more lethal to soldiers than combat.

Typhoid fever is treatable with antibiotics; however, it still kills 150,000 people a year, being most prevalent in South Asia.

When fever once enters, want soon follows

WILLIAM BUDD, *Typhoid Fever: Its Nature, Mode of Spreading, and Prevention* (1873)

A country doctor from Somerset, William Budd (1811–1880), nearly died of typhoid when in the navy as a young man and studied the disease in his community in the 1830s. He was unable to get his work published for

*two decades, although while working in Bristol in the 1840s and after
studying the work of John Snow in London (see page 151), he successfully
averted a large outbreak by making improvements to the water supply.
Ultimately, his demonstration that the disease was not transmitted
through a miasma or fetid air but was contagious and transmitted in the
excreta of infected people and through the hands of those who attended
the sick, proved a major step to the identification of the infectious agent,*
Salmonella typhi, *in 1880.*

No one can know what they really imply who has not had experience of
this fever in his own home. The dreary and painful night-watches – the
great length of the period over which the anxiety is extended – the long
suspense between hope and fear, and the large number of the cases in
which hope is disappointed and the worst fear is at last realized, make
up a sum of distress that is scarcely to be found in the history of any
other acute disorder. Even in the highest class of society, the introduction
of this fever into the household is an event that generally long stands
prominently out in the record of family afflictions. But if this be true
of the mansions of the rich, who have every means of alleviation which
wealth can command, how much more true must it be of the cottages
of the poor, who have scant provision even for the necessaries of life,
and none for its great emergencies. Here, when fever once enters, want
soon follows, and contagion is not slow to add its peculiar bitterness
to the trial.

As the disease is, by far, most fatal to persons in middle life, the
mother or father, or both, are often the first to succumb, and the young
survivors being left without support, their home is broken up and their
destitution becomes complete....

In its ordinary course, human life has few such consummations of
misery as this....

Having been by accident thrown much in the way of this fever, I have
long felt that it is impossible to bear a part in the calamities of which it is
the source, without becoming possessed with a burning desire to devote
the best powers of the mind to the discovery of means by which such
calamities may be prevented.

From the fact, already referred to, of its being so much more deadly to grown-up persons, this disease has a relation to pauperism which is almost peculiar to itself....

If it be true of diseases in general, that all prevention must be based on an intimate knowledge of their causes, how much more true must it be of that great group of diseases which is the work of definite and specific agents, having not only the power of breeding within the body, but capable, for limited periods at least, of existing externally to it? For it is clear, that, in such a case, a thing against which we may be impotent so long as it infects the body itself, may present, on its issue from the body, the conditions of an easy conquest.

That Typhoid Fever is a true member of this group, or in other words, that it is, in its essence, a contagious or self-propagating fever, was proved long ago.

It is scarcely to the credit of the medical profession that this great truth should still be disputed....

But...the great majority, not of the laity only, but of the profession also, still remain anti-contagionists. And this, moreover, is not only true of the rank and file, but distinguished men, who have gained great credit and wide acceptance as teachers of medical science, are to be found, who appear to lean to the same side....

In the discussions on the cause of typhoid fever which filled so large a space in the public papers, both lay and medical, for many weeks together, on a recent memorable occasion, the idea of contagion in connection with the disease was almost universally either ignored or repudiated....

The practice of both had been confined to large cities.

This direct opposition of opinion to fact in a matter of such vital importance, and so open to observation, is as perplexing as it is discouraging. And the more so, because the property of contagion, of which the proof is so clear, so far from being new to disease, is already familiarly known as the common property of a great family group, of which this fever repeats, in unmistakable traits, the family characteristics.

The search for Typhoid Mary

GEORGE SOPER, 'The Curious Case of Typhoid Mary' (1939)

Once it became clear that typhoid was indeed contagious and passed in water contaminated with the excreta of infected people, it became possible to control its transmission through tracking and tracing the source of an outbreak. New York-based sanitation engineer George Soper (1870–1948) famously demonstrated this by identifying an Irish cook, Mary Mallon (who quickly became known as 'Typhoid Mary'), as an asymptomatic carrier and the source of an outbreak in a wealthy New York town in 1906. She was held in quarantine against her will for more than twenty years.

I first saw Mary Mallon thirty-two years ago in 1907. She was then about forty years of age and at the height of her physical and mental faculties. She was five feet six inches tall, a blond with clear blue eyes, a healthy color and a somewhat determined mouth and jaw. Mary had a good figure and might have been called athletic had she not been a little too heavy.... I think she was born in the north of Ireland....

My discovery of Typhoid Mary was the outcome of an investigation made in the winter of 1906–7 into an outbreak of typhoid fever in the house of Mrs George Thompson, at Oyster Bay, N.Y., the preceding summer. The place had been rented to a New York banker, General William Henry Warren, who had occupied it with his family of three, and seven servants for the summer months. Late in August an explosion of typhoid had occurred in which six of the eleven persons in the household were taken sick. The epidemic had been studied immediately after it occurred by persons who were regarded as experts, but the cause had not been positively ascertained. It was thought by the owner that unless the mystery could be cleared up, it would be impossible to find tenants for the coming season.

It will be remembered that in those days typhoid fever was far more common than it is today and that knowledge of its transmission was less complete.... Typhoid was believed to be due generally to polluted water or milk, or, in the opinion of some, to putrefying organic matter and sometimes to sewer gas....

It happened that in 1907 I had had a good deal of experience with typhoid fever. This began when as an undergraduate student passing my Christmas holidays at Warrensburg in the Adirondacks, I had the temerity to move two typhoid patients and their families out of a house which had a long history of communicable disease and, with the consent of the owner, burn it to the ground. My experience grew with my years.

Eventually I was called on to investigate and put a stop to many epidemics, numbering the City of New York and the State of New York among my clients. I was called an epidemic fighter....

Having undertaken to see if there had been any carriers in the Oyster Bay house before the outbreak there occurred, I soon came, through the process of exclusion, to the cook. But where was she? She had left soon after the epidemic and that event had occurred over six months ago. I tried to find out everything I could about her, but there was not much to learn. Mrs Warren said she was a good plain cook, her wages were forty-five dollars a month, and she had been obtained from Mrs Stricker's. Stricker's was a well-known employment agency on Twenty-eighth Street. The cook had not fraternized with the other servants and they knew little about her. She was not particularly clean. Her name was Mary Mallon. That was about all....

It was not at first clear how the family could have been infected from the cook, granting that she was a carrier, for, where there are so many servants, there is little food that a cook handles which is not subsequently raised to a temperature sufficient to make it harmless. I found, however, that on a certain Sunday there was a dessert which Mary prepared and of which everybody present was extremely fond. This was ice-cream with fresh peaches cut up and frozen in it. I suppose no better way could be found for a cook to cleanse her hands of microbes and infect a family....

When at length I caught up with her, which was some four months after I started out on the Oyster Bay epidemic, Mary was working as cook in an old-fashioned, high-stoop house on Park Avenue on the west side, two doors above the church at Sixtieth Street. The laundress had recently been taken to the Presbyterian Hospital with typhoid fever and the only child of the family, a lovely daughter, was dying of it.

I had my first talk with Mary in the kitchen of this house. I suppose it was an unusual kind of interview, particularly when the place is taken into consideration. I was as diplomatic as possible, but I had to say I suspected her of making people sick and that I wanted specimens of her urine, feces and blood. It did not take Mary long to react to this suggestion. She seized a carving fork and advanced in my direction. I passed rapidly down the long narrow hall, through the tall iron gate, out through the area and so to the sidewalk. I felt rather lucky to escape.

THIRD PLAGUE PANDEMIC

This outbreak of bubonic and pneumonic plague – known as the 'third pandemic', following the Plague of Justinian (see page 34), and the Black Death and Great Plague (see pages 56 and 119) – began in Yunnan province in China in the 1870s, spread to India where it killed over 12 million, and thence to every continent, carried on trains and steamships. The epidemic it caused in California began in San Francisco in 1900; in 1924 it killed thirty-seven in Los Angeles and resulted in the demolition of many run-down blocks. The pandemic finally abated in the mid-20th century.

Today, plague remains endemic in Central and North America, but the identification of the pathogen *Yersinia pestis* (named for Alexandre Yersin, the Swiss-French bacteriologist who identified the bacillus in 1894) made it possible to develop an effective vaccine. The subsequent discovery that the bacillus was transmitted by fleas that normally live on rodents clarified how the disease spreads, making public health measure more effective, then finally, the development of antibiotics made it readily treatable.

The plague in China

C. A. GORDON, *Reports of the Medical Officers to the Chinese Imperial Maritime Customs Service* (1884)

A British medical officer to the Chinese imperial customs service, C. A. Gordon, reported the initial outbreak of plague in Yunnan, south-west China, in the 1870s.

In the Report on Amoy for the half-year ending 31 March 1878, there is an article on the Plague in China, prepared chiefly from notes by Mr Rocher, of the Chinese Customs Service. These notes are believed to prove the existence of bubonic plague in China, that of late years the disease spread over a large area of the empire, and that it did not in reality disappear, as believed by some writers.

In Yunnan the sickness known as Yang-tzu, otherwise Plague, carries off yearly many victims in that province. It appears to have been imported from Burma. Its early history is imperfectly traced, but since the outbreak of the rebellion in that province it has spread among the population of it.

A belief was expressed that its cause existed in exhalations from the ground, because rats and other animals that live in it or much upon it, suffered in an especial manner. After animals had suffered, the disease spread to man. Then the people employ such 'sanitary' measures as purifying their houses, lighting fires in every room and abstaining from pork. The reporter states that in Yunnan he has seen many persons attacked by the disease, but few recovered. In places where the plague passes but lightly through, the mortality may be estimated at 4 per cent; in places where it stops for some time, whole families disappear one after another and the general population is decimated. In some districts the inhabitants, to avoid the pestilence, abandon their houses and harvests, and camp out on the heights, where, however, in some instances the epidemic follows them. The dead are usually left exposed, unburied; thus the Fung-shui is not desecrated by their interment – but the odour from decomposing bodies is intense.

In 1871, 1872 and 1873, the epidemic in Yunnan began about the period of rice-planting – that is, in May or June. During summer, which is also the rainy season, the disease continues, but in a mild form; after the rains have ceased, however, it becomes most active and deadly. Instead of visiting every village in its direct progress, it would pass some completely by, visiting places near to and on either side of them, to return several months afterwards to those forgotten spots, when elsewhere it would appear to have died away. After having devastated villages in the plains, it often ascended mountains, and there affects severely the aborigines. It was constant among the Imperial troops during the years named, while they were operating against the Mahometan rebels. One is inclined to believe that the disease is imported by men and women who descend into the valleys to barter, or work at certain seasons at the harvest, as it is chiefly the mountains adjoining the plains that are visited by the disease.

Strict hygiene

JAMES LOWSON, 'The Epidemic of Bubonic Plague in Hongkong, 1894' (1897)

The Scottish physician James Lowson (1866–1935) was sent to Hong Kong to help with the epidemic there in 1894. He criticized both the hospital authorities for failing to identify the disease at first, and the colony's authorities for being slow to introduce public health provisions such as isolating sufferers, disinfecting properties and ensuring rapid burials. In the hospital, he helped the Japanese bacteriologist Shibasaburo Kitasato to identify the bacillus responsible for the disease and to have his results published in The Lancet. *Separately the Swiss-French bacteriologist Alexandre Yersin was working in Hong Kong, and reported his own discovery of the bacillus, a few days after Kitasato, to the French Académie de Sciences.*

At the beginning of the epidemic every precaution that we could think of was taken to prevent the infection of attendants. Most of these precautions were useful and necessary, while others proved to be more in the nature of luxuries. As our knowledge and experience progressed we were able to bring down our requirements to fine lines. Plenty of fresh air was a *sine qua non* both for patients and attendants. At first, attendants were allowed to smoke as they pleased; and, as a couple of rabbits died in two days after inoculation by blood from our first case, nurses had strict orders to be careful of all wounds and scratches on their fingers, and to see that they were dressed with antiseptic at once. They were ordered to use eucalyptus or carbolic acid solution on their handkerchiefs more especially when the hospitals were crowded. Faeces were disinfected by quicklime or carbolic acid as were all dressings. At the Slaughter House Hospital, Jeyes' fluid was used as the disinfectant all along. If at any time the wards smelt badly or the stillness and closeness of the atmosphere became oppressive, some eucalyptus oil evaporated over small lamps had a wonderful effect in alleviating the nauseated feeling that sometime come over the attendants. In the beginning nausea was sometimes brought on by the cigars and pipes which were freely used....

During an epidemic personal cleanliness should be carefully observed by those who have any work to do which takes them close to the infected district. A bath should be taken immediately after coming out of an affected area, some disinfectant being used in the water. A change of clothes is essential, and those that are discarded should be removed immediately and exposed to the fresh air. They may be put through the steam sterilizer, but it will be found that free exposure to air in the sunlight will be sufficient.

With regard to those who are employed on cleaning or disinfecting houses, free smoking should be allowed...preferable to smoking would be the use of respirators with exit and entrance valves, and a sprinkling of thymol or menthol over the entrance valves. If smoking goes on, then a carbolic mouth-wash should also be insisted on. As regards stimulants, these should be dispensed carefully but not too freely; the nauseating character of the work in a dirty town sometimes suggests an occasional glass of whisky or other alcoholic stimulant.

When it is realized that the floating population of Hong Kong practically escaped scot-free, it is a matter of regret that a suggestion to form water-camps for the inhabitants of Taipingshan was not acted upon....

If ever this Colony has had reason to congratulate itself it was when we were able to procure well-trained British nurses. I think the greatest compliment that I can pay these ladies is to say that, had it not been for their presence there could have been no well-run epidemic hospital during last summer. Amateur nurses at the beginning of an epidemic, or indeed at any stage where there is a rush, are worse than useless and multiply the worries of a medical officer *ad infinitum*. Not only this but all outsiders took care to give our hospitals a wide berth.

When the hospitals were crowded, it was often a matter of difficulty for the medical officers employed to keep their meals in their stomachs. It would have been much harder if they had had to remain in constant attendance all the time as our sisters had to do. There is something especially awe-inspiring in plague which seems to appal the onlooker. Cholera and smallpox make a spectator aware of the existence of a severe disease, but to witness rows of plague patients dying off in a hospital has, I am sure, a much more depressing effect on by-standers than the two diseases I have mentioned.

Plague in prison

WALDEMAR HAFFKINE, 'Remarks on the Plague Prophylactic Fluid' (1897)

The Ukrainian-born bacteriologist Waldemar Haffkine (1860–1930) worked at the Pasteur Institute in Paris to develop a cholera vaccine before travelling to India in the autumn of 1896, where in three months he produced the first vaccine against bubonic plague. After first testing the vaccine on himself, he trialled it on inmates of a prison undergoing a plague epidemic. He reported the successful results in the British Medical Journal *on 12 June 1897. Millions of Indians received his vaccine over the following decade.*

On 23 January 1897, the plague broke out in Her Majesty's House of Correction, Byculla, Bombay, while the number of inmates was 345. Between 23 and 29 January, nine cases with five deaths occurred. On the morning of 30 January, six more cases took place, of which three prove fatal. In the afternoon 154 prisoners belonging to the same batches as the rest, and living with them in perfectly identical conditions, volunteered to undergo the preventive inoculation and received 3 c.cm of the mixture of sediment and fluid described above. One of these men had a swollen gland at the time of inoculation, and two others developed glands on the same evening within a few hours of inoculation. These three cases proved also fatal.

From the next morning a difference showed itself in the susceptibility and mortality of the inoculated when compared with the non-inoculated. Between 31 January and 6 February, twelve cases occurred among the non-inoculated prisoners, of which six proved fatal; whereas among the inoculated prisoners, just two cases occurred, both of which recovered.

If repeated observations in similarly precise conditions confirm the results in the Byculla Gaol, the plague prophylactic will appear to influence the disease in men in a very advanced stage of incubation, the period of the latter being in plague between two and seven days, whereas the prophylactic will appear to act in some twelve to fourteen hours, arresting or mitigating the disease in individuals infected several days before.

Between 10 January and 6 May 1897, 11,362 individuals from the infected areas have been inoculated by the above processes, with the following occurrences (which do not include those in the Byculla House of Correction detailed above). The fatal occurrences were twelve: namely three patients who were already unwell at the time of inoculation; three patients who contracted the disease within twelve hours after inoculation; two patients who fell ill within three days after inoculation; four patients attacked 15–25 days after inoculation. The attacks with recoveries numbered thirty-three.

Figures relating to the general population are not available for an exact comparison with the death rate from plague in the corresponding classes of non-inoculate persons. A rough estimate, however, would seem to show that the inoculated have suffered to an extent about twenty times smaller than the non-inoculated living under the same conditions and exposed to the same chance of infection.

Identifying fleas as the vector

W. G. LISTON, *Reports on Plague Investigations in India* (1911)

The British army doctor W. G. Liston (1873–1950) worked in the Bombay plague laboratory, where he was able to show that the disease was transmitted by fleas associated with the rodent population.

On 7 March [1903] a servant was attacked by plague. Dead rats had been seen near his quarters a day or two previously. The man was removed to hospital and the servants' quarters evacuated. The man died on 9 March. Nothing further occurred in the servants' quarters till the 16th when a dead rat was found in one of the empty rooms. The rat was examined bacteriologically and was found to have died of plague. Six guinea-pigs were brought to this house, and on the evening of the 16th two of these were placed in the room in which the rat had died. Two others were placed in a similar room in a neighbouring house, which was at the time occupied, and two others in an empty room of similar construction to the room in which the rat had died. Neither of these latter two rooms had been infected with plague.

On the morning of the 17th the guinea-pigs were chloroformed and examined in the usual manner. No fleas were found on the four guinea-pigs from the two non-infected rooms. Ten rat fleas were taken on the two guinea-pigs in the infected room. The guinea-pigs were marked and returned to the laboratory, and the fleas reserved for dissection and examination. Three of the ten showed numerous plague germs in their stomachs. One of the two guinea-pigs which were placed in the infected room was decidedly ill on 21 March. It was worse on the 22nd and a large bubo could be made out in the right groin. The guinea-pig died on 25 March, i.e. nine days after exposure to infection. A pure culture of plague was obtained. None of the other guinea pigs suffered in any way.

The important point of this experiment was that rat fleas, which had apparently fed on a plague-sick rat, could be captured on an animal which was not a normal host for that flea....

To sum up, then, rat fleas can always be found in infected houses; these fleas will take to an animal which is not their normal host. Some of those fleas have been shown to be infected with large numbers of plague germs in their stomachs, and these germs, far from being destroyed by the digestive juices of the stomach, seemed to be multiplying and in a healthy state. Many of the guinea-pigs on which these rat fleas were found died of plague, while other animals placed in uninfected quarters were not attacked by rat fleas and did not suffer or die from plague....

About 6 or 7 April, rats began to die in large numbers in a chawl or block of tenement houses. Suddenly the deaths among rats ceased, and on 11 April the people became troubled with fleas. The fleas became so numerous that they had to quit their rooms and sleep on the verandah. While living in the verandah on 17 April, one of the inhabitants of the particular room in which the fleas were taken became infected with plague. Another case occurred on the same day in a room adjoining. The people who inhabited the room where the above case occurred were induced by Mr Lord to collect some of the fleas from their persons which they said troubled them, and he sent the collection to me on 20 April. An examination of this collection was most instructive. Now I must tell you that on previous occasions, of 246 fleas which were caught on man under normal conditions, I had found only one rat flea, *pulex cheopis*. But of the collection of thirty fleas caught on man under the circumstances above recorded, no less than fourteen were rat fleas.

SMALLPOX: FROM TREATMENT TO ERADICATION

While smallpox continued to be devastating, treatment improved in the West. The noted English doctor of the Restoration period, Thomas Sydenham, was at the forefront of studying how it spread and devising more effective methods of treatment. Shortly thereafter, inoculation, also known as variolation, began to promise immunity. The practice – which involved collecting infectious material from a patient and using it to infect another in order to provoke a mild outbreak followed by immunity – had developed in Asia and was widespread in the Ottoman Empire, where Lady Mary Wortley Montagu, wife of the British ambassador, experienced it herself and brought the practice back to the West. As the practice slowly spread in Europe, the threat of a devastating epidemic there declined (though it still killed 400,000 people annually and was the cause in a third of all cases of blindness).

In North America the colonists were slower to adopt the new practice, and the Native Americans were not given the opportunity. As a result, smallpox continued to play a key role in North American history in the 18th century. In 1753 the British commander Lord Jeffrey Amherst, wanting to 'extirpate this execrable race', urged the use of blankets deliberately infected with smallpox to be put in the hands of Native Americans; whether or not his orders were followed, smallpox remained a devastating disease for many indigenous communities – not least perhaps because they followed disastrous treatment regimes. It also played a role in the American War of Independence, weakening the Continental Army at vital moments.

In 1796, the British doctor Edward Jenner, noting that those who had contracted the mild cowpox disease from cows did not catch smallpox, inoculated a boy with matter from a cox-pox blister and demonstrated that this gave him immunity to smallpox. This 'vaccination', much safer than variolation, proved a breakthrough and despite initial scepticism, brought the disease under control in the West.

In the 20th century, smallpox was identified as a disease that could be entirely eradicated through mass vaccination, and this was done in the 1960s and 1970s under the auspices of the World Health Organization (WHO);

in 1980 it was declared eradicated in the wild, and in 2020 remained the only disease to have been defeated in this manner.

Every house has a practitioner in the art of killing mankind

THOMAS SYDENHAM, *Observationes Medicae* (1669)

The influential English doctor Thomas Sydenham (see page 103) was particularly noted for his work on smallpox, studying its transmission and epidemiology as well as observing the disease in detail. He emphasized the importance of devising a treatment that was based on an expert understanding of the progress of the disease, denouncing the more cavalier approach of many doctors and nurses at the time.

As to what may be the essence of smallpox, I am, for my own part... wholly ignorant; this intellectual deficiency being the misfortune of human nature, and common to myself and the world at large. Nevertheless, when I carefully weigh the evidence, it suggests to me the idea of inflammation; of an inflammation specifically different from all others; of an inflammation both of the blood and humours. In clearing herself of this, Nature is at work during the first two or three days, striving at the digestion and concoction of the inflamed particles, with the intention of afterwards discharging them upon the surface of the body, for the sake of maturation, and finally of expelling them from her boundaries under the form of little abscesses.

We must, then, if we wish to make our *methodus medendi* [method of healing] the superstructure to a foundation in principles, recognize two periods in this disease; first, the period of separation; second, the period of expulsion.

The first of these two periods is generally passed in a febrile ebullition, which usually is completed within the first three or four days. During this stage, Nature is employed upon picking out and gathering together those inflamed elements which fret the blood, in making them over to the fleshy parts of the body, and in depositing them therein. This being accomplished, she returns to her former repose, having allayed the tumult which was excited, during her operations, in the blood.

When the ebullition has thus brought about the separation, the process of expulsion begins, and this continues during the remainder of the disease, by means of the little abscesses in the solid parts. These, inasmuch as they agree with a true abscess in character, pass through all the stages, viz. those of crudity, maturation and excrescence. If all this is done properly, matters are safe. Upon its being done properly, however, all the chance of cure depends. Everything goes wrong when this is faulty. Now, this last-named process, or that of expulsion, takes up more time than the other. It has to do its work in a thicker and denser medium, and on one more remote from the fountain of life. Whereas the separation takes place in a subtle and fluid body, and in the very focus of Nature.

With these premises, two indications of treatment present themselves. 1. The ebullition of the blood must be kept to a regular rate, so that it neither hurry over the work of separation too quickly and too violently; nor yet check it by any torpidity of movement. Still less must it work it out insufficiently. 2. The little abscesses, or pustules, must be carefully kept up, so that they may go through their proper stages, void the matter that they contain, and, finally, themselves disappear....

It is particularly dangerous for the patient to be over-heated during the period of secretion, while the fever is going on, and before the appearance of the pustules. It is no less dangerous for it to happen during any other stage of the complaint; more especially, however, is it mischievous at the approach of the expulsive epoch, while the pustules are yet crude....

It is clear that the disease and practice are equally uncertain. Hereupon, I venture to assert that the physician who has much to do with smallpox runs many risks with his reputation. The vulgar are ever in the habit of ascribing deaths to the officiousness of the attendant; while physicians themselves catch greedily at opportunities for slander. They make out their case before incompetent judges, and procure most uncharitable verdicts. They act thus in order that they may build up a name for themselves upon the ruined reputations of others; a proceeding disgraceful to even honest artisans, doubly disgraceful to scholars.

The aforesaid difficulties explain why over-active and officious nurses so often cause failures. It is a hard problem, and above the capacity of females, to determine the precise degree of the requisite heat, especially when other things have also to be considered, e.g. the age of the patient, his manner of life, the season of the year, &c. These are points for the sagacious and prudent physician.

I must now go over part of the ground again, and come more closely to our practice. The moment that undoubted signs of smallpox have shown themselves, I forbid the patient wine, meat and the open air. His ordinary drink is weak small beer, with a toast put in to take the chill off. His food is oatmeal porridge, barley broth, roasted apples and the like; articles which are neither hot nor cold, and which give no trouble to the digestion. I have no objection to a form of diet that is common in the country, and which consists of a roasted apple mashed with milk, only it must be taken at intervals, moderately and with the chill off the milk. Hot regimen I forbid altogether. I forbid also all such cordials as are used by some under the rash notion of propelling the pustules towards the skin before the fourth day....

From these statements it is easy to answer the common question, as to why so many of the poor survive, and so many of the rich sink under an attack of smallpox: that is, comparatively speaking. This can be referred to one cause only, viz., the want of opportunity on the part of the poor man for hurting himself by a nice and delicate regimen. Their *res angusta domi* [straitened circumstances] as well as their more countrified manner of life ensures this. Still, even among the vulgar, many more have died of smallpox, since they learned the use of mithridate, diascordium, decoction of hartshorn, &c., than there did during the previous ages less learned but more wise. Nowadays, every house has its old woman, a practitioner in an art which she never learnt, to the killing of mankind.

I went abroad, by his direction, till I was blind

THOMAS DOVER, *The Ancient Physician's Legacy to His Country (1684)*
Thomas Dover (1660–1742), a future doctor and author of The Ancient Physician's Legacy to His Country, *described his treatment for smallpox at Sydenham's hands in 1684. Sydenham distinguished between different forms of the disease (the 'flux' and 'anomalous' varieties of smallpox, plus a milder form of the disease which he called 'distinct').*

While I lived in Dr Sydenham's house, I had myself the smallpox, and fell ill on the twelfth day. In the beginning I lost twenty-two ounces of blood [from bloodletting]. He gave me a vomit, but I find by experience purging much better. I went abroad, by his direction, till I was blind, and then took to my bed. I had no fire allowed in my room, my windows were constantly open, my bedclothes were ordered to be laid no higher than my waist. He made me take twelve bottles of small beer, acidulated with spirit of vitriol, every twenty-four hours. I had of this anomalous kind [of smallpox] to a very great degree, yet never lost my senses one moment.

The oriental art of inoculation

LADY MARY WORTLEY MONTAGU, letter to a friend, 1 April 1717

The wife of the British ambassador to the Ottoman Empire, Lady Mary Wortley Montagu (1689–1762) had lost her own brother and herself had been disfigured by the disease in the 1710s. In Constantinople, she observed the effectiveness of inoculation as it was widely practised there, and subjected both herself and her children to it, as she remarked to a friend in this letter. On returning to England in 1720, she campaigned to have inoculation adopted more widely, and despite scepticism about what was seen as an oriental practice, it slowly caught on, with the royal family leading the way.

Apropos of distempers, I am going to tell you a thing that will make you wish yourself here. The smallpox, so fatal and so general among us, is here entirely harmless by the invention of ingrafting, which is the term they give it. There is a set of old women who make it their business to perform the operation every autumn, in the month of September, when the great heat is abated. People send to one another to know if any of their family has a mind to have the smallpox: they make parties for this purpose, and when they are met (commonly fifteen or sixteen together), the old woman comes with a nut-shell full of the matter of the best sort of smallpox, and asks what vein you please to have opened. She immediately rips open that you offer to her with a large needle (which gives you no more pain than a common scratch), and puts into the vein as much matter as can lie upon the head of her needle, and after that binds up the little wound with a hollow bit of shell; and in this manner opens four or five veins. The Grecians have commonly the superstition of opening one in the middle of the forehead, one in each arm and one on the breast, to mark the sign of the cross; but this has a very ill effect, all these wounds leaving little scars, and is not done by those that are not superstitious, who choose to have them in the legs, or that part of the arm that is concealed.

The children or young patients play together all the rest of the day, and are in perfect health to the eighth. Then the fever begins to seize them and they keep their beds two days, very seldom three. They have very rarely above twenty or thirty in their faces, which never mark; and in eight days' time they are as well as before their illness. Where they are wounded there remain running sores during the distemper, which I don't doubt is a great relief to it.

Every year thousands undergo this operation, and the French ambassador says pleasantly, that they take the smallpox here by way of diversion, as they take the waters in other countries. There is no example of anyone that has died in it, and you may believe I am well satisfied of the safety of this experiment, since I intend to try it on my dear little son.

I am patriot enough to take pains to bring this useful invention into fashion in England, and I should not fail to write to some of our doctors very particularly about it, if I knew any one of them that I thought had virtue enough to destroy such a considerable branch of their revenue for the good to mankind. But that distemper is too beneficial to them not to expose to all their resentment the hardy wight that should undertake to put an end to it. Perhaps, if I live to return, I may, however, have courage to war with them. Upon this occasion admire the heroism in the heart of your friend.

The heart of man is an unfathomable abyss

GIACOMO CASANOVA, *Story of My Life* (1790s)

The famous Italian libertine Giacomo Casanova (1725–1798) had a lifelong friendship with Bettina Gozzi, the sister of his tutor – and the young woman who gave him his first experience of sex, at the age of eleven. In his Story of My Life, *he described how, as a young man, he watched at the bedside of his usually lively, free-thinking friend as smallpox brought her close to death.*

After supper the servant informed me that Bettina had gone to bed with violent feverish chills, having previously had her bed carried into the kitchen beside her mother's....

The next day Doctor Olivo found her very feverish, and told her brother that she would most likely be excited and delirious, but that it would be the effect of the fever and not the work of the devil. And truly, Bettina was raving all day, but Dr Gozzi, placing implicit confidence in the physician, would not listen to his mother, and did not send for the Jacobin friar. The fever increased in violence, and on the fourth day the smallpox broke out. Cordiani and the two brothers Feitrini, who had so far escaped that disease, were immediately sent away, but as I had had it before I remained at home.

The poor girl was so fearfully covered with the loathsome eruption, that on the sixth day her skin could not be seen on any part of her body. Her eyes closed, and her life was despaired of, when it was found that her mouth and throat were obstructed to such a degree that she could swallow nothing but a few drops of honey. She was perfectly motionless; she breathed and that was all. Her mother never left her bedside, and I was thought a saint when I carried my table and my books into the patient's room. The unfortunate girl had become a fearful sight to look upon; her head was dreadfully swollen, the nose could no longer be seen, and much fear was entertained for her eyes, in case her life should be spared. The odour of her perspiration was most offensive, but I persisted in keeping my watch by her.

On the ninth day, the vicar gave her absolution, and after administering extreme unction, he left her, as he said, in the hands of God. In the midst of so much sadness, the conversation of the mother with her son, would, in spite of myself, cause me some amount of merriment. The good woman wanted to know whether the demon who was dwelling in her child could still influence her to perform extravagant follies, and what would become of the demon in the case of her daughter's death, for, as she expressed it, she could not think of his being so stupid as to remain in so loathsome a body. She particularly wanted to ascertain whether the demon had power to carry off the soul of her child. Doctor Gozzi, who was an ubiquitarian, made to all those questions answers which had not even the shadow of good sense, and which of course had no other effect than to increase a hundred-fold the perplexity of his poor mother.

During the tenth and eleventh days, Bettina was so bad that we thought every moment likely to be her last. The disease had reached its worst period; the smell was unbearable; I alone would not leave her, so sorely did I pity her. The heart of man is indeed an unfathomable abyss, for, however incredible it may appear, it was while in that fearful state that Bettina inspired me with the fondness which I showed her after her recovery.

On the thirteenth day the fever abated, but the patient began to experience great irritation, owing to a dreadful itching, which no remedy could have allayed as effectually as these powerful words which I kept constantly pouring into her ear: 'Bettina, you are getting better; but if you dare to scratch yourself, you will become such a fright that nobody will ever love you.' All the physicians in the universe might be challenged to prescribe a more potent remedy against itching for a girl who, aware that she has been pretty, finds herself exposed to the loss of her beauty through her own fault, if she scratches herself.

At last her fine eyes opened again to the light of heaven; she was moved to her own room, but she had to keep her bed until Easter. She inoculated me with a few pocks, three of which have left upon my face everlasting marks; but in her eyes they gave me credit for great devotedness, for they were a proof of my constant care, and she felt that I indeed deserved her whole love. And she truly loved me, and I returned her love, although I never plucked a flower which fate and prejudice kept in store for a husband. But what a contemptible husband!

Two years later she married a shoemaker, by name Pigozzo: a base, arrant knave who beggared and ill-treated her to such an extent that her brother had to take her home and to provide for her.

The practice of inoculation divided people

BENJAMIN FRANKLIN

The American polymath Benjamin Franklin (1706–1790) lost a son to smallpox in 1736, as he described in his autobiography. Thereafter he became a leading proponent of inoculation, working with doctors on both sides of the Atlantic to face down the religious objections of sceptics with convincing evidence of the value of the procedure.

The Autobiography of Benjamin Franklin (1771)

In 1736 I lost one of my sons, a fine boy of four years old, by the smallpox, taken in the common way. I long regretted bitterly, and still regret that I had not given it to him by inoculation. This I mention for the sake of parents who omit that operation, on the supposition that they should never forgive themselves if a child died under it; my example showing that the regret may be the same either way, and that, therefore, the safer should be chosen.

Franklin's Preface to William Heberden's Some Account of the Success of Inoculation for the Small-Pox in England and America (1759)

Having been desired by my greatly esteemed friend Dr William Heberden FRS, one of the principal physicians of this city, to communicate what account I had of the success of inoculation in Boston, New England, I some time since wrote and sent to him the following paper, viz.

'About 1753 or '54, the smallpox made its appearance in Boston, New England. It had not spread in the town for many years before, so that there were a great number of the inhabitants to have it. At first, endeavours were used to prevent its spreading, by removing the sick, or guarding the houses in which they were; and with the same view inoculation was forbidden; but when it was found that these endeavours were fruitless, the distemper breaking out in different quarters of the town, and increasing, inoculation was then permitted.

'Upon this, all that inclined to inoculation for themselves or families hurried into it precipitately, fearing the infection might otherwise be taken in the common way; the numbers inoculated in every neighbourhood spread the infection likewise more speedily among those who did not choose inoculation; so that in a few months, the distemper went through the town, and was extinct; and the trade of the town suffered only a short interruption, compared with what had been usual in former times, the country people during the seasons of that sickness fearing all intercourse with the town.

'As the practice of inoculation always divided people into parties, some contending warmly for it, and others as strongly against it; the latter asserting that the advantages pretended were imaginary, and that the surgeons, from views of interest, concealed or diminished the true number of deaths occasioned by inoculation, and magnified the number of those who died of the smallpox in the common way: it was resolved by the magistrates of the town to cause a strict and impartial enquiry to be made by the constables of each ward, who were to give in their returns upon oath.... Their several returns being received, and summed up together, the numbers turned out as follows,

Had the Smallpox in the common way		Of these died		Received the distemper by inoculation		Of these died	
Whites	Blacks	Whites	Blacks	Whites	Blacks	Whites	Blacks
5,059	485	452	62	1,974	139	23	7

'It appeared by this account that the deaths of persons inoculated, were more in proportion at this time than had been formerly observed, being something more than one in a hundred. The favourers of inoculation however would not allow that this was owing to any error in the former accounts, but rather to the inoculating at this time many unfit subjects, partly through the impatience of people who would not wait the necessary preparation, lest they should take it in the common way; and partly from the importunity of parents prevailing with the surgeons against their judgment and advice to inoculate weak children, labouring under other disorders.... The surgeons and physicians were also suddenly oppressed with the great hurry of business, which so hasty and general an inoculation and spreading of the distemper in the common way must occasion, and probably could not so particularly attend to the circumstances of the patients offered for inoculation.

'Inoculation was first practised in Boston by Dr Boylstone in 1720. It was not used before in any part of America, and not in Philadelphia till 1730. Some years since, an enquiry was made in Philadelphia of the several surgeons and physicians who had practised inoculation, what numbers had been by each inoculated, and what was the success. The result of this enquiry was, that upwards of 800 had been inoculated at different times, and that only four of them had died. If this account was true, as I believe it was, the reason of greater success there than had been found in Boston, where the general loss by inoculation used to be estimated at about one in 100, may probably be from this circumstance; that in Boston they always keep the distemper out as long as they can, so that when it comes, it finds a greater number of adult subjects than in Philadelphia, where since 1730 it has gone through the town once in four or five years, so that the greatest number of subjects for inoculation must be under that age.

'Notwithstanding the now uncontroverted success of inoculation, it does not seem to make that progress among the common people in America, which at first was expected. *Scruples of conscience* weigh with many, concerning the *lawfulness* of the practice: and if one parent or near relation is against it, the other does not choose to inoculate a child without free consent of all parties, lest in case of a disastrous event, perpetual blame should follow. These *scruples* a *sensible Clergy* may in time remove. The *expense* of having the operation performed by a surgeon, weighs with others, for that has been pretty high in some parts of America; and where a common tradesman or artificer has a number in his family to have the distemper, it amounts to more money than he can well spare. Many of these, rather than own the *true motive* for declining inoculation, join with the scrupulous in the cry *against it*, and influence others. A small pamphlet wrote in plain language by some skilful physician, and published, directing what preparations of the body should be used before the inoculation of children, what precautions to avoid giving the infection at the same time in the common way, and how the operation is to be performed, the incisions dressed, the patient treated and on the appearance of what symptoms a physician is to be called, &c. might by encouraging parents to inoculate their own children, be a means of removing that objection of the expense, render the practice much more general, and thereby save the lives of thousands.'

The doctor, after perusing and considering the above, humanely took the trouble of writing the following *Plain Instructions*, and generously, at his own private expense, printed a very large impression of them, which was put into my hands to be distributed *gratis* in America. Not aiming at the praise which however is justly due to such disinterested benevolence, he has omitted his name; but as I thought the advice of a nameless physician might possibly on that account be less regarded, I have without his knowledge here divulged it. And I have prefixed to his small but valuable work these pages, containing the facts that gave rise to it; because *facts* generally have, as indeed they ought to have, great weight in persuading to the practice they favour. To these I may also add an account I have been favoured with by Dr Archer, physician to the smallpox hospital here, viz.

Inoculated in this Hospital since its first institution to 31 Dec. 1758	Persons 1,601
Of which number have died	6
Patients who had the smallpox in the common way in this hospital	3,856
Of which number have died	1,002

By this account it appears, that in the way of inoculation there has died but *one* patient in 267, whereas in the common way there had died more than *one* in *four*.... I have also obtained from the Foundling Hospital (where all the children admitted, that have not had the smallpox, are inoculated at the age of five years) an account to this time of the success of that practice there, which stands thus, viz.

Inoculated, boys 162, girls 176, in all	338
Of these died in inoculation, only	2
(And the death of one of those two was occasioned by a worm fever)	

On the whole, if the chance were only as *two* to *one* in favour of the practice among children, would it not be sufficient to induce a tender parent to lay hold of the advantage? But when it is so much greater...surely parents will no longer refuse to accept and thankfully use a discovery God in his mercy has been pleased to bless mankind with; whereby some check may now be put to the ravages that cruel disease has been accustomed to make, and the human species be again suffered to increase as it did before the smallpox made its appearance.

A melancholy example of the ruin brought on an Indian nation

JOHN FERDINAND DALZIEL SMITH, *A Tour in the United States of America* (1784)

John Ferdinand Dalziel Smith (1745–1814) was a Scottish-born doctor who emigrated to Virginia and fought with the loyalists, returning to Britain in 1780. In his Tour in the United States of America, *he described his encounter with one of the Native American tribes in South Carolina that had been virtually wiped out by smallpox.*

This day I had the hour of being introduced to the king or chief of the Catawba nation, whose Indian appellation I cannot recollect but his English name is Joe. He appeared to be a strong, straight, well-looking, robust fellow, little or no way distinguishable from the rest otherwise than in the accidental gifts of his person; for he seemed to me the likeliest, best made and handsomest man in the nation.

I was not a little surprised to find that they all spoke English very intelligibly, and they informed me that they understand and pronounce it as well as their own language.

This once numerous, powerful and even lately very respectable nation is now dwindled away almost to nothing, there being at this time no more than sixty or seventy warriors in the whole, as such they are as would excite the derision and contempt of the more western savages, for these are in a kind of state of civilization which the Indians consider as enervating effeminacy and hold it in the utmost abhorrence.

The Catawbas afford a melancholy example, and striking but insuperable proof of the ruin and fatality brought on any Indian nation by the intemperance and vicinity of the settlements of the whites.

This astonishing havoc and depopulation, which is indeed most alarming, grievous and awful, and truly painful for humanity to reflect upon, has been occasioned in great measure by the introduction of the smallpox and spirituous liquors.

Their injudicious treatment of that infectious malady generally renders it fatal, for they make use of hot stimulating medicines to promote a most profuse diaphoresis [sweating], in the height of which, while reeking with sweat and dissolving in streams of warm moisture, they rush out into the open air, quite naked, and suddenly plunge into the deepest and coldest stream of running water that can be found, immersing their whole body in the chilling flood.

It may well be supposed that if their recovery was doubtful before, this renders it totally impossible, and the poor unfortunate victims fall sacrifices to the most wretched ignorance and folly.

Defeated by the smallpox

CALEB HASKELL, diary entries while outside Quebec City, 1775/6

Smallpox weakened not only the Native Americans, but also the New World white population. In 1775 during the American War of Independence, the Continental Army attacked Quebec City, hoping to weaken the British position in the north and induce the French Canadians to support their cause. The attack was a failure, in large part because of a smallpox outbreak in the American army as recorded by Caleb Haskell, a Massachusetts-born fife player, who was one of its victims. The following winter George Washington took the decision to have his entire army inoculated while resting at Valley Forge.

Tuesday, 12 December 1775 Exceedingly cold. Our guards were moved down towards the city; but little firing on either side today. At night I was on guard. We moved our cannon down to our batteries; getting in readiness to storm the city.

Wednesday, 13 December Today the enemy kept a continual firing with cannon and small arms. At night we were employed mounting our cannon on our breastworks. We had a number of shells thrown at us in our breastworks. At midnight we were beat off by the snow.

Thursday, 14 December The enemy keep up a continual firing upon us in our breastworks.... Employed tonight in getting in readiness to play upon the city in the morning.

Friday, 15 December Early this morning a hot cannonading began on both sides, which lasted several hours. We sent a flag to the city, but were refused. The firing began again and lasted till dark. We had one of our carriages cut down, and one man killed on our breastworks.

Saturday, 16 December Had but little firing today. We had one man killed with grape shot. I am unwell, and have been for three days unfit for duty.

Sunday, 17 December I was ordered to the hospital. A bad storm; could not go.

Monday, 18 December Myself and four more of our company were carried to the Nunnery hospital. All still on both sides.

Tuesday, 19 December Today three of those who came to the hospital with me broke out with the smallpox; I have the same symptoms.

Wednesday, 20 December This morning my bedfellow, with myself, were broke out with smallpox; we were carried three miles out in the country out of the camp; I am very ill.

Thursday, 21 December The smallpox spreads fast in our army.

Friday, 22 December Poor attendance; no bed to lie on; no medicine to take; troubled much with a sore throat.

Saturday, 23 December My distemper works very bad. Does not fill out.

Sunday, 24 December I feel much better today; am able to sit up much of the day.

Monday, 25 December Christmas; a pleasant day. We have nothing from the camp.

Tuesday, 26 December There were two men brought here today with the smallpox.

Wednesday, 27 December A man in our room died today with the smallpox. I am getting better every day.

Thursday, 28 December All the houses in the neighbourhood are full of our soldiers with the smallpox. It goes favourably with the most of them.

Friday, 29 December We have nothing from the camp.

Saturday, 30 December My distemper leaves me fast. I went to the door today.

Sunday, 31 December Heard from the camp that General Montgomery intended to storm the city soon. A bad snowstorm. One of our company died of smallpox about twelve o'clock tonight.

Monday, 1 January 1776 About four o'clock this morning we perceived a hot engagement at the city by the blaze of the cannon and small arms, but could hear no report by reason of the wind and storm, it being a violent snowstorm. We supposed that General Montgomery had stormed the city. Just after daylight all was still. We are fearful and anxious to hear the transactions of last night.

This morning I took my clothes and pack on my back, being very weak and feeble after the smallpox. Returned to the camp. Found all my officers and three of my messmates and almost all the company taken or killed, and the rest in great confusion. Could get no particular account of the siege till the afternoon....

Thus we were defeated, with the loss of our general and upwards of four hundred of our officers and men killed or taken. Every captain in Colonel Arnold's party was killed or taken, and but four of his men escaped and they invalids.

Annihilation of the smallpox must be the final result
EDWARD JENNER

A hero of the battle against smallpox, Edward Jenner (1749–1823) was a country doctor in Gloucestershire, England, who became interested in the transmission of diseases between species. It had been known for some time that women in contact with cows infected with the relatively mild cowpox seemed immune to smallpox; Jenner was able to demon-strate this, as he described in two works, An Inquiry into the Causes and Effects of the Variolae Vaccinae, *and* On the Origin of the Vaccine Inoculation. *His success led directly to widespread vaccination.*

An Inquiry into the Causes and Effects of the Variolae Vaccinae (1798)
In the present age of scientific investigation, it is remarkable that a disease of so peculiar a nature as the cowpox, which has appeared in this and some of the neighbouring counties for such a series of years, should so long have escaped particular attention. Finding the prevailing notions on the subject, both among men of our profession and others, extremely vague and indeterminate, and conceiving that facts might appear at once both curious and useful, I have instituted as strict an inquiry into the causes and effects of this singular malady as local cir-cumstances would admit....

The deviation of man from the state in which he was originally placed by nature seems to have proved to him a prolific source of diseases. From the love of splendour, from the indulgences of luxury and from his fond-ness for amusement, he has familiarized himself with a great number of animals, which may not originally have been intended for his associates.

The wolf, disarmed of ferocity, is now pillowed in the lady's lap. The cat, the little tiger of our island, whose natural home is the forest, is equally domesticated and caressed. The cow, the hog, the sheep and the horse, are all, for a variety of purposes, brought under his care and dominion.

There is a disease to which the horse, from his state of domestication, is frequently subject. The farriers have termed it 'the grease'. It is an inflammation and swelling in the heel, from which issues matter possessing properties of a very peculiar kind, which seems capable of generating a disease in the human body (after it has undergone the modification which I shall presently speak of), which bears so strong a resemblance to the smallpox, that I think it highly probable it may be the source of that disease.

In this dairy country a great number of cows are kept, and the office of milking is performed indiscriminately by men and maid servants. One of the former having been appointed to apply dressings to the heels of a horse affected with 'the grease', and not paying due attention to cleanliness, incautiously bears his part in milking the cows, with some particles of the infectious matter adhering to his fingers. When this is the case, it commonly happens that a disease is communicated to the cows, and from the cows to the dairymaids, which spreads through the farm until most of the cattle and domestics feel its unpleasant consequences.

This disease has obtained the name of the cowpox. It appears on the nipples of the cows in the form of irregular pustules. At their first appearance they are commonly of a palish blue, or rather of a colour somewhat approaching to livid, and are surrounded by an erysipelatous inflammation [bacterial infection of the skin]. These pustules, unless a timely remedy be applied, frequently degenerate into phagedenic ulcers, which prove extremely troublesome. The animals become indisposed, and the secretion of milk is much lessened. Inflamed spots now begin to appear on different parts of the hands of the domestics employed in milking, and sometimes on the wrists, which quickly run on to suppuration, first assuming the appearance of the small vesications [blisters] produced by a burn. Most commonly they appear about the joints of the fingers, and at their extremities; but whatever parts are affected, if the situation will admit, these superficial suppurations put on a circular form, with their edges more elevated than their centre, and of a colour distantly approaching to blue. Absorption takes place, and tumours appear in each axilla. The system becomes affected – the pulse is quickened; and shiverings succeeded by heat, with general lassitude and pains about the loins and limbs, with vomiting, come on. The head is painful, and the patient is now and then even affected with delirium....

The lips, nostrils, eyelids and other parts of the body, are sometimes affected with sores, but these evidently arise from their being heedlessly rubbed or scratched with the patient's infected fingers. No eruptions on the skin have followed the decline of the feverish symptoms in any instance that has come under my inspection, one only excepted, and in this case a very few appeared on the arms: they were very minute, of a vivid red colour and soon died away without advancing to maturation, so that I cannot determine whether they had any connection with the preceding symptoms.

Thus the disease makes its progress from the horse to the nipple of the cow, and from the cow to the human subject.

Morbid matter of various kinds, when absorbed into the system, may produce effects in some degree similar; but what renders the cowpox virus so extremely singular, is, that the person who has been thus affected is for ever after secure from the infection of the smallpox; neither exposure to the variolous effluvia, nor the insertion of the matter into the skin, producing this distemper.

On the Origin of the Vaccine Inoculation (1801)

I was struck with the idea that it might be practicable to propagate the disease by inoculation, after the manner of the smallpox, first from the cow, and finally from one human being to another. I anxiously waited some time for an opportunity of putting this theory to the test. At length the period arrived. The first experiment was made upon a lad of the name of Phipps, in whose arm a little vaccine virus was inserted, taken from the hand of a young woman who had been accidentally infected by a cow.

Notwithstanding the resemblance which the pustule, thus excited on the boy's arm, bore to variolous inoculation, yet as the indisposition attending it was barely perceptible, I could scarcely persuade myself the patient was secure from the smallpox. However, on his being inoculated some months afterwards, it proved that he was secure. (This boy was inoculated nearly at the expiration of five years afterwards with variolous matter, but no other effect was produced beyond a local inflammation around the punctured part upon the arm.)

This case inspired me with confidence; and as soon as I could again furnish myself with virus from the cow, I made an arrangement for a series of inoculations. A number of children were inoculated in succession, one from the other; and after several months had elapsed, they were exposed to the infection of the smallpox; some by inoculation, others by variolous effluvia, and some in both ways; but they all resisted it.

The result of these trials gradually led me into a wider field of experiment, which I went over not only with great attention, but with painful solicitude. This became universally known through a Treatise published in June 1798. The result of my further experience was also brought forward in subsequent publications in the two succeeding years, 1799 and 1800. The distrust and scepticism which naturally arose in the minds of medical men, on my first announcing so unexpected a discovery, has now nearly disappeared. Many hundreds of them, from actual experience, have given their attestations that the inoculated cowpox proves a perfect security against the smallpox; and I shall probably be within compass if I say, thousands are ready to follow their example; for the scope that this inoculation has now taken is immense. A hundred thousand persons, upon the smallest computation, have been inoculated in these realms. The numbers who have partaken of its benefits throughout Europe and other parts of the globe are incalculable: and it now becomes too manifest to admit of controversy, that the annihilation of the smallpox, the most dreadful scourge of the human species, must be the final result of this practice.

Anti-Vaccination Society of America
USA, late 19th century
Scepticism about vaccination has been a constant on both sides of the Atlantic ever since Jenner, especially so in Britain after infant vaccination was made compulsory in 1853. After widespread and prolonged protest, penalties for non-compliance were removed in 1898, and a 'conscientious objection' clause introduced to permit parents to opt out. In the United States, an anti-vaccination movement was established in 1879. It has taken several forms: a libertarian objection to compulsory invasion of the body of a child; a religious objection to the introduction of animal matter into the human body; a general mistrust of scientific expertise; and a fear of side effects more dangerous than the original disease.

Help End Compulsory Vaccination!

We want our children to go to school without first having to be vaccinated.

The law says our children must go to school. This is our law. We, the people, approve this law.

Another law prevents the child from entering school without being vaccinated. If parents object to vaccination they are jailed and fined for not sending their child to school.

This is not our law. We, the people, do not approve of it.

It conflicts with the educational law. It discriminates against the public schoolchild. The law does not apply to private and parochial schools.

It discriminates against the school child in the larger cities. The law applies only to cities of the first and second classes.

Help us destroy this discriminatory law.

Help us end this outrage against our children.

VACCINATION DESTROYS HEALTH AND LIFE

Vaccination is the forcible introduction into the body of an individual of putrid pus squeezed from the festering sores on the abdomen of a sick cow which has previously been infected with smallpox.

VACCINE IS PUS. It is septic (poisonous) matter. It produces inflammation, fever, discomfort, suppuration and ulceration, intense itching, enlargement of the glands of the armpit and neck, skin eruptions of various kinds, abscesses, erysipelas, cellulitis, syphilis, tetanus (lock jaw), blood poisoning, sleeping sickness, infantile paralysis, meningitis, leprosy and death. It causes latent tuberculosis to become active.

Winning over the 'fetisheurs'

WILLIAM H. FOEGE, *House on Fire: The Fight to Eradicate Smallpox* (2011)

In 1959, WHO began a plan to eradicate smallpox worldwide, led by American doctor D. A. Henderson; after a slow start the programme was intensified in 1967, with the help of American physician William H. Foege (b. 1936), who led the campaign on the ground in Africa and India. He described his work in House on Fire: The Fight to Eradicate Smallpox.

In West Africa, variolation was performed by practitioners called *fetisheurs*. In 1969, while visiting Benin (then called Dahomey), I spent a day with one practitioner. He looked like a typical village person but was better dressed. He exuded the confidence of a person who knows more than those around him, though without the arrogance often seen in city dwellers who returned to their villages for a visit. He enjoyed talking, and through an interpreter answered my most probing questions with candour and clarity. Indeed, he reminded me of an attending physician teaching a medical student.

The *fetisheur*, it became clear, knew exactly what he was doing. When a person had smallpox, the family would consult him. He would instruct the patient on what he or she needed to do to recover. The *fetisheur* knew that the mortality rate for smallpox in his area was between 20 and 25 per cent. He also knew that most of his patients would therefore recover, regardless of treatment. The *fetisheur* was rewarded by the family either way. If the patient died, he simply informed the family that the patient had not followed his very specific instructions.

Fetisheurs, he explained, used visits to patients as opportunities to collect scabs which they kept in bottles in a dark place, having discovered that sunlight and heat render the virus impotent. If no smallpox had occurred for some time and a *fetisheur* needed business, he could seed an outbreak by what amounted to covert variolation. He would grind scabs into a paste, coat thorn branches with the paste and place these in doorways where they would scratch unsuspecting passers-by. Even a single 'take' could start a new outbreak.

In due course, the practitioner introduced me to his two students, who were serving two-year 'residencies' to learn the trade. The knowledge of smallpox and its transmission was impressive. In their efforts to understand and communicate about the cause of the disease, however, the *fetisheurs* did not use what we in the West would call a scientific approach. Rather, they told patients that they had contracted the disease because they were being punished for some previous offence. When I asked why babies, too young to have committed misdeeds, sometimes contracted the disease, the three men responded almost in unison: the baby was being punished for something the parents had done.

The disappearance of smallpox from West Africa was bad for business and the *fetisheurs* did not give up their entire smallpox enterprise without a fight. Multiple *fetisheurs* visited the last smallpox patient in Benin in order to harvest scabs, but they were unable to propagate the virus and smallpox disappeared despite their best efforts. Adapting to market chances, some began to consult on cases of chickenpox, with a high success rate for recovery.

Declaration of Global Eradication of Smallpox

World Health Organization, 33rd World Health Assembly, 8 May 1980

The final case of smallpox in the community was in Somalia in 1977, when hospital cook Ali Maow Maalin developed the disease and recovered. However, the following year, a British medical photographer Janet Parker died of the disease, which she caught in the laboratory at Birmingham University where research on the virus was being conducted. Two years later, smallpox was declared to be globally eradicated. Small stocks of the variola virus are kept in the United States and Russia.

The Thirty-Third World Health Assembly, on this eighth day of May 1980, Having considered the development and results of the global programme on smallpox eradication initiated by WHO in 1958 and intensified since 1967; Declares solemnly that the world and all its peoples have won freedom from smallpox which was a most devastating disease seeping in epidemic form through many countries since earliest times, leaving death, blindness and disfigurement in its wake and which only a decade ago was rampant in Africa, Asia and South America;

Expresses its deep gratitude to all nations and individuals who contributed to the success of this noble and historic endeavour;

Calls this unprecedented achievement in the history of public health to the attention of all nations, which by their collective action have freed mankind of this ancient scourge and, in so doing, have demonstrated how nations working together in a common cause may further human progress.

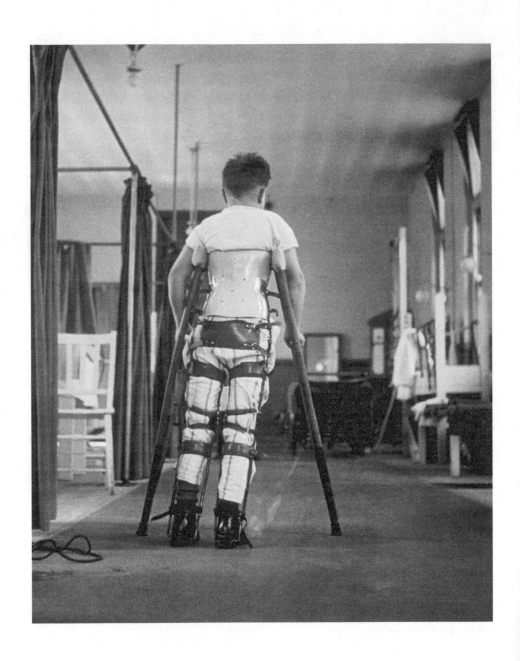

A child suffering from polio learns to walk again with the aid of a
special support at Queen Mary's Hospital, London, 1947.

PART V
THE 20TH CENTURY

The 20th century saw a sea-change in the pandemic threat that societies faced, and in the way they prepared for them and dealt with them.

With improved knowledge of pathogens and means of transmission, pandemics were no longer mysterious or acts of God, but natural events that could be anticipated, prepared for and under normal conditions mitigated by civil and military authorities. Equally, with growing availability of vaccines, antibiotics and other drugs, outbreaks could be confined and treated more effectively than ever before.

As a result, epidemics of many of the old infectious diseases gradually became limited to places disrupted by war or natural disaster, or developing countries unable to afford the infrastructure or health services required. Instead, pathogens such as influenza and polio aroused new fears; these were not diseases of poverty but could strike at the heart of the family life, even of the well to do.

While many countries invested in public health schemes and preventive medicine, international cooperation was also possible for the first time, mainly under the auspices of the World Health Organization, set up after the Second World War to collect accurate data about disease around the world, to create an early warning system for new epidemics, and to coordinate international efforts to eradicate diseases, for which smallpox and polio have seen the most successful programmes to date.

On the other hand, some older and highly infectious pathogens, particularly influenza, grew in importance, able to spread quickly across the globe thanks to the growth in fast mass transport. The ability of the flu virus to mutate quickly, and to transfer from its reservoirs in the animal kingdom to humans, made it a growing threat, and by the end of the 20th century it had become clear that global preparations were required for the next flu pandemic.

'SPANISH FLU'

Influenza – a highly infectious respiratory disease, caused by several types of influenza virus that have a natural reservoir in the world's bird population but periodically jump to humans, sometimes via pigs – had been described by Hippocrates in the 5th century BC, and from the 16th century there have been many reported epidemics. It has recurred in many forms and sometimes with great intensity since the late 19th century as the continually mutating virus means that neither exposure to the disease nor vaccination confer long-term immunity. Devastating attacks by influenza viruses in modern times have included the 'Russian flu' of 1889–90, which killed perhaps 1 million, mainly in Russia; Asian flu of 1957–58 (see page 243), which infected perhaps 500 million and killed about 2 million; Hong Kong flu of 1968–69 which killed about 1 million (see page 248); and the 2009 pandemic, which killed about half a million. In addition, outside of these pandemics, seasonal flu typically kills half a million people each year.

The most dramatic pandemic, however, was undoubtedly that of 1918–20, which affected every continent, infected between a third and a half of the world population and had an exceptionally high mortality rate, which resulted in an estimated 50 million deaths within a few months. 'Spanish flu' occurred in three waves, of which the second, beginning in the autumn of 1918, was the deadliest. The spread of this H1N1 virus was made possible by the unique conditions of the mass armies that brought together previous disparate populations in the First World War: it was first observed in army camps in the United States, and spread in the crowded British Army camp at Étaples in northern France, in 1917; however, it has sometimes been speculated that the virus was introduced to both continents by labourers from China. The virus acquired its name only because, whereas combatant nations in the First World War were reluctant to publicize it, the neutral Spain had no such restrictions on the press and therefore its outbreak in early 1918 was the first to come to public attention. The press, though, had fewer qualms about reporting outbreaks among the armies of their enemies.

Unusually, men in the prime of life, as well as the obviously vulnerable very young and very old, were badly hit; between 10 and 20 per cent of those who contracted it would die, sometimes within hours, if not days, of the first symptoms; it spread very fast, both geographically and within a community; its cause was unknown; there was no cure; and preventive measures were crude. A vaccine was tried, but to little effect, as it targeted not the as-yet unknown influenza virus but a bacillus that commonly caused serious secondary symptoms. In Britain, 228,000 people died, mostly in the period September to December 1918. The United States lost as many as 675,000 people; in India, fatalities totalled between 12 and 17 million.

Despite all this, the pandemic was not met with a strong public reaction. Initially, it was treated as something of a joke; at a time when the public was inured to mass death in the trenches, the pandemic may have seemed more of the same. In Britain, it was never discussed in Cabinet or mentioned in Parliament until October 1918. There was little analysis in the press, nor was it much covered by artists or writers. Public health measures – such as closing cinemas and schools or requiring people to wear masks in the street – were introduced to varying degrees in different places, but their value was debated even among health professionals.

The Spanish Epidemic: 700 Deaths in 10 Days

The Times, 3 June 1918

While there had been reports of 'Spanish flu' in the British press since the spring of 1918, none had taken the outbreak seriously, until this report in The Times of early June.

The unknown disease which appeared in Madrid a fortnight ago spread with remarkable rapidity. Owing to its benign character it was at first, together with its victims, the subject of much good-natured badinage and pleasant writing in the newspapers. Today the complaint has passed the joking stage. It is reported that there are well over 100,000 victims in Madrid alone, and the numbers are increasing daily. It has reached most of the provincial capitals and Morocco, where it has attacked the Spanish garrison. So rapid has been its advance, especially in thickly populated centres, that the public services have been seriously disorganized.

Further bacteriological information must be awaited

Report in the *British Medical Journal*, 8 June 1918

The medical establishment struggled to identify the true cause of the disease. In 1892 the bacterium known as Bacillus influenzae, *or Pfieffer's bacillus, was identified by German physician Richard Pfieffer and was widely believed to be the cause of influenza until the 1930s when the virus was finally isolated. This analysis was published in the* British Medical Journal *in June 1918.*

The widespread epidemic of an acute catarrhal affection in Spain, which was stated in our last issue to be most probably influenza and attended by little or no mortality, is now reported to have caused 700 deaths in ten days, but if the number of cases has been as large as reported the case mortality must have been very low.

The Times of 3 June quoted Dr Pittaluga to the effect that the disease attacks the respiratory rather than the abdominal organs; that relapses frequently occur within a few days; and that, although the disease is clearly of the character of influenza, bacteriological examination has not resulted in the discovery of the influenza bacillus, but has revealed an organism described as the parameningococcus.

It is well known that the *Bacillus influenzae* is quite commonly absent in cases clinically characteristic of influenza, and that *Micrococcus catarrhalis*, which has some superficial resemblance to the parameningococcus, is very commonly found. Although, as recent reports of the Medical Research Committee have shown, an epidemic of meningococcus carriers may reach a very high percentage among contacts, we are not cognizant of any previous outbreak of cerebro-spinal fever in any degree comparable in extent to the epidemic in Spain. Before coming to any conclusion it is obvious that further bacteriological information must be awaited.

Dropping on parade like flies

WILFRED OWEN, letter to his mother, 24 June 1918

In June 1918, the war poet Wilfred Owen (1893–1918) was in Scarborough with his regiment, after a period of treatment for shell shock. He returned to frontline duties on the Western Front in September and was killed on 4 November. His letter to his mother, written on 24 June, suggests he was putting a brave face on an already alarming situation.

STAND BACK FROM THE PAGE! and disinfect yourself. Quite 1/3 of the Battalion and about 30 officers are smitten with the Spanish Flu. The hospital overflowed on Friday, then the Gymnasium was filled, and now all the place seems carpeted with huddled blankcted forms. Only the very bad cases have beds. The boys are dropping on parade like flies in number. Priestley and the Adjutant are the two latest cases....

The thing is much too common for me to take part in. I have quite decided not to! Scottie, whom I still see sometimes, went under today, and my servant yesterday. Imagine the work that falls on unaffected officers.

Influenza Spreading in Germany: Berlin Industries Affected

The Times, 3 July 1918

In contrast to the minimal coverage of the flu in Britain, The Times *was quite happy to report its impact on the German war effort.*

Spanish influenza is increasing in Germany to an alarming extent. Many large industries in Berlin are suffering from the illness of their employees. In two weeks the number of patients on the books of the Berlin local sickness insurance office has increased from 10,000 to 18,000. From 200 to 300 new patients are reported daily. In the greater part of Bavaria 'Spanish influenza' prevails, and cases are increasing daily in Munich. The epidemic is also reported from Nuremberg, Regensburg, Passau, Ingolstadt, Landshut and various other places. Another Berlin report says that a large number of patients suffering from influenza were received on Monday into the larger Berlin hospitals. Conferences have been held at main Headquarters in which all the high army medical authorities participated, to discuss means of preventing the spread of the epidemic to the front.

We eat it, sleep it and dream it

N. ROY GRIST, letter sent from Camp Devens, Boston,
29 September 1918

US Army physician N. Roy Grist, based at Camp Devens outside Boston, described the desperate situation that faced him to a fellow physician

Burt in a letter written at the end of September 1918. A new wave of the flu in the United States occurred among returned soldiers in Boston on 27 August; the disease reached Camp Devens on 8 September. Three weeks after that, more than 10,000 cases of flu had been seen among the 45,000 men stationed in the camp on their way to France.

These men start with what appears to be an attack of *la grippe* or influenza, and when brought to the hospital they very rapidly develop the most viscous type of pneumonia that has ever been seen. Two hours after admission they have the mahogany spots over the cheek bones, and a few hours later you can begin to see the cyanosis extending from their ears and spreading all over the face, until it is hard to distinguish the coloured men from the white. It is only a matter of a few hours then until death comes, and it is simply a struggle for air until they suffocate. It is horrible. One can stand it to see one, two or twenty men die, but to see these poor devils dropping like flies sort of gets on your nerves....

It's more comfortable when one has a friend about.... I want to find some fellow who will not 'talk shop' but there ain't none, no how. We eat it, sleep it and dream it, to say nothing of breathing it sixteen hours a day. I would be very grateful indeed if you would drop me a line or two once in a while, and I promise you that if you ever get into a fix like this, I will do the same for you.

It was sure pitiful to see them die

LUTIANT VAN WERT, letter sent from Washington DC,
   17 October 1918

Lutiant Van Wert, a Native American woman, volunteered as a nurse in Washington DC. In this letter, she wrote to a friend at the Haskell Institute, a school for Native American students in Kansas, about the flu epidemic in the capital.

Dear friend Louise,
So everybody has the 'Flu' at Haskell? I wish to goodness that Miss Keck and Mrs McK would get it and die with it. Really, it would be such a good riddance, and not much lost either! As many as ninety people die every day here with the 'Flu'. Soldiers too are dying by the dozens. So far, Felicity,

C. Zane and I are the only ones of the Indian girls who have not had it. We certainly consider ourselves lucky, too, believe me. Katherine and I just returned last Sunday evening from Camp Humphreys 'Somewhere in Virginia', where we volunteered to help nurse soldiers sick with the influenza. We were there at the camp ten days among some of the very worst cases and yet we did not contract it. We had intended staying much longer than we did, but the work was entirely too hard for us, and anyway the soldiers were all getting better so we came home to rest up a bit....

When I was in the officers' barracks, four of the officers of whom I had charge, died. Two of them were married and called for their wife nearly all the time. It was sure pitiful to see them die. I was right in the ward alone with them each time, and oh! The first one that died sure unnerved me – I had to go to the nurses' quarters and cry it out. The other three were not so bad. Really, Louise. Orderlies carried the dead soldiers out on stretchers at the rate of two every three hours for the first two days we were there.

Two German spies posing as doctors were caught giving these Influenza germs to the soldiers and they were shot last Saturday morning at sunrise. It sure is a horrible thing, it is hard to believe and yet such things happen almost every day in Washington....

Washington is certainly a beautiful place. The Washington Monument is within walking distance of the Interior Department where we work.... But the place is closed temporarily on account of this 'Flu' ... All the schools, churches, theaters, dancing halls etc are closed here also. There is a Bill in the Senate today authorizing all the war-workers to be released from work for the duration of this epidemic. It has not passed the House yet but I can't help but hope it does. If it does, I can find plenty of things at home to busy myself with, or I might accidentally take a trip to Potomac Park. Ha! He!

Wear the mask to cover the nose and the mouth

St Paul Pioneer Press, 6 November 1918

The St Paul Pioneer Press, *the newspaper for St Paul, Minnesota, offered helpful advice on how to wear a mask against the flu. Masks were not always obligatory, and many doctors opposed them as unnecessary, but they proved popular with the public, and with businesses that identified a new market.*

The outside of a face mask is marked with a black thread woven into it. Always wear this side away from the face. Wear the mask to cover the nose and the mouth, tying two tapes around the head above the ears. Tie the other tapes rather tightly around the neck. Never wear the mask of another person. When the mask is removed...it should be carefully folded with the inside folded in, immediately boiled and disinfected. When the mask is removed by one seeking to protect himself from the influenza it should be folded with the inside folded out and boiled ten minutes. Persons considerably exposed to the disease should boil their masks at least once a day.

No one was able to get out of bed for days

IMTALE GRILLO, account of the flu epidemic in New Jersey, 1918

A member of a first-generation Italian-American family in New Jersey, Imtale Grillo described how his family suffered the flu in 1918, but all survived.

My grandfather, Antonio Grillo and my mother, Frances told me stories about how our family survived the 1918 flu, but that many of their neighbors did not.

My grandparents had emigrated from Palermo, Sicily, in 1912 and had not really learned to speak English yet. They lived on the farm in East Vineland, New Jersey. The family consisted of my grandfather, grandmother, my mother, who was six at the time, and two or three younger brothers.

The farm was near an intersection with the Mays Landing Highway and soldiers traveling home from the war would stop to ask for water. Although they could not understand the soldiers, they always gave them water or allowed them to drink water from the well.

In 1918, a few days after some soldiers had stopped for water, the entire family got sick. Antonio thought the soldiers had made the water bad. The entire family was sick with high fever, vomiting and diarrhea. Mum said that she and her brothers were all in their parents' bed together and everyone was so sick, that no one was able to get out of bed for days.

Down the road from their farm was a couple who spoke English. The man came to their house to check on them. He killed several chickens from their chicken coup, made chicken soup and then spoon fed each one of the family. This man helped my grandparents to the outhouse, cleaned them up, changed the bed sheets, cleaned the children and put all the dirty sheets and clothing in a pile outside.

After they all recovered, other neighbors said this man had come to their home to check on them, too, and offered or gave them chicken soup.... After the flu was over, they went to the man's house but it was empty. No one knew if the couple had moved away or if both had died, but their kindness has never been forgotten.

Death of an avant-garde pioneer

BLAISE CENDRARS, interview, 1950

The French poet Guillaume Apollinaire (1880–1918), one of the key figures of the Parisian avant-garde world, was close to both Picasso and Braque and is said to have invented the term Cubism. In 1914 he volunteered for the French Army, and was wounded two years later. In early November 1918 he met the poet Blaise Cendrars (1887–1961) in Paris and they discussed the flu epidemic; a few days later Apollinaire succumbed to it, dying on 9 November. Cendrars described the burial on 13 November.

The final absolution having been given, the casket of Apollinaire left the church of St Thomas Aquinas, draped in a flag, Guillaume's lieutenant helmet on the *tricolor*, among the flowers and wreaths. A guard of honour, a squad of soldiers, arms at their sides, led the slow convoy, the family behind the carriage, his mother, his wife, in their mourning veils, the poor Jacqueline, who had escaped the epidemic which had taken Guillaume, but who was still weak, the intimate friends of Apollinaire, Picasso, all the other great friends of Guillaume, all of literary Paris, Paris of the arts, the press. But as it reached the corner of Saint-Germain, the cortège was besieged by a crowd of noisy celebrants of the Armistice, men and women with arms waving, singing, dancing, kissing, shouting deliriously....

It was fantastic, Paris celebrating. Apollinaire lost. I was full of melancholy. It was absurd.

To the People of New South Wales

Government of New South Wales, 3 February 1919

The worst of the flu reached Australia in early 1919; in Sydney 40 per cent of the population caught the virus. Public health measures were decided at state level. The weakness of this was evident and after the pandemic had passed, a federal Department of Health was established. This edict, though, was issued by New South Wales premier William Holman (1871–1934).

A danger greater than war faces the State of New South Wales and threatens the lives of all. Each day the progress of the battle is published in the Press. Watch out for it. Follow the advice given and the fight can be won. Already efforts made by the government have had the effect of keeping the New South Wales figures down. But everybody is not yet working, so from today on the government insists that the many shall not be placed in danger by the few, and that
EVERYONE SHALL WEAR A MASK.
Those who are not doing so are not showing their independence – they are only showing their indifference for the lives of others, for the lives of the women and the helpless little children who cannot help themselves.

CABINET DECISIONS
At a special meeting of the Cabinet held yesterday, the following recommendations were adopted:

1. Long-distance trains – no need to restrict railway travel in New South Wales as yet, although it may be necessary to do so at any moment.
2. Hotels, bars, restaurants, tea houses: not to be closed at the present time but the 250 cubic feet regulation to apply to them.
3. Retail shops: space regulation to apply; also prohibition of bargain and clearing sales, and a recommendation that orders be telephoned.
4. Church services: prohibition of both indoor and outdoor services.
5. Auction rooms: prohibition of all sales in rooms.
6. Libraries: reading rooms to be closed down.
7. Billiards rooms: to be closed.
8. Race meetings: prohibited.
9. Theatres, music halls, indoor public entertainments: prohibited.
10. Beaches: no restrictions to be placed upon the free uses of the

beaches on the ground that the risk of infection is likely to be more than counterbalanced by the benefits that will ensue.

11. Open air meetings in the domain and other places: prohibited.
12. Churches and schools outside the County of Cumberland: not to be closed. Local authorities not to act on own initiative but to be asked to refer to Public Health Department in every instance.

The Day of Masks: Gauze Versus the Microbe
Sydney Morning Herald, 4 February 1919
The day after New South Wales introduced compulsory masks, the Sydney Morning Herald *reported on the impact on citizens of wearing them in the midsummer heat.*

Sydney was officially supposed to be masked yesterday.

Generally speaking citizens responded cheerfully enough to the order of the government. But it was a very hot day, and as the hours passed it is to be feared that a very material section of the community, who found it necessary to move about the streets, were much less cheerful behind their masks than they were at an earlier stage of acquaintance with the innovation. There is no doubt about one effect of wearing a mask on a person whose affairs involve much locomotion. It imposes a rather trying test upon both his temper and his endurance. After an hour or so there is an overwhelming sense of partial suffocation, a feeling of intense heat and an almost unconquerable yearning for surreptitious inhalations of atmosphere without the intervention of gauze.

Dying by Hundreds: The Influenza Scourge in Cape Town
Matron of the Cape Town General Hospital, *The Times*,
    6 January 1919

Some 300,000 people may have died in three months in South Africa from the flu, which was probably brought by black labourers returning from the Western Front. Despite a brief quarantine, they were free to travel in early October.

We have had a most terrible time in Cape Town, and, in fact, all over South Africa with Spanish influenza. It has upset everything; the rush in Cape Town has been so dreadful that everyone who was not ill has been worked to the limit. At first we laughed and joked about the 'flu', but in a few days people began to be ill by the dozens; the sickness was very violent, very short and very fatal. Before the first week was out, they were dying as if with a plague, by the scores, and later by the hundreds. The deaths started at 20 a day, and before many days were over mounted up to 500 and even 600 a day. In two weeks 6,000 people died, and Cape Town was like a city of the dead.

In the hospital here we were crowded out, and all the staffs short. On night duty it was terrible; at times we had 400 patients, and several times I only had 10 night-nurses on duty. My nurses worked like heroes.... Young nurses, most of them, we were all working at more than our best, the dead and dying all round, and death in a terrible form too, many shrieking to the last in a terrible delirium. Yet my nurses never faltered; they knew it was almost impossible for them to escape getting it; still, steady, brave, loyal girls, they never failed me, and at times I had to ask such big things of them; none ever said 'No.'... Out of a staff of 110, only 12 or 14 escaped the disease. All the doctors were down at one time or another; we lost one doctor and one of the porters. Although many of the nursing staff were very near death, we saved them all. Things have eased down now. The nurses are nearly all on duty again now, and the past six weeks is like a bad dream that could surely never have been real.

People do not appreciate the risks they run

GEORGE SOPER, 'The Lessons of the Pandemic', May 1919

As soon as the pandemic had abated, public health officials – one of whom described it as 'both destroyer and teacher' (see page 8) – considered what lessons could be learned. US Sanitary Corps officer George Soper (see also page 180) published his views in Science Magazine *in May 1919.*

The most astonishing thing about the pandemic was the complete mystery which surrounded it. Nobody seemed to know what the disease was, where it came from or how to stop it. Anxious minds are inquiring today whether another wave of it will come again.

The fact is that although influenza is one of the oldest known of the epidemic diseases, it is the least understood. Science which by patient and painstaking labor has done so much to drive other plagues to the point of extinction has thus far stood powerless before it. There is doubt about the causative agent and the predisposing and aggravating factors....

Three main factors stand in the way of prevention: First, public indifference. People do not appreciate the risks they run. The great complexity and range in severity of the respiratory infections confuse and hide the danger. The infections vary from the common cold to pneumonia. They are not all separate entities by any means. An attack which begins as a coryza or rhinitis may develop into a pharyngitis, tonsilitis, laryngitis, bronchitis or pneumonia. The gravity increases with the progress toward the lungs. The infection sometimes seems to begin in the chest, sometimes in the throat, sometimes in the head....

For the specific infections such as diphtheria, measles, scarlet fever and influenza...the symptoms at the beginning may be identical with those of the common cold and the true nature of the disease escape notice until the patient shows unmistakable and alarming symptoms. By that time other persons may be infected.

The second factor which stands in the way of prevention is the personal character of the measures which must be employed. The enteric infections can be controlled by procedures of a general sort which impose no great restriction upon the conduct of the individual, but this is not true of the respiratory infections. The waste products of influenza containing the infective virus are not deposited in a vessel or sewerage system where they can be properly dealt with as in typhoid. The excreta of the nose and throat are projected into the air and allowed to pollute the hands, the food, the clothing and, in fact, the entire environment of the infected person. This is done unconsciously, invisibly, unsuspectingly. General methods directed against this kind of germ distribution must necessarily be of limited value. The kind of preventive measures which must be taken in order to control the respiratory infections devolve upon the persons who are already infected, while those who are liable to contract the disease can do little to protect themselves. The burden is placed where it is not likely to be well carried. It does not lie in human nature for a man who thinks he has only a slight cold to shut himself up in rigid isolation as a means of protecting others on the bare chance that his cold may turn out to be a really dangerous infection.

Third, the highly infectious nature of the respiratory infections adds to the difficulty of their control. The period of incubation varies considerably; in some infections it may be as short as a day or two. And the disease may be transmissible before the patient himself is aware that he is attacked....

As late as the pandemic of 1889–90 it was thought by many that the cause of the influenza outbreak was in some way connected with world conditions and quite independent of human intercourse. Today there are some who think that the extraordinarily cold winter of 1917–18 followed by the hot summer was largely responsible for the recent pandemic. Others believe that the great war precipitated the plague. Not a few think that the infection was spontaneously developed in many places at about the same time.... The weight of evidence now available indicates that the immediate cause of the great pandemic of 1918 was an infective virus which passed from person to person until it had spread all over the world....

The steps which should be taken to suppress the disease if it breaks out afresh are such as seem best for the maintenance of general health and protection from respiratory infections as a class. If doubt arises as to the probable efficacy of measures which seem so lacking in specificity it must be remembered that it is better for the public morale to be doing something than nothing....

First as to the things which it is desirable not to do. It is not desirable to close theaters, churches and schools unless public opinion emphatically demands it. It is not desirable to make the general wearing of masks compulsory. Patients should not be masked except when traveling from one point to another – they need air. Suspects should wear masks until their cases are positively diagnosed.

Influenza patients should be kept separate from other patients. A case of influenza should be dealt with as though it was as contagious as a case of smallpox: there is danger in the presence of the sick, in his eating utensils, in his clothes and in the air into which he coughs and sneezes, if indeed these respiratory symptoms are present. He is to be regarded as much more seriously ill than his visible symptoms perhaps indicate.

It is worthwhile to give more attention to the avoidance of unnecessary personal risks and to the promotion of better personal health. The writer's idea of the most essential things to remember are embodied in the following twelve condensed rules which were prepared in September:

1. Avoid needless crowding – influenza is a crowd disease.
2. Smother your coughs and sneezes – others do not want the germs which you would throw away.
3. Your nose, not your mouth was made to breathe through – get the habit.
4. Remember the three C's – a clean mouth, clean skin and clean clothes.
5. Try to keep cool when you walk and warm when you ride and sleep.
6. Open the windows – always at home at night; at the office when practicable.
7. Food will win the war if you give it a chance – help by choosing and chewing your food well.
8. Your fate may be in your own hands – wash your hands before eating.
9. Don't let the waste products of digestion accumulate; drink a glass or two of water on getting up.
10. Don't use a napkin, towel, spoon, fork, glass or cup which has been used by another person and not washed.
11. Avoid tight clothes, tight shoes, tight gloves – seek to make nature your ally not your prisoner.
12. When the air is pure, breathe all of it you can – breathe deeply.

The worst catastrophe since the Black Death

EDWIN O, JORDAN, 'The Present Status of the Influenza Problem', November 1925

An alternative viewpoint was offered a few years later by American public health scientist Edwin O. Jordan (1866–1936) in the American Journal of Public Health.

It is now clear that the first estimates of the loss of life caused by the influenza pandemic of 1918 were too low. The disclosures of the census of British India of 1921 and other data make an estimate of 20,000,000 deaths in the whole population of the world probably not wide of the mark. This is incomparably the worst catastrophe of the sort that has visited the human race since the Black Death of the Middle Ages. In modern times the ravages of neither Asiatic cholera nor the bubonic plague can vie with those of influenza....

Nothing is more certain than that we shall some day have another visitation of this destructive infection. It is a commonplace that if it were to descend upon us tomorrow we, as public health workers and students of disease, should be little if at all better equipped to deal with it than we were seven years ago. It is conceivable, however, that if we occasionally remind ourselves of the gaps in our knowledge we shall be in a position to study more advantageously the manifestations of the disease even in the presence of an epidemic period....

The mode of transmission of influenza must remain more or less obscure until we can identify and determine the location in the human body of the exciting agent. In the meantime cogent reasons compel us to believe that the disease is spread mainly if not altogether by human contact in the early stages of the malady or perhaps before symptoms are manifested. The rapidity of spread and other features can hardly be explained in any other way than by supposing that the virus is contained in and disseminated from the upper respiratory tract. Mouth spray and finger-to-mouth infection appear the most likely means of transmission.

It cannot be said that any method of community protection has been worked out. Vaccination against the secondary invaders might conceivably be of value, but the variety of the potentially pathogenic organisms in the respiratory tract is so great and the practical difficulties in the way of administering efficient vaccination on a worldwide scale during an influenza outbreak seem so insuperable that we can hardly make it the basis of a protective campaign. Face masks, however efficient under special conditions, are of limited applicability. Chlorine and similar gases have not yet been proved of decisive prophylactic value. Perhaps the most demonstrably useful methods of protection are certain forms of quarantine and isolation. Under conditions of modern life these are not readily applicable. Isolation such as may be practiced in institutions is sometimes entirely effective....

There are probably certain advantages in simply retarding the advent of influenza into a particular group, since the organisms accompanying the influenza virus may not be either so numerous or so virulent as at the height of the pandemic. No one can hope to prevent altogether another pandemic of influenza by methods of quarantine and isolation. It is believed, however, that something can be done to lower the attack rate in favorably situated small groups, to protect some individuals altogether and to lessen the exaltation of virulence on the part of the accessory microbes. Mortality may be lowered even if morbidity is not greatly affected. Difficult to apply and uncertain of success as it may be, the minimizing of contact seems at present to offer the best chance we have of controlling the ravages of influenza.

POLIOMYELITIS

This infectious viral disease, which causes a sudden onset of muscle weakness, usually in the legs but also sometimes in the neck and diaphragm, can cause death. While its roots are in antiquity and polio victims are depicted in ancient Egyptian art, it has been endemic in much of the world, whereas outbreaks in the 20th century – mostly occurring in cities and in the summer – reached epidemic proportions, affecting half a million people a year in Europe, Australasia and the United States. An outbreak in the USA that began in New York in 1916 killed 6,000 and left another 20,000 paralysed. With a general assumption that the disease was spread by coughs, sneezes and flies, this outbreak was blamed on immigrant children, specifically from Naples, who were perceived to be 'dirty'. Although most of those affected by polio were infants and young children, adults were also susceptible: most famously, the future US president Franklin D. Roosevelt, who in 1921 was diagnosed with the disease, which left his legs permanently paralysed. In 1938 he set up the National Foundation for Infantile Paralysis, later renamed the March of Dimes and given a wider brief to improve the health of mothers and babies in the United States.

The poliovirus was isolated in 1931, and the first vaccine was developed in 1955 by Jonas Salk, who trialled the vaccine on two million American children. When asked who owned the patent, he replied 'There is no patent... Could you patent the sun?' An oral vaccine followed in 1961, and the last case in the United States was seen in 1979.

In 1988, the World Health Organization (WHO) and UNICEF began a global effort at mass vaccination, aiming to eradicate the disease completely. Despite setbacks – some related to infections caused by the oral vaccine itself, and other to suspicions, especially in Islamic countries, of a vaccine that appeared to be related to Western powers and culture – by 2020 polio was declared eradicated in the wild in Africa, and only a few hundred cases remained anywhere in the world, all in Afghanistan and Pakistan.

Debility of the lower extremities

MICHAEL UNDERWOOD, *A Treatise on the Diseases of Children,*
  Volume II (1784)

The London surgeon and male-midwife Michael Underwood (1737–1820) was a founder of modern paediatrics, having published A Treatise on the Diseases of Children *in 1784, written for use in the home as well as for doctors. It included the first description of the symptoms and treatment of polio – a disease that coincidentally the novelist Walter Scott, then an infant, had contracted a few years earlier and which left him permanently lame.*

The disorder intended here is not noticed by any medical writer within the compass of my reading, or is not so described as to ascertain the disease. It is not a common disorder anywhere, I believe, and seems to occur seldomer in London than in some other parts.

Nor am I enough acquainted with it to be fully satisfied, either in regard to the true cause, or seat of the disease, either from my own observation, or that of others: I shall therefore only describe its symptoms, and mention the several means attempted for its cure.

It seems to arise from debility, and usually attacks children previously reduced by fever; seldom those under one, or more than four or five years old. It is a chronical or lingering complaint, and not attended with pain, fever, nor any manifest disease; so that the first thing observed is a debility of the lower extremities, which gradually become more infirm, and after a few weeks are unable to support the body. There are no signs of worms, nor other foulness of the bowels, therefore mercurial purges have not been of any use; neither has the bark, nor hot, nor cold-bathing. Blisters, or caustics on the bottom of the back and hip-joint, and volatile and stimulating applications to the legs and thighs, have been chiefly depended upon; though there is no appearance of any enlargement of any of the joints of the back, nor of suppuration in the external parts.

When only one of the lower extremities has been affected, the above means, in two instances out of five or six, entirely removed the complaint: but when both have been paralytic, nothing has seemed to do any good but irons to the legs, for the support of the limbs, and enabling the patient to walk. At the end of four or five years, some have by this means got better, in proportion as they have acquired general strength: but even some of these, where the debility has not been entirely removed, have been disposed to fall afterwards into consumption of the lungs. On this account it may be suspected, that the complaint is sometimes owing to scrofula.

I have seen a similar debility seize grown people, especially women, after some very long illness, and has continued a year, or more; during which time they were utterly incapable of walking without the help of crutches. These cases, however, have always been attended with great pain in the commencement of the complaint, though without tumour of the limbs; and have been benefited by the external use of the waters at Bath.

Do children have greater exposure or greater susceptibility?
WADE H. FROST, 'Poliomyelitis (Infantile Paralysis): What is Known of its Causes and Modes of Transmission', *Public Health Reports*, 14 July 1916

The epidemiology of polio was carefully tracked in early 20th-century America and discussed during the severe epidemic of 1916. While it was clear that children were more susceptible than adults, no good explan-ation for this was forthcoming; the popular notion that the disease was spread by dirt was debunked by the science, but it remained a powerful notion in society at large.

The close study of epidemics has shown that the incidence of poliomyelitis is proportionately about the same among persons living under good and those living under poor hygienic conditions. This practically eliminates from consideration as of great importance in the causation of the disease such factors as are intimately associated with poor hygienic conditions

– such factors, for example, as insufficient and improper food, overcrowding, personal uncleanliness and association with verminous insects.

No constant difference in regard to the incidence of poliomyelitis has been observed between the different races and nationalities constituting the population of areas where the disease has been epidemic. Nor has any constant relation been shown between the incidence of the infection and the topographic features of the various sections of the affected areas.

In one respect, however, poliomyelitis is constantly and very strikingly selective in its incidence, namely, in respect to age, its greatest incidence being always among children, especially those in the first half decade of life. Children under five years of age, constituting, in this country, from 9 to 12 per cent of the total population, furnish usually from 50 to 90 per cent of the cases of poliomyelitis. In some epidemics the disease is almost as prevalent proportionately in children between the ages of five and fifteen as in those under five years of age, but adults (those past the second decade), constituting usually over 50 per cent of the total population, seldom furnish more than 10 per cent of the cases, usually a very much smaller proportion. In the Buffalo epidemic of 1912 the incidence of poliomyelitis in children under five years of age was fifty times greater in proportion to their number than in persons from five to twenty-four years of age, while the whole population over twenty-four years of age, more than 50 per cent of the total inhabitants of the city, remained entirely immune from attack. As to the significance of this characteristic age incidence of poliomyelitis, its enormously greater incidence in children, it must indicate on the part of the children, either a generally greater exposure to the infective agent or else a greater susceptibility to its effects.

So far as I am aware it has never been satisfactorily demonstrated that the children in any large epidemic focus were considerably more exposed to any probable source of infection than were the adults of the corresponding families. To be sure a number of suggestions have been made as to possible ways in which children might be generally more exposed to certain sources of infection than adults. For example, children drink milk more generally and more freely than do adults, but in every considerable epidemic of poliomyelitis of which I am aware, where the data collected have been sufficient, milk supplies could be quite definitely excluded as probable vehicles of infection. Moreover, milk-borne epidemics of other infectious diseases, as typhoid fever and scarlet fever, while character-ized by a high rate of incidence in children, are not so strikingly – almost exclusively – confined to children as are epidemics of poliomyelitis. Even the proof that poliomyelitis is characteristically a milk-borne infection would not, therefore, offer an altogether satisfactory explanation of its very excessive incidence in children under five years of age and of the almost complete immunity of adults.

Again, on the hypothesis that poliomyelitis may be transmitted by biting insects, it has been suggested that children are more exposed to infection in this way because of their scantier summer clothing and their inability to ward off such insects as readily as do adults. It seems altogether improbable that these considerations are sufficient to account for an incidence fifty times greater in children than in young adults; and, as a matter of fact, epidemic diseases known to be transmitted by biting insects (yellow fever, bubonic plague, typhus fever) are not, in nonimmune populations, characteristically children's diseases.

It has also been suggested that the infection may be commonly contracted from the dust of streets and dwellings, and that children, by reason of their habit of crawling and playing on the ground, are greatly more exposed to infection from this source than are adults. Especially as regards street dust it appears very doubtful that children, as a class, are greatly more exposed than adults, since the latter travel more widely over dusty streets. It certainly seems quite improbable that the expo-sure of children to dust infection is so enormously greater than that of adults as to account for the peculiar age incidence of poliomyelitis, assuming dust as the chief vehicle of infection. Finally, because of their less cleanly and individualistic personal habits, children are probably more exposed than are adults to direct contagion through infectious secretions, yet experience teaches that contagious diseases in a nonim-munized, generally susceptible population are not disproportionately prevalent in children....

On the whole it may be said that epidemiologic studies up to this time have failed to demonstrate greater exposure of children than of adults to the infective agent of poliomyelitis, and that the hypotheses put forward to explain an assumed greater exposure are not competent to explain it. The only hypothesis which appears to satisfactorily explain the enormously greater incidence among children is that they are, in general, more readily susceptible to the infection than are older persons.

'I am the Baby Killer!'

Newark Evening News, 12 June 1916

Whatever the informed opinion of the experts, dirt was popularly blamed for the outbreak of polio in New York in 1916, and affected areas were carefully cleaned and sanitized. This poem and associated illustration blamed the housefly for the spread of polio among young children.

No Fairy-Tale Hobgoblin

I am the baby-killer!
I come from garbage-cans uncovered,
From gutter pools and filth of streets,
From stables and backyards neglected,
Slovenly homes – all manner of unclean places
I love to crawl on babies' bottles and baby lips;
I love to wipe my poison feet on open food
In stored and markets, patronized by fools.

New York 1916

New York Times, 26 July 1916

The 1916 epidemic in New York killed six thousand. Public health officers imposed quarantines on homes where someone was diagnosed with polio and required the affected person to be isolated in hospital, often against the will of the parents or family. As the New York Times *reported on 26 July, the fear of infection extended to health workers as much as the general public.*

Unable to obtain a physician, he put the boy into an automobile and drove to the Smith Infirmary, but the child died on the way and the doctors at the hospital would not receive the body.... He drove around Staten Island with the boy's body for hours looking for some one who would receive it.

Locked in an iron lung

RICHARD LLOYD DAGGETT, *Not Just Polio*, 2010

Richard Lloyd Daggett (b. 1940) grew up in Los Angeles where he con-
tracted polio as an early teenager. He has written extensively on disabil-
ity, and is president of the Polio Survivors Association. Like many other
children whose breathing was affected, he was put into an 'iron lung'
or negative-pressure ventilator where the air pressure is periodically
reduced and then raised in order to expand and contract the patient's
chest, forcing air in and out of the lungs. This life-saving device, in
which the patient had to lie almost entirely enclosed and immobile,
became the symbol of the devastating impact of polio on young lives.
Prototype devices were developed in the late 1910s, and they became
widely used from 1928; by the late 1950s, thousands were in use in the
USA and Europe. Today, less restrictive positive-pressure ventilators
are far more commonly used.

I woke up one morning in 1953 with a very painful, stiff neck and back. I
was thirteen years old, and I'd never known anything like this. I stayed in
bed until mid-morning when my mother called my father at work. He came
home and they took me to see...the doctor who did some tests, mostly to
do with my reflexes. He said I should be taken to the Los Angeles County
General Hospital.

We arrived at County General and entered the Communicable Disease
Ward. I was assigned a bed and they began giving me more tests. Every
time a doctor came by he would ask me to try sitting up in bed without
using my arms. This seemed to have some special significance. I did this
about a dozen times and had no difficulty.

In the afternoon they did a spinal tap. They told me it was a test to
see if I had polio. Everyone in the early 1950s had seen March of Dimes
posters with iron lungs and kids with leg braces and crutches, but I didn't
think any more about polio than I did about getting hit by a truck. I don't
remember my parents making much of a fuss over it either.

The tap itself was very painful, but what hurt even more was trying to
get in the knees-to-chin position that a tap required. They kept asking me
to bend forward more but the pain in my back was really intense.

That night my legs began to ache, and shortly after midnight I started to have trouble sitting up. I needed to urinate and I could see a urinal on the nightstand next to my bed. I tried to reach for it but my arms wouldn't cooperate. With great effort I finally reached it but I was completely exhausted.

I wasn't sure how a person was supposed to feel if they had polio, but not being able to sit up told me I had it. I distinctly remember saying to myself, 'Uh-oh. I think I have it.' When my parents came to visit the next day I told them the same thing. I said it almost apologetically. I knew my parents didn't want to hear this.

In the late evening they wheeled me into a small room where they started an IV. Then some people in surgical gowns wheeled me to another room that looked like a dentist's office. Here they performed a tracheotomy....

The operation was performed with a local anesthetic. I was wide awake and I could watch the doctors bending over me as they worked. The one who seemed to be the leader wore goggles over his glasses because, he said, 'It keeps the patient's breath from fogging my glasses up.' Everybody in the room obviously knew what they were doing to me. Everybody in the room but me!

Up until this time I had moments of apprehension but I was never really frightened. Of course I wondered what was happening but, except for the spinal tap, nothing that had been done was very painful and everybody acted like things were going fine. Then the doctor doing the tracheotomy made one final cut and air started sucking in and out of the hole he made in my windpipe. I thought he must have done something wrong. I tried to ask them what had happened but every time I tried to talk more air bubbled up out of the hole. Now I really was frightened.

When they finished the operation they put me in a tank respirator, more commonly known as an iron lung. As my head was sliding through the opening, I vomited. I tried to apologize but the words wouldn't come out. And blood seemed to be all over the place. My blood!...

The next thing I remember was waking up in a large room. There was a mirror over my head, and in the mirror I could see a row of large black bellows across the room. They were going up and down. I didn't know much about respirators but I figured one of them must be making me breathe. I tried to figure which one it was by timing my breathing with the motion of each bellows. None of them seemed to match my breathing pattern. It wasn't until later in the day, when my mirror was adjusted upward, that I realized those bellows were all attached to the underside of other respirators. I couldn't see mine because it was beneath me.

I was in a Drinker-Collins 'iron lung'. The Drinker machines were bluish green and had the bellows on the bottom of the respirator.... An iron lung helps a person breathe by creating a rhythmic negative pressure within the tank. This negative pressure creates a partial vacuum and the patient's chest wall expands trying to fill this vacuum. When the chest expands the patient draws in air, mimicking natural breathing. The pressure and rate can vary for each patient. Those of us with significant paralysis of our breathing muscles often had additional air forced into our lungs through a tracheostomy. The tracheostomy can also be used to suction mucous from our lungs. I'm sure the tracheostomy saved my life.

After a few days I got used to the routine: two shots in the morning, one at noon, one at night. I had blood taken for tests every third day, usually out of my leg or groin. Ouch! Some people might think that if a person can't move, then they can't feel either. Let me clear that up right now. Polio does not affect your senses. You are able to feel everything....

I couldn't swallow, so they inserted a tube through my nose and down into my stomach to feed me, and I still had the intravenous tube in my arm....

My mother drove to the hospital to visit almost every afternoon and both parents came in the evening. I'm sure it was a difficult time for them. I was their youngest child, and I was very, very ill with bulbospinal polio, the most severe form of this disease. I learned later that, in addition to polio, I had a life-threatening case of pneumonia.

It was probably more difficult for all the parents. Imagine entering a room filled with these huge metal tanks. The tanks are making their whooshing sound. All you can see are heads sticking out one end of each tank, and you know that one of these heads belongs to your child.

Islamic Advisory Group for Polio Eradication

FINAL COMMUNIQUÉ FROM MEETING IN JEDDAH, 26–27 February 2014

While the mass vaccination programme against polio that began in 1988 proceeded smoothly in many parts of the world, in others it raised suspicions. In the Islamic world, doubts persisted in many places as to whether vaccination was acceptable under Sharia law; and these were compounded by fears that the programme was a Western plot that used contaminated vaccine to sterilize Muslims. These fears seemed to many to be borne out in 2011 when it was revealed that the CIA had used a vaccination campaigner to confirm the presence of Osama Bin Laden in the Pakistan compound where, shortly after, he was killed by American troops. In response, in 2014 a group of Islamic nations, meeting in Jeddah in Saudi Arabia, asserted the importance of vaccination to Muslims. By 2020 the few remaining cases of polio in the wild occurred in the predominantly Muslim countries Afghanistan and Pakistan.

Having noted that of 403 polio cases reported in eight countries in 2013, that a large number of them were from Pakistan, Somalia, Nigeria, Syria and Afghanistan;

Having recognized the progress made in Afghanistan and Nigeria in 2013, with more than a 60 per cent decline in polio cases compared to 2012; and the challenges faced by the polio eradication programme in Pakistan and Somalia that resulted in an increase in the number of children paralysed by polio virus infection in these countries;

Acknowledging the urgency of rapidly stopping the transmission of polio virus in the polio-affected countries, and recognizing the need to prevent further spread of polio virus and avoid more outbreaks of this disease;

Noting the violence to which health workers are subjected in some polio-affected countries, which prevents them from performing their duties, poses a threat to their lives, and has a detrimental effect on immunization programmes, on the effectiveness of health workers and on the acceptance of parents, and which poses a major constraint to reaching the target children;

Recognizing that there are still misconceptions about the purpose of vaccination campaigns, that those misconceptions have a serious impact on the acceptance by some communities of polio vaccination and on reaching children in those communities;

We, having examined the different religious, cultural, social and health aspects of polio eradication, having reviewed the doubts and suspicions that were raised, and building on our knowledge, and the information provided by the trusted medical experts – declare as follows:

1. We strongly reaffirm the importance of Islamic solidarity in combating polio and our support for global polio eradication efforts; and acknowledge that it fully conforms to Islamic principles and religious rulings.

2. We commend 54 states among the OIC's [Organisation of Islamic Cooperation's] 57 Member States for their success in stopping the spread of polio virus using Oral Polio Vaccines (OPV) given their safety and effectiveness, and the government of the Kingdom of Saudi Arabia for vaccinating all Haj and Umra visitors from polio-affected countries.

3. We express serious concern that the vast majority of children afflicted by polio-paralysis in 2013 were from the Islamic world, and we are distressed at the state of these innocent children who now suffer from lifelong disability which could have been prevented.

4. We appeal to all communities, governments, civil society and religious organizations to place the highest priority on the health and welfare of children and ensure that all children have access to the needed health services, including vaccine, knowing that children are the future of the Ummah and are incapable of protecting themselves; it is thus the duty of all parents and local communities to protect their children from all diseases, particularly polio and lifelong paralysis that could ensue. We also call for all governments' commitment to provide the needed health services and social protection to the people.

5. We strongly condemn any misuse of public health activities for purposes other than the promotion of health and prevention of disease, and we call on all organizations and parties to maintain strict neutrality in the planning and implementation of all public health activities, including polio vaccination campaigns.

6. We condemn the attacks launched against health workers, as they contravene Islamic teachings and human values, and demand that governments, local societies, civil societies and religious organizations extend all necessary assistance to ensure the safety

and security of all health workers who carry out their duties to protect our children from fatal diseases; we also call upon all governments, philanthropic, local and international organizations to appreciate the services offered by those who were killed among them while discharging their duties and to provide support to their families who suffered the consequences, by establishing specialized funds for this purpose.

7. We express thanks to the governments of the states concerned for the efforts exerted to protect health workers, and strongly encourage the adoption of more measures to ensure full protection of the vaccination campaign in all areas that are difficult to access.

8. We appeal to political and religious leadership in the Islamic world to expedite work to support the efforts aimed at putting an end to violent campaigns and lifting all kinds of bans imposed on vaccination activities in the states concerned.

9. We invite the media to provide full opportunity to experts in the field of health and religion to speak about issues of societal concern regarding the activities of polio vaccination, and to prepare and publish comprehensive reports on the issue, including awareness programmes aimed at correcting misconceptions, especially in areas deprived of health services. We appeal to media and community organizations not to publish misinformation or rumours that may cause confusion among parents and expose the lives of millions of children to danger, and to seek to obtain accurate information.

Anti-vaxxers in the West

JUDITH SHAW BEATTY, 'My Polio Story is an Inconvenient Truth to those who Refuse Vaccines', 8 June 2016

In 2016, American childhood polio sufferer Judith Shaw Beatty found herself the victim of online trolls who were sceptical of the value of vaccination or the intentions of those who promote it.

I was diagnosed with paralytic poliomyelitis, which is experienced in less than 1 per cent of poliovirus infections. Not only did it immobilize me completely from the neck down, it also attacked my lungs. It was 1949: August, a popular month for polio, and I was six years old.

A few weeks before, we had moved from the outskirts of New York City to Rowayton, Connecticut, a small town of 1,200 people.... I was playing with other children at a lawn party and developed such a terrible headache we had to go home. When I woke up the next morning, my legs were so weak I couldn't stand on them and I could barely lift my arms. It took all day for the doctor to visit the house and examine me, and that night I was taken to the Englewood Hospital in Bridgeport and put in an iron lung....

About four years ago, my story was published online and then shared by people on Facebook. I became active in advocating for the importance of vaccines and, for the first time, learned that there were people out there who opposed vaccinations of any kind.

I've been hearing from them ever since. Either they declare that I never really had polio, or else they insist that polio is still around and has new names because the vaccine was ineffective and that this is part of a cover-up by 'big pharma'. Other people, in an effort to shut me up, angrily point out that they know someone who was permanently paralyzed by the polio vaccine or injured by it in some unspecified way, as though that should be a reason for getting rid of the vaccine altogether. Now, these same people are claiming that it was DDT that created the polio epidemics, even though there is evidence that polio existed in ancient Egypt and that more recent epidemics preceded the introduction of DDT.

The lack of compassion expressed by these people is startling. I've never interacted with a vaccine refuser who cared one way or the other about my life as a polio survivor. They don't want to hear about it because I'm an inconvenient truth, just like all the other polio survivors I know. On Facebook, I'm lectured and attacked by arrogant people who claim they know a lot more than I do about polio.

Polio and Covid-19: multi-tasking in rural Somalia

DR FATIMA ISMAIL AND COLLEAGUES, 'Somalia's Polio Teams Help
  Combat Covid-19', Polio Global Eradication Initiative, May 2020

*Dr Fatima Ismail, a Somali doctor, works for a polio disease surveillance
network, tracking outbreaks of the disease and part of the vaccination
and eradication programme. In 2020 her team had to be redirected to
address the Covid-19 pandemic.*

It's only 50 kilometres to the mountain village, but the journey took more
than three hours. We were bouncing in the car. The polio volunteer had
found an acute flaccid paralysis (AFP) case.

Here in Somalia, thousands of polio programme frontline staff are
now also supporting the effort against Covid-19. Rapid response teams
– disease surveillance officers, community health care workers and volunteers — have been trained to educate people about the virus and to
test suspected cases.

In the villages, they know us as their polio teams, and once they see
us, they expect us to give them information about polio. So we give them
information about Covid-19 too. Social mobilizers tell them about Covid-19
symptoms, how to prevent getting infected, physical distancing, cleaning
the hands very well with running water and soap.

We've trained our surveillance people on case definition and how to
collect samples correctly. It's the same infrastructure. Then, when we
have collected the samples from the patient, we send it to the laboratory
in Hargeisa.

The logistical challenges haven't changed. This is the rainy season
and the roads are terrible. You can't get to certain places you normally get
to, because of the situation on the road. Most of our vehicles can't make
it through the mud.

Despite the challenges, our teams are committed to continuing their
polio work in tandem with the Covid-19 response. It is critical that polio
surveillance continues during the pandemic, as Somalia is also fighting
outbreaks of vaccine-derived polio type 2 and 3. With polio vaccination
campaigns temporarily paused, we must be able to track any spread of
poliovirus and get ready to respond as soon as it is safe to do so.

So we are still doing polio surveillance at the same time as we do surveillance for Covid-19. My colleagues used to say that the polio surveillance system is the strongest disease surveillance system. What gives me hope is when I look behind and I see what we have done with the polio teams, the impact we've had on so many lives. We face everything and we overcome it.

ASIAN FLU AND HONG KONG FLU

Two flu pandemics of the mid-20th century infected vast numbers world-wide and caused millions of deaths – in the United States causing more deaths than the Korean and Vietnam Wars together – but without causing serious disruption to the world economy.

The Asian flu of 1957–58, an outbreak of avian influenza, broke out in Guizhou in China in 1956, and spread across the world via Singapore and Hong Kong, from which it travelled to the United States and the United Kingdom in June 1957. As the *New York Times* commented, 'Wherever it occurs, flu strikes quickly, it spreads as rapidly as man travels.'

Work on a vaccine started very quickly and was successful by the end of the year, but despite the vaccination programme a second wave still occurred in 1958, by which time it was estimated that 9 million people had been infected in Britain – many of them schoolchildren or the elderly; 5.5 million required medical attention and 14,000 died. By the time the Asian flu strain of H2N2 virus had disappeared by the late 1960s, it had caused about 2 million deaths, including about 70,000 in the USA.

The Hong Kong flu epidemic of 1968–69, caused by the highly infectious H3N2 strain of the influenza A virus, a mutation from H2N2, caused another million deaths worldwide. The first record of the outbreak in Hong Kong appeared in July 1968 and quickly spread to Singapore and Vietnam, from which it was taken to North America by returning US Marines, as well as to Australia and Europe. Worldwide deaths peaked in late 1968 and the virus seemed to disappear in early 1969 but returned late in the year. In the United States, the second wave was less virulent than the first; in Europe and elsewhere, the opposite was true.

In the United States, almost 34,000 people died, including Hollywood star Tallulah Bankhead and CIA director Allen Dulles. President Lyndon B. Johnson caught the disease as did Vice-President Hubert Humphrey (immediately after his narrow defeat in the 1968 presidential elections in November at the hands of Richard Nixon).

The Hong Kong flu yielded a relatively low death rate, partly because populations may have retained some immunity since the Asian flu, while improved medical care gave better support to the very ill. The H3N2 virus still resurfaces every year.

Few preventive measures were taken to curb the pandemic beyond asking people to wash their hands and keep surfaces clean. Homely cures – aspirin, lemon drinks and whisky – were recommended for as long as possible. There was no quarantine; workplaces, schools and colleges remained open, as did theatres, cinemas and sports arenas.

Hospitals, however, found themselves under severe strain. Very ill patients needed ventilation and some hospitals were forced to cancel surgeries, even life-saving procedures, through inadequate blood supplied. When hospitals were overrun, sufferers were sent home and told to rest. In Germany, refuse collectors had to help the undertakers to bury bodies because of the overwhelming demand, while in Berlin corpses had to be stored in tunnels.

The experience of the two pandemics allowed the establishment of a sophisticated global system for collecting and disseminating information about flu epidemics, with the World Health Organization (WHO) at its heart.

I survived the Asian flu

HARVEY MORRIS and MARIA MORANDINI, 'Asian flu v. coronavirus', *News Decoder*, 5 March 2020

Harvey Morris, later a foreign correspondent for Reuters and the Financial Times, *experienced Asian flu as a child in England. Maria Morandini experienced the flu while at school in Italy.*

Harvey Morris

It was *The Times* that first reported in April 1957 that an influenza epidemic had affected thousands in the British colony of Hong Kong. As it spread through Asia, a million in India were affected by June.... It then rapidly swept around the world.

One symptom among young boys was a profuse nosebleed. That's what took me eventually by ambulance to the local emergency ward. A kindly nurse stuffed my nostrils with bandage and after that I was on the mend.

Schools remained open. A fellow classmate – we were both 11 at the time – recalled... 'Half the teaching staff were victims and...the timetable collapsed. We spent our time in mixed class groups supervised by random teachers. We were told to read and wait for symptoms.'

Maria Morandini

I was in boarding school in Italy in 1958 when the Influenza Asiatica struck. I was 11. I remember the not-very-large infirmary being full. No masks, no hand sanitizers. Beds were 3 to 4 feet apart. The doctor came once a day; the one nurse more often. We played cards and chess. I remember sleeping a lot and having trouble breathing deeply. I also remember my bones being 'heavy'. Nobody died. There were 175 girls 6 to 18 years in the boarding school; the teachers and most of the staff lived outside. I was told that 15 per cent of the residents had been infected. The school did not close down, nor was there ever mention of social distancing.

> **Sensible advice on the BBC is needed to help the NHS function effectively in times of crisis**
>
> H. V. REEVES, letter to the *British Medical Journal*, 9 November 1957
> *In a letter published in the* British Medical Journal, *a British GP expressed his frustration with what he regarded as scare stories about the flu epidemic in the press, which had led to an unnecessary workload for family doctors.*

SIR,

During the present influenza epidemic I have been impressed by the impact made upon a large section of the population by the headlines in certain popular newspapers and by advertisements on ITV. The several remedies advertised on the latter medium suggest that the doctor should be called or informed, and on several visits I have been told that that was the sole reason for my visit. Newspaper headlines giving brief details of occasional tragic happenings have added to the state of anxiety of patients and relatives. These factors have, I believe, contributed considerably to the excessive number of calls.

I would like to suggest that, in such times, a few minutes on BBC television by a member of a responsible body, such as the BMA [British Medical Association], would go a long way towards putting events in their true perspective, allaying anxiety and suggesting that home remedies should be given a short trial. The concessions made concerning the 'first certificate' [allowing the sufferer to claim sickness benefit] should also be broadcast, and this alone would save many otherwise unnecessary visits. I know that this latter information has been put in the local press two or more weeks after the epidemic started, but I have yet to meet a patient who has read it. Some sensible advice on the medium that is now almost universal would go a long way towards helping the NHS to function efficiently, even in times of crisis.

I am. etc.

H. V. REEVES

Walton-on-Thames

Remembering the 1957 Asian flu pandemic

CLARK WHELTON, *City Journal*, 13 March 2020

In 2020, Clark Whelton, a New York-based writer, recalled the experience of having Asian flu in the 1950s, and contrasted the low-key public response of the 1950s to the more comprehensive public health measures imposed for Covid-19.

In October 1957 I spent a week in my college infirmary with a case of the H2N2 virus, known at the time by the politically incorrect name of 'Asian flu'. My fever spiked to 105°, and I was sicker than I'd ever been. The infirmary quickly filled with other cases, though some ailing students toughed it out in their dorm rooms with aspirin and orange juice. The college itself did not close, and the surrounding town did not impose restrictions on public gatherings. The day that I was discharged from the infirmary, I played in an intercollegiate soccer game, which drew a big crowd.

It's not that Asian flu...wasn't a serious disease. And yet, to the best of my knowledge, governors did not call out the National Guard, and political panic-mongers did not blame it all on President Eisenhower. College sports events were not cancelled, planes and trains continued to run, and Americans did not regard one another with fear and suspicion, touching elbows instead of hands. We took the Asian flu in stride. We said our prayers and took our chances.

Today, I look back and wonder if an oblivious America faced the 1957 plague with a kind of clueless folly. Why weren't we more active in fighting this contagion? Could stricter quarantine procedures have reduced the rate of infection and lowered the death toll? In short, why weren't we more afraid?...

For [people like me] who grew up in the 1930s and 1940s, there was nothing unusual about finding yourself threatened by contagious disease. Mumps, measles, chicken pox and German measles swept through entire schools and towns; I had all four. Polio took a heavy annual toll, leaving thousands of people (mostly children) paralyzed or dead. There were no vaccines. Growing up meant running an unavoidable gauntlet of infectious disease. For college students in 1957, the Asian flu was a familiar hurdle on the road to adulthood. For everyone older, the flu was a familiar foe. There was no possibility of working at home. You had to go out and face the danger.

Why were we not better prepared?

J. CORBETT MCDONALD, letter to UK Epidemic Observation Unit, 1957
In Britain, public health expert J. Corbett McDonald wrote to the Royal College of General Practitioners' Epidemic Observation Unit in late 1957, complaining that the lessons of the Spanish flu were yet to be fully taken on board.

Although we have had thirty years to prepare for what should be done in the event of an influenza pandemic, I think we have all been rushing around trying to improvise investigations with insufficient time to do it properly. We can only hope that people will have taken advantage of their opportunities and at the end it may be possible to construct an adequate explanation of what happened.

Flu arrives in Hong Kong, 1968

W. K. CHANG, 'National Influenza Experience in Hong Kong, 1968', *WHO Bulletin* (1969)

Like the Asian flu pandemic of 1957, the Hong Kong flu of 1968 is thought likely to have originated in China. Hong Kong physician W. K. Chang described Hong Kong's unique situation, in contact with the otherwise isolated Maoist China at the time of the Cultural Revolution.

Ever since our virus laboratory started functioning as a National Influenza Centre of the World Health Organization in 1963, we have been aware of the emergence of influenza virus mutants in this part of the world. Eleven years after the Asian influenza epidemic, a new virus variant was isolated in the summer of 1968 in Hong Kong. The origin of this variant is not known. There was no official information on an influenza epidemic from the health authorities of mainland China, but prior to the outbreak in Hong Kong, travellers reported an increased incidence of influenza-like infections in the neighbouring Chinese province. For various reasons, virus isolations were not carried out on arriving travellers to confirm these reports. Hong Kong is one of the few places which communicates freely with the Chinese mainland. Cargo boats and trains daily bring in food supplies as well as passengers. Local residents are free to go to their native villages and return, provided they possess a re-entry permit. Hence, the place is vulnerable to the spread of influenza in the event of an epidemic in mainland China. On the other hand, Hong Kong, being a free port and a busy tourist centre, is also an effective place for virus exchange with other parts of the world by air and sea....

An epidemic broke out in mid-summer of 1968. It was first observed on 13 July, when there was a sudden increase of patients with influenza-like symptoms at the government clinics. The epidemic soon reached its maximum intensity in the week of 27 July and gradually subsided in the following three weeks. Altogether, the outbreak lasted for about six weeks. It was reported that the disease affected all age-groups and the clinical symptoms were considered mild, lasting for three to five days. There were no observable excess deaths during the epidemic.

The flu taught me to have a social conscience

ROGER MCNEILL, letter to *North Shore News*, 26 April 2020

Roger McNeill from Vancouver wrote to his local newspaper in 2020 about his experience of flu as a teenager in 1968, and its far worse impact on an older generation that had already endured two world wars and the Great Depression.

Even among my aging baby boomer cohorts, I have met few who recall it. I remember because I caught it.

I was in high school and to this day recall lying on my bed for ten days while my fever topped out at 104°F. My parents, heedless of their own safety, brought me cold drinks and a few small bowls of oatmeal, all I could manage to swallow.

I returned to school two weeks later and ten pounds lighter. One of my friends who was a bit chubby told me he wished he had caught the virus so he could have lost weight too. That sums up our attitude at the time.

It was a novel high-fever flu you soon forgot about, especially if you never caught it. If someone had asked me to weigh the benefits of hygienic measures against lost economic productivity, I would have scratched my head. I was more concerned about important decisions such as whether to buy a Honda or a Yamaha motorcycle or if the Beatles were better than the Stones. I was unaware at the time that one million people died from the virus and even if someone had told me, it would have worried me less than being unnoticed by most of the girls in the school....

With a quarter of the students off sick, there was some talk about closing down the high school for a couple of weeks to let the virus clear, but that was the only public health measure even discussed.

The only deaths were mostly among seniors and no one fussed about this inconsequential segment of the population. After all, old people were going to die soon anyways, right?

Who were those senior citizens who died and were quickly forgotten by younger generations? Most of them were First World War veterans or their spouses and siblings – the survivors of a Canadian armed contingent who faced unimaginable horrors in the trenches and muddy killing grounds....

On the home front, the women ran the farms, businesses and essential services for years, all while raising their families. After the First World

War, their generation survived the worst pandemic on record, the worst depression and another world war while building this peaceful prosperous country I am so thankful for today.

If there is one idea I can take away from my experience with the Hong Kong flu pandemic, it is that however self-involved we may have been as teenagers, now is the time to act with a greater social conscience and show the value we put on the faceless victims of COVID-19.

Let us persist until we win this war.

How good is our influenza surveillance?

ALEXANDER D. LANGMUIR and JERE HOUSWORTH, 'A Critical Evaluation of Influenza Surveillance', *WHO Bulletin* (1969)

In 1969, Alexander D. Langmuir and Jere Housworth of the US Department of Health, Education and Welfare considered the successes and failures of WHO's influenza surveillance system, as revealed by the Hong Kong flu pandemic of the previous year, and called for less reliance on qualitative data.

Surveillance of influenza has become a global reality. The rapidity with which the epidemic in Hong Kong was recognized and the new strain of virus isolated and characterized confirms the wisdom and leadership of Dr C. H. Andrewes and the group that conceived and organized the World Influenza Programme at the end of the Second World War. This programme set the pattern for expanded surveillance activities now being undertaken by the World Health Organization. It is worthy of note, however, that the World Influenza Programme was in operation years before even the term 'surveillance' with its present connotation was in general use.

In the face of this impressive array of current and relevant data, it is difficult to be critical of influenza surveillance. Patently the present system is a highly effective communications network with hundreds of competent participants working jointly towards a common goal. Clearly also the prompt availability of increasingly sophisticated surveillance data has led health authorities in many nations to plan and attempt to carry out major control efforts....

Dr R. G. Sharrar has described the introduction of Hong Kong influenza to the USA – its pre-epidemic seeding and the extent and severity of the epidemic as it developed during the early winter. A very large amount of data was collected, evaluated and promptly disseminated to the health profession and the public in the spirit of modern surveillance. Yet, in spite of all these data, neither can we account for the unusual severity of our epidemic, nor do we have the essential facts to formulate logical alternative possibilities. Our information regarding the occurrence of influenza is largely qualitative. Schools close, absenteeism increases, medical services become taxed, virus isolations and serological identifications are made in great numbers, and daily accounts appear in our newspapers and on television. We know we have an epidemic and we know its specific cause, but we have few quantitative measures of incidence, age- and sex-specific attack rates, and character and severity of complications. Furthermore, we have only crude data regarding mortality. We do not know what proportion of excess deaths occurs among reasonably active and productive citizens in contrast to deaths among persons who are already invalids suffering from severely debilitating pre-existing disease. Despite this serious deficiency we base our recommendations for vaccine use largely on mortality experience. We undertake major efforts to produce influenza vaccine in large amounts, but we have no meaningful information regarding its actual distribution. We do not know to what extent it actually reaches persons at highest risk....

In studying influenza surveillance reports from many countries, one is immediately aware of a serious limitation in the comparability of data. The methods of reporting, the fashions of nosology [classification of diseases], the systems of medical care, and the availability and use of laboratory diagnostic services vary so widely that it is difficult to compare the extent and severity of epidemics in different countries. For example, it is claimed that the recent epidemic in the USA was unusually severe. We know this to be true in relation to our own past experience, and clearly our epidemic was more severe in terms of mortality than the epidemics in England and Wales and in Czechoslovakia, as has been shown in earlier papers, but there are few data with which to compare our experience in a quantitative way with that in most other countries.

Doctors administer oxygen to a Covid-19 patient in West Middlesex University Hospital's Accident and Emergency department, 2020.

PART VI
PANDEMICS IN A GLOBALIZED WORLD

In the past forty years, the world has seen not only the emergence of many new infectious agents, from HIV to Ebola to coronavirus, but also the growing danger of a fast and disastrous global spread, which has brought the pandemics that these pathogens can cause to the very top of the political agenda in an entirely novel manner. All these aspects – the new pathogens, the rapid spread and the global response – are features of a globalized world that mean nowhere on Earth can any longer be considered remote.

Environmental change – deforestation, insecticide use, commercial agriculture and factory farming – has altered the ecology for many older pathogens that have survived for millennia in animal reservoirs and only occasionally crossed to humans, and created an environment in which new pathogens can emerge unnoticed. Once these pathogens have crossed to humans, urbanization means they can become established quickly, while rapid mass transport allows them to spread around the world in a matter of hours.

Since the Second World War, the need for a global response to public health issues has been led by organizations such as the World Health Organization and other NGOs; protocols have been established and governments have considered the knock-on effects of a major pandemic and rehearsed their responses, both in terms of health care and a wider social response.

While this preparation – and the parallel rise in genetics and a global scientific community that can share knowledge instantly – should result in a world that is better prepared than ever before, it is also the case that pandemic preparation is at the mercy of politicians' priorities and what they would call 'the art of the possible'.

AIDS

AIDS (acquired immunodeficiency syndrome) was an entirely unknown disease when it appeared among the gay community of New York and California in the early 1980s, and the initial medical and political response was tentative. As the untreatable syndrome spread and expanded into other communities, resources were directed towards identifying the cause and seeking drugs that could arrest its progress. The causative agent proved to be a retrovirus, human immunodeficiency virus (HIV), which was shown to be spread through bodily fluids and blood, and could remain in the body for a long time without symptoms until it caused the immune system to fail, permitting a range of opportunistic infections and cancers to develop. Usually causing death if left untreated, AIDS has been one of the deadliest pandemics in history.

The virus is believed to have been endemic in chimpanzees in the Congo region, to have passed to humans in about 1920 and moved to the coastal town of Kinshasa, before being spread around the world in the 1970s; it has been estimated that hundreds of thousands of people may have been infected worldwide before the first cases of AIDS came to light.

In the 1980s, the US government was criticized for its slow response – indeed by 1989, at the end of President Ronald Reagan's eight years in power, almost 90,000 Americans had died without him having shown any significant interest in the problem. In the mid-1980s, however, the first antiretroviral therapy (ART) could prevent the condition developing into AIDS, and from this point the epidemic gradually became more manageable in the West. In other regions the lack of availability of cheap drugs meant its spread was unrestricted, causing particular havoc in sub-Saharan Africa, where 75 per cent of cases globally were to be found in the early 21st century, and where the majority of transmission was from mother to baby.

By 2020, AIDS was estimated to have been responsible for over 30 million deaths globally, and almost 40 million people were HIV-positive (living with the HIV virus). Of these, between half and two-thirds have access to ART.

An unknown disease in Los Angeles

DR MICHAEL GOTTLIEB, *CDC Morbidity and Mortality Weekly Report*, 3 July 1981

In July 1981, Dr Michael Gottlieb (b. 1947) published a paper that announced that otherwise healthy young men were dying from infection with a usually benign pneumonia parasite. He also noted that they were all gay. As a result, the unknown disease was initially called gay-related immune deficiency (GRID) – giving it a stigma that was hard to shake off in much of conservative America.

In the period October 1980–May 1981, five young men, all active homosexuals, were treated for biopsy-confirmed *Pneumocystis carinii* pneumonia at three different hospitals in Los Angeles, California. Two of the patients died. All five patients had laboratory-confirmed previous or current cytomegalovirus (CMV) infection and candidal mucosal infection....

The diagnosis of *Pneumocystis* pneumonia was confirmed for all five patients ante-mortem by closed or open lung biopsy. The patients did not know each other and had no known common contacts or knowledge of sexual partners who had had similar illnesses. The five did not have comparable histories of sexually transmitted disease. Four had serologic evidence of past hepatitis B infection but had no evidence of current hepatitis B surface antigen. Two of the five reported having frequent homosexual contacts with various partners. All five reported using inhalant drugs, and one reported parenteral drug abuse. Three patients had profoundly depressed numbers of thymus-dependent lymphocyte cells and profoundly depressed *in vitro* proliferative responses to mitogens and antigens. Lymphocyte studies were not performed on the other two patients.

1,112 and Counting

LARRY KRAMER, *New York Native*, March 1983

This article by playwright Larry Kramer (1935–2020) in the March 1983 edition of the New York Native, *a magazine for the gay community, challenged the reluctance of the US public health authorities to investigate the new disease, and the simultaneous denial of what was happening on the part of much of the gay community.*

If this article doesn't scare the shit out of you, we're in real trouble. If this article doesn't rouse you to anger, fury, rage and action, gay men may have no future on this earth. Our continued existence depends on just how angry you can get.

I repeat: our continued existence as gay men upon the face of this earth is at stake. Unless we fight for our lives, we shall die. In all the history of homosexuality we have never before been so close to death and extinction. Many of us are dying or already dead.

There are now 1,112 cases of serious Acquired Immune Deficiency Syndrome. When we first became worried, there were only 41. In only twenty-eight days, from 13 January to 9 February 1983, there were 164 new cases – and 73 more dead. The total death tally is now 418. Twenty per cent of all cases were registered this January alone. There have been 195 dead in New York City from among 526 victims. Of all serious AIDS cases, 47.3 per cent are in the New York metropolitan area.

These are the serious cases of AIDS, which means Kaposi's sarcoma, *Pneumocystis carinii* pneumonia and other deadly infections. These numbers do not include the thousands of us walking around with what is also being called AIDS: various forms of swollen lymph glands and fatigues that doctors don't know what to label or what they might portend.

The rise in these numbers is terrifying. Whatever is spreading is now spreading faster as more and more people come down with AIDS.

Leading doctors and researchers are finally admitting they don't know what's going on. I find this terrifying too – as terrifying as the alarming rise in numbers. For the first time, doctors are saying out loud and up front, 'I don't know.'

For two years they weren't talking like this. For two years we've heard a different theory every few weeks. We grasped at the straws of possible cause: promiscuity, poppers, back rooms, the baths, rimming, fisting, anal intercourse, urine, semen, shit, saliva, sweat, blood, blacks, a single virus, a new virus, repeated exposure to a virus, amoebas carrying a virus, drugs, Haiti, voodoo, Flagyl, constant bouts of amebiasis, hepatitis A and B, syphilis, gonorrhea.

Hospitals are now so filled with AIDS patients that there is often a waiting period of up to a month before admission, no matter how sick you are. And, once in, patients are now more and more being treated like lepers as hospital staffs become increasingly worried that AIDS is infectious.

Suicides are now being reported of men who would rather die than face such medical uncertainty, such uncertain therapies, such hospital treatment and the appalling statistic that 86 per cent of all serious AIDS cases die after three years' time.

If all of this had been happening to any other community for two long years, there would have been, long ago, such an outcry from that community and all its members that the government of this city and this country would not know what had hit them.

Why isn't every gay man in this city so scared shitless that he is screaming for action? Does every gay man in New York want to die?

No matter what you've heard, there is no single profile for all AIDS victims. There are drug users and non-drug users. There are the truly promiscuous and the almost monogamous. There are reported cases of single-contact infection.

All it seems to take is the one wrong fuck. That's not promiscuity – that's bad luck.

There have been no confirmed cases of AIDS in straight, white, non-intravenous-drug-using, middle-class Americans. The only confirmed straights struck down by AIDS are members of groups just as disenfranchised as gay men: intravenous drug users, Haitians, eleven hemophiliacs (up from eight), black and Hispanic babies, and wives or partners of IV drug users and bisexual men.

Of all serious AIDS cases, 72.4 per cent are in gay and bisexual men.

Now we're arriving at the truly scandalous. For over a year and a half the National Institutes of Health [NIH] has been 'reviewing' which from among some $55 million worth of grant applications for AIDS research money it will eventually fund.

It's not even a question of NIH having to ask Congress for money. It's already there. Waiting. NIH has almost $8 million already appropriated that it has yet to release into usefulness.

There is no question that if this epidemic was happening to the straight, white, non-intravenous-drug-using middle class, that money would have been put into use almost two years ago, when the first alarming signs of this epidemic were noticed.

Every hospital in New York that's involved in AIDS research has used up every bit of the money it could find for researching AIDS while waiting for NIH grants to come through. These hospitals have been working on AIDS for up to two years and are now desperate for replenishing funds. Important studies that began last year are now going under for lack of money. Important leads that were and are developing cannot be pursued. New York University Hospital, the largest treatment center for AIDS patients in the world, has had its grant application pending at NIH for a year and a half.

The NIH would probably reply that it's foolish just to throw money away, that that hasn't worked before. And, NIH would say, if nobody knows what's happening, what's to study?

Gay men pay taxes just like everyone else. NIH money should be paying for our research just like everyone else's. We desperately need something from our government to save our lives, and we're not getting it.

The gay press has been useless. If we can't get our own papers and magazines to tell us what's really happening to us, and this negligence is added to the negligent non-interest of the straight press, how are we going to get the word around that we're dying? Gay men in smaller towns and cities everywhere must be educated, too. Has the *Times* or the *Advocate* told you that 29 cases have been reported from Paris?

I am sick of closeted gays. It's 1983 already, guys, when are you going to come out? By 1984 you could be dead. Every gay man who is unable to come forward now and fight to save his own life is truly helping to kill the rest of us. As more and more of my friends die, I have less and less sympathy for men who are afraid their mommies will find out or afraid their bosses will find out or afraid their fellow doctors or professional associates will find out. Unless we can generate, visibly, numbers, masses, we are going to die.

I am sick of everyone in this community who tells me to stop creating a panic. How many of us have to die before you get scared off your ass and into action? Aren't 195 dead New Yorkers enough? Every straight person who is knowledgeable about the AIDS epidemic can't understand why gay men aren't marching on the White House. Over and over again I hear from them, 'Why aren't you guys doing anything?' Every politician I have spoken to has said to me confidentially, 'You guys aren't making enough noise. Bureaucracy only responds to pressure.'

I am sick of people who say 'it's no worse than statistics for smokers and lung cancer' or 'considering how many homosexuals there are in the United States, AIDS is really statistically affecting only a very few'. That would wash if there weren't 164 cases in twenty-eight days. That would wash if case numbers hadn't jumped from 41 to 1,112 in eighteen months. That would wash if cases in one city – New York – hadn't jumped to cases in fifteen countries and thirty-five states. That would wash if cases weren't coming in at more than four a day nationally and over two a day locally. That would wash if the mortality rate didn't start at 38 per cent the first year of diagnosis and climb to a grotesque 86 per cent after three years. Get your stupid heads out of the sand, you turkeys!

I am sick of guys who moan that giving up careless sex until this blows over is worse than death. How can they value life so little and cocks and asses so much? Come with me, guys, while I visit a few of our friends in Intensive Care at NYU. Notice the looks in their eyes, guys. They'd give up sex forever if you could promise them life.

I am sick of 'men' who say, 'We've got to keep quiet or they will do such and such.' They usually mean the straight majority, the 'Mora'; Majority, or similarly perceived representatives of them. Okay, you 'men' – be my guests: you can march off now to the gas chambers; just get right in line.

And I am very sick and saddened by every gay man who does not get behind this issue totally and with commitment – to fight for his life.

AIDS in Gay Men

San Francisco Department of Public Health, May 1983
The initial advice to gay men about AIDS was to limit the number of sexual partners and to use condoms, as expressed in a brochure put out by San Francisco Department of Public Health in May 1983. The stress on accurate information was important at a time that press coverage remained patchy and sensationalist.

If you are a gay man living in the San Francisco Bay Area you have probably heard something about AIDS already. There is a lot of information filtering through the gay community now – much of it true and valuable and some of it not true and therefore misleading. For example, it is true that we have learned much about the disease since it appeared two years ago, especially in terms of transmission. Its cause and cure, however, are still obscure. And it is also true that AIDS has killed a third of the over-200 gay men diagnosed so far in the San Francisco Bay Area. It is not true, though, that AIDS is some sort of 'gay plague', singling out the 'promiscuous' homosexual lifestyle. Gay men were simply the first group in which the condition was diagnosed. And it is not true that the situation is hopeless.

AIDS has been diagnosed in several, not always distinct population groups besides gay men or bisexuals: Haitians, intravenous drug users and their sexual partners and children, hemophiliacs and other blood product recipients. But about 70 per cent of the reported cases are gay men and about a fifth of these cases are in San Francisco. Half the reported cases are in New York City with most of the others distributed in major urban centers such as Los Angeles, Miami, Houston and Chicago. Through 1 July 1983, more than 1,600 cases may be reported from the United States. Mortality is high, with approximately 75 per cent of cases dead within two years after appearance of symptoms. Medical researchers are working intensively on prevention and treatment in medical centers throughout the country.

WHAT YOU CAN DO:

RISK REDUCTION There is no evidence that casual contact of the general public with AIDS patients in elevators, waiting rooms or other public places leads to spread of the disease. Similarly, no AIDS has been found in health workers who care for patients with AIDS, as a result of their work. Medical evidence to date supports the theory that AIDS is transmitted through intimate contact or blood transfusion. The shared use of needles when shooting up 'recreational' drugs is another important way of transferring infection between people. Not surprisingly, AIDS' high incidence and mortality have created a great deal of concern in San Francisco's gay population. We must learn to cope with the feelings of anger, anxiety, fear and sadness which AIDS has brought into our lives. One way to do this is to take advantage of the information we have or strongly suspect about the transmission of AIDS. Much of the prevention we need can only be done by us ourselves, in changing some details of our own lifestyles.

We propose the following guidelines:

DECREASE THE NUMBER OF DIFFERENT SEXUAL PARTNERS IN YOUR LIFE. This does not mean that you must limit your amount of sex, but limit the number of different partners.

CHOOSE HEALTHY PARTNERS. In other words, if someone has symptoms of illness (especially those which we indicated as possible AIDS symptoms) or complains about vague feelings of unwellness without apparent signs, it would be a good idea not to have sex with that person at that time. A partner who has many different sex contacts may expose you to a high and significant risk, even though you have decreased the number of different sex contacts in your own life. Ideally, you should know enough about a potential sex partner to be able to make an informed decision.

USE CONDOMS. As you can never be really sure your sex partner is healthy, each of you has a vital interest in seeing that a condom is used.

AVOID SEXUAL ACTIVITY THAT MAY CAUSE BLEEDING. Refrain from sex that may tear, pierce or abrade delicate tissues. Anorectal tissues, even hemorrhoids, can easily be stretched or torn by fisting and other vigorous sexual acts, causing bleeding which may not be apparent to either party, and introducing AIDS infection through the torn tissues. Even cuts, sores or abrasions on the hands and arms can be an entry port for infection in the fister. Basically, sex of any kind which involves the possibility of bleeding – even in the smallest amounts – should be avoided.

ELIMINATE (OR AT LEAST MINIMIZE) RECREATIONAL DRUG USE. Many drugs popular with gays (and non-gays of course) can damage the immune system. Shooting heroin, speed and cocaine with a shared needle is especially damaging. Snorting cocaine and poppers can also lower one's resistance to infection. Steroid injections can also have this result when taken inappropriately for body-building purposes. Alcohol, marijuana and other street drugs can blur your ability to make good decisions about your sexual conduct; when taken in excess they damage your overall good health.

DO GOOD THINGS FOR YOUR MIND AND BODY. The old-fashioned advice about good health is still true: proper rest, nutrition and exercise are essential for good health. Learn to manage stress in ways that increase well-being (exercise and relaxation) as opposed to those that do not (alcohol and drugs).

All we have are memories and pictures

ANON, *Gay Star News*, 2015

In 2015, Gay Star News *published a number of anonymous stories of survivors of the 1980s AIDS crisis.*

I'm a 62-year-old gay man. I thankfully made it through the epidemic that started in the early 80s and went right through the mid-90s. You ask what it was like? I don't know if I can even begin to tell you how many ways AIDS has affected my life, even though I never caught the virus.

By the early 80s, I had what I would consider a really large circle of friends and acquaintances and once the epidemic really started to hit, it was not uncommon to find out three, four or more people you knew had died each month. We set up informal and formal support groups to look after our friends who took sick. Feeding them when they would eat. Changing them. Washing them. Acting as go-between with families who 'were concerned' about their sons, nephews, brothers, etc., but wouldn't lend a hand to help because AIDS was, you know, icky.

After they passed, there were memorial services to plan with no real time to grieve because when one passed, you were needed somewhere else to begin the process all over again.

I kept a memory book/photo album of everyone I knew that died of AIDS. It's quite large to say the least. Who were these guys? These were the people I had planned to grow old with. They were the family I had created and wanted to spend the rest of my life with as long as humanly possible but by the time I was in my late 40s, every one of them was gone except for two dear friends of mine.

All we have left of those days are each other, our memories and pictures. I hope that statement doesn't come off as pitiful though. I am fit, active, healthy and you know what? I enjoy every single day of my life. I enjoy it because most of my friends can't. In my own personal way, I want to honor their lives by living and enjoying mine.

AIDS and haemophilia

JEANNE WHITE-GINDER, 'Who Was Ryan White?', Ryan White HIV/
    AIDS Program

*In the early days of AIDS research, haemophiliacs were identified as an
at-risk group. One such was Ryan White (1971–1990), from Kokomo in
Indiana, who was diagnosed with AIDS following a blood transfusion
aged thirteen in December 1984. Given six months to live, he insisted
on returning to school and fought a long court battle to do so against
his school authorities and other parents. This gained national attention, and Ryan became the face of public education about his disease.
He died in April 1990. A few months later Congress passed the Ryan
White Comprehensive AIDS Resources Emergency (CARE) Act, which
provided federal support for people living with HIV/AIDS. His mother
Jeanne White-Ginder described the experience.*

Ryan was diagnosed with AIDS on 17 December 1984. He was one of the
first children, one of the first hemophiliacs to come down with AIDS, and
it was a time where there was hardly any information on AIDS. I was living
in Kokomo, Indiana, and Ryan was attending Western Middle School, and it
was something that I really didn't even believe he had. I felt like, 'How could
he have AIDS?' He was a hemophiliac since birth, and I just felt like 'How
could he be one of the first ones?' I felt like somehow, in some way, it was
going to be something else. I really never really believed he had AIDS for quite
a while. At that time, of course, he had no precautions, or anything. There
were no precautions at the hospital. And all of a sudden the CDC [Centers
for Disease Control and Prevention] shows up and the CDC started putting
in all kind of precautions, you know: the gloves, the gowns, the masks and
so forth, and started talking to the nurses and so forth. It became apparent
just like overnight that all of a sudden things were different.

They only gave him three to six months to live. So I thought every
cough, every fever, I worried that it was going to be his last. And I really
never thought he'd be healthy enough to go to school. But as he started
getting healthy, as he started gaining weight, he started to ask, 'Mom,'
he said, 'I want to go to school, I want to go visit my friends. I want to see
my friends.' So I really kind of put him off for a while and finally he just
said, 'Mom, I want to go to school, I want to go visit.'

It was a long process we had to go through: he didn't go to school for about a year and a half. He was worried about taking the 7th grade over again, and he didn't want people to think he was dumb, because he was a very smart and intelligent kid. So it was a long process. We thought it would take one court hearing, and we'd have all these medical experts in so to speak, and then everybody would be educated, but it didn't happen that way.

It was really bad. People were really cruel, people said that he had to be gay, that he had to have done something bad or wrong, or he wouldn't have had it. It was God's punishment, we heard the God's punishment a lot. That somehow, some way he had done something he shouldn't have done or he wouldn't have gotten AIDS.

Then we moved to Cicero, Indiana, and there, the community welcomed us. And it was all because a young girl, named Jill Stuart, who was president of the student body, who decided to bring in the medical experts and talk to the kids, and then the kids went home then and educated their parents. So Ryan was welcomed, he got to go to school, he got to go proms and dances. He even got a job. It was kind of funny, he came home once after he turned 16 and told me he had a job for the summer. I thought, 'Oh my gosh. Who is going to hire you, knowing who you are?' I said, 'What are you going be doing,' and he said, 'I'm working at Maui's Skateboard shop. I'm going to be putting together skateboards.' And I said, 'How much are they going to pay you?' and he said '$3.50 an hour.' I said, 'Ryan, that won't even buy your gas to Indianapolis and back.' He said, 'Mom, you don't get it. I got a job just like everyone else does.' So it was really important to Ryan, to just be one of the kids, and to just fit in. He never bragged or anything about who he was, or what he got to do, he just wanted to be around his friends.

A lot of people will say, 'Your son was such a hero' and all that, but to me, he was my son. And you know, sometimes it's so confusing, because he was my little boy, and to share him with everybody, because he wasn't perfect, but at the same time, he was my son.

At the time when Ryan was diagnosed with AIDS, we heard of so many drugs coming out, and none of them was worth nothing. By the time you heard of one, there would be another one out, and you would never get the research for one. And none of them worked. And so even in the early

90s, when I was hearing there was hope, I kind of thought, 'You know, we had that hope, too, but they didn't pan out.' But they did pan out! The biggest contribution I think that Ryan made is, and I didn't know it at that time, that his legacy would be that people are getting their drugs and their treatment and that people are living with AIDS.

The war to defeat AIDS is a war to defeat the humiliation of the African people

'Castro Hlongwane, Caravans, Cats, Geese, Foot & Mouth and
 Statistics', March 2002

The vast majority of HIV/AIDS sufferers in the world live in Southern Africa, and international organizations such as the United Nations launched campaigns for education about the disease, access to health care and ART. In the early 2000s, much of this was thwarted by the South African president Thabo Mbeki (b. 1942) who took a sceptical view of much Western science – in particular, denying that AIDS was necessarily caused by HIV alone but was part of a wider issue relating to poverty and the systematic subjugation of Africa and African values by the West, and advocating traditional African medicine. He banned retroviral drugs in South African hospitals, including a programme to stop pregnant women passing the virus onto their babies, and he has consequently been held responsible for hundreds of thousands of premature deaths. In March 2002 an anonymous paper on the subject was submitted to the annual congress of the ruling African National Congress (ANC); Mbeki is said to have been closely involved in writing it.

For some strange reason, Africa, among the poorest continents of the world, is not supposed to talk about these diseases of poverty and to focus on their eradication. **We are urged from all sides to break the silence about HIV/AIDS and maintain perfect silence about the diseases of poverty.**

To what do we owe these strange goings-on!

The war to defeat AIDS is also a war to defeat the humiliation and dehumanization of the African people.

This humiliation and dehumanization 'is not a pretty thing when you look into it too much'.

When the humiliated and dehumanized speak of it too much, some friends of the African judge such conversation as not being a pretty thing. Discussion then becomes impossible.

The war to defeat AIDS is a difficult struggle because it is not only a struggle against the conditions that produce ill health and unnecessary death among millions of Africans, challenging as this struggle is.

It is a difficult struggle also because it has to be waged against some friends of the African, who find that the truth is not a pretty thing.

Asserting that they stand on irrefutable scientific knowledge, these particular friends of the Africans, and the Africans themselves, are horrified beyond measure that the Africans will perish, consumed by an HIV/AIDS pandemic which is sweeping across the face of Sub-Saharan Africa.

Statistics are produced regularly to show rapidly growing HIV infections and rapidly growing deaths from HIV/AIDS on our continent.

Our friends claim that millions of Africans, in increasing numbers, are infected with a highly mutant and indestructible Human Immunodeficiency Virus. They say that this HI Virus is communicated from person to person through heterosexual intercourse and from mother to child.

To stop the spread of the virus, they say that the Africans should abstain from sexual intercourse or use condoms.

They also say that HIV-positive mothers should be given drugs to stop the transmission of the virus. Their babies, too, should be given the same drugs, presumably to kill the virus if the mother has nevertheless transmitted it.

They urge that in the event of rape, the victims should also be given drugs, in case the rapist/s is or are carriers of the HI Virus.

They argue that all the above conforms, unequivocally, to the best available scientific knowledge. It is therefore unquestionable. Diagnosis, prevention and treatment are all based on immutable scientific truths that were agreed by the global scientific community twenty years ago.

It is then said that to question any of the above, or to ask any questions whatsoever, is to commit the sacrilege of questioning science itself and take on the guilt of the perpetration of the high crime of genocide.

The message is simple to understand and communicate. If it moves – clothe it in a condom! If it was naked – destroy its diseased emission with drugs!

The message is also simple in another way. The assertion is made that scientific discoveries about HIV and AIDS were proclaimed two decades ago. At the moment of the proclamation, the science of AIDS came to a standstill. It was frozen at this particular moment into an unquestionable and unchangeable monument to scientific thought.

Accordingly, further scientific inquiry into this matter is impermissible.

Such scientific knowledge as was possible two decades ago must be supported by all and sundry, including scientists, as part of a religious dogma. Accordingly, to establish his or her credentials, everybody must answer the bald question – do you believe that HIV causes AIDS! **Belief** about a scientific matter, and not empirical evidence, thus becomes the criterion of truth....

No longer will the Africans accept as the unalterable truth that they are a dependent people that emanates from and inhabits a continent shrouded in a terrible darkness of destructive superstition, driven and sustained by ignorance, hunger and underdevelopment, and that is victim to a self-inflicted 'disease' called HIV/AIDS.

For centuries we have carried the burden of the crimes and falsities of 'scientific' Eurocentrism, its dogmas imposed upon our being as the brands of a definitive, 'universal' truth.

Against this, we have, in struggle, made the statement to which we will remain loyal – that we are human and African!

Because we are human, we shall no longer permit control by a colonial mother who claims for herself the right unceasingly to restrain us from reclaiming our dignity.

We *shall* overcome!

There is so much more to life

'ELIZABETH', 'Living with HIV', avert.org

With the widespread availability of cheap antiretroviral treatment, a diagnosis of HIV-positive stopped being a death sentence and allowed millions of people to lead a normal life. Nevertheless, this requires access to adequate health care and a society that offers good education for both sexes and understands there need be no stigma attached to the diagnosis. Many NGOS have been involved in developing these things in Africa and other affected parts of the world. This anonymous story from Africa is typical of an individual coming to terms with the diagnosis and reconstructing her life.

I had finally graduated from college, after years of working full-time and being a single mother. Then I met the man I thought I'd spend the rest of my life with. Six months after our first sexual encounter, I was taken to the emergency room with a high fever and spots all over my body. It was then that I was diagnosed.

I didn't handle the news well. I thought my life was over. The disease was still a mystery to me and I worried that I had given the virus to my husband. I was terrified to tell him. What would I do if he left me? Who would love me? But I told him and he took the news almost with an 'oh well' attitude.

I went to my follow up appointments and I am grateful that I had kind and understanding doctors. I received a crash course in HIV and learned what it means to be undetectable. I also learned that my new husband had a very high load, which meant it was more likely he gave it to me. I was prepared to tell him our love would overcome it all. What I didn't expect was to find out later that he was already aware of his status long before we ever said 'I do'.

This news destroyed me.

Needless to say, our marriage ended and I was now a single mother, positive and alone. I had moved to a new state, was working a part-time job and struggling to make ends meet. I was living in fear of someone finding out or worse, of dying and leaving my son alone.

Eventually it was my faith that got me through. I decided this would not ruin me. I returned to my hometown, reconnected with family and friends, starting seeing an amazing doctor and met an even more amazing man. He's negative and eleven years and two kids later, he still makes me glad I didn't give up on love.

I know there's still a ridiculous amount of misinformation and stigma around HIV. I've even experienced unprofessional behaviour from doctors but I refuse to let it change who I am. I am living my positive life positively. There's so much more to life.

EBOLA

Ebola virus disease (EVD), also known as Ebola haemorrhagic fever, is a rare disease that kills between 50 and 90 per cent of infected people. It is highly contagious and spread through contact with body fluids. Virtually all known cases have been in sub-Saharan Africa; a handful have involved infection in Western laboratories or are associated with infected health care workers returning from Africa to the West. The Ebola virus is thought to be carried in certain species of fruit-bat, and perhaps to have been transferred to humans in West Africa by eating bushmeat. Thus, in part, the virus's transfer from bats to humans can be attributed to the environmental degradation that reduced the bats' rainforest habitat and the population pressure that drove humans to kill chimps for their meat.

The disease was first identified in 1976, in two outbreaks in Africa, one of which was near the Ebola River in the Democratic Republic of the Congo (DRC). Between 2013 and 2016, a large occurrence of Ebola in West Africa (Guinea, Liberia and Sierra Leone) resulted in almost 30,000 cases and over 11,000 deaths; the World Health Organization (WHO) declared the epidemic the most severe public health emergency of modern times. It proved particularly dangerous for health workers, who comprised 10 per cent of the dead in the West African outbreak. It was eventually contained, however, as a result of a vast humanitarian response led by the United Nations, with military support from the USA, France and Britain, though at considerable cost to the fragile economies of the affected countries.

A further outbreak began in the DRC in 2017. No effective treatments have been discovered, but a vaccine was licensed for use in late 2019.

The Ebola outbreak in Liberia
GARRETT INGOGLIA, *Huffington Post*, 10 September 2014
Garrett Ingoglia, an American worker with the health-focused relief organization Americares, described the mood in Liberia in October 2014, one year into the West African outbreak.

When traveling to areas devastated by earthquakes and violent storms, the physical damage is often apparent even before you step off the plane.

But here in Liberia where the death toll has surpassed 2,000 and continues to climb, there are no flattened buildings or tent camps filled with survivors. Signs of the crisis are more understated. In front of every building, hand-washing stations spill out a diluted chlorine solution. Police at checkpoints stop vehicles so they can check temperatures. And murals graphically depicting Ebola's symptoms scroll along sidewalks and roads.

The virus has the whole country on edge and everyone is more guarded. It is a matter of survival. There is no shaking hands, no hugging and no kissing. All the schools in the country are closed. Parents are telling their children not to play with their friends, to stay home. Many foreign-owned businesses have closed their doors, laying off workers, while other Liberian families suffer as the breadwinners become ill, and customers stay home out of fear.

Traumatized by watching their co-workers succumb to the virus, many health workers are staying home, too. Without them, hospitals have closed or scaled back services. As I walk through empty hospital wards, it's clear the lack of health workers has brought medical care to a virtual standstill for a population of 4 million. Patients still need care for malaria, typhoid and complicated childbirth – conditions that can prove deadly, too – but the degradation of an already weak health care system has left many of those conditions unattended. While good data is not available, many speculate that the increase in deaths from treatable diseases due to the breakdown of the health system has been more devastating than Ebola itself.

The Ebola treatment units (ETUs) are the cornerstones of the Ebola response strategy in Liberia. I recently visited one in a rural part of the country. There are 200 staff including doctors, nurses, cooks, decontamination crews, sanitation workers and ambulance drivers. There are workers to maintain the latrines, hand-washing stations, the incinerator that burns used safety equipment and the morgue for burying the dead. There are visitors, too: families come to see their loved ones stricken with Ebola, talking to them through a mesh screen. Almost everything you need is right there on site, or at a nearby university campus that's serving as a dormitory for the medical crews. Workers shuttle blood samples to Monrovia for testing – an agonizing wait for patients who get the diagnosis two or three days later.

I am not wearing the full protective gear shown on news reports. Those are only required for the medical professionals treating high-risk patients, who are carefully separated from the rest of the unit. When their shift is over, those doctors and nurses are sprayed with a chlorine solution before and after they remove their layers of protective equipment. The equipment is then incinerated, except for certain re-usable items, such as the goggles and boots, which are disinfected and re-used. This laborious process goes on around the clock. With seventeen more treatment centres planned, the need for trained health workers – and personal protective equipment – is going to increase dramatically.

Liberians were already struggling with the everyday grind of poverty and the devastation of the recent civil war when the epidemic struck. They are reacting with a mix of fear and a sort of weary determination that this is yet another crisis to overcome. Liberia alone won't be able to stop the outbreak from spiraling out of control. It is going to take a combined effort of governments, non-governmental organizations, multilateral organizations and the private sector coming together to support Liberians and halt this epidemic. And once that is accomplished, it is going to take an even greater – and much more sustained effort – to restore and improve the health system of Liberia so that it doesn't happen again.

The battle for hearts and minds in the DRC

GILLIAN McKAY, London School of Hygiene and Tropical Medicine, 2019

In 2019, the British researcher Gillian McKay supported WHO in combating the Ebola outbreak in the DRC, which had caused more than 2,000 deaths. She found that the problems of containing the outbreak were less technical ones than in overcoming the people's scepticism of Western organizations.

People ask me when I'm deploying out to Ebola outbreaks, 'Aren't you scared?' and the answer is usually, 'No, not really, I'm pretty good at this.' Which must sound a bit strange. But after working for nine months on the big West African outbreak back in 2014 and 2015, and then doing my doctoral study on reproductive health during outbreaks of Ebola, it's my speciality. So, when I was asked to go to the DRC to support the infection prevention and control team in the current Ebola outbreak, I thought I was right in my zone. Turns out, there is so little about stopping Ebola that is about technical solutions. It is almost entirely about local contextual factors, and I found the learning curve very steep.

The current outbreak is happening mostly in North-Kivu... [where] there are more than 100 armed groups, a deep mistrust of the Congolese government and poor health infrastructure. Put together, these elements make fighting an outbreak of a deadly disease incredibly difficult.

We have new innovations that we didn't have during the West Africa outbreak, including a very effective vaccine and experimental treatments to improve survival among those who have the disease. But these tools are only useful when the responders can access the people in need, and when sick people have enough confidence in the response and the health system to seek care. In a conflict-affected setting with a population that has been highly marginalized for years, neither of these things are guaranteed....

I hadn't anticipated how scared and alone the health workers were feeling. They told me they often feel like the enemy of the people, because if someone comes to their facility with Ebola symptoms (i.e. fever, vomiting, fatigue) they have to call the case investigation teams to assess whether the person in fact has Ebola. After doing this, the health workers can be threatened or attacked by local people, in retaliation for 'collaborating' with the response.

Community members feel that health facilities are places where you'll catch Ebola, because they often have stock-outs of essential items such as gloves, and many don't have running water. Another common complaint is that the response, including big SUVs and large numbers of outsiders, is too loud and disruptive, and why can't Ebola be more discreetly managed?

Finding a vaccine

THOMAS GEISBERT, *Discover* magazine, 30 November 2015

Work on a vaccine had begun in the mid-2000s, but attracted little interest and funding before the West African outbreak of 2013–16. Thomas Geisbert, a virologist at the University of Texas, contributed to the development of the vaccine that was finally licensed for use in December 2019. The first human trials had been held in 2014 in Guinea, and it was also tested in the DRC in 2017–18.

272

After 9/11, there was a lot of concern that Ebola could be used as a bio-terror agent, and the National Institutes of Health put a lot of money into biodefense. But there wasn't any money for product development or the financial incentive for Big Pharma to get involved because who were you going to sell your drug to? We made tremendous progress as a field, but everything just sat there until this outbreak. I felt a real sense of frustration watching this outbreak because we had something sitting on the shelf that might have saved lives. But the silver lining is that we now have the public's attention.

The VSV vaccine is extremely robust and has tremendous potential to be used to control an outbreak and contain its spread rather than to vaccinate large populations. To contain, manage and control an outbreak in Africa, you need a vaccine that requires just one injection and that works quickly. The vaccine works fast, within seven to ten days. It was shown to protect up to 50 per cent of primates after exposure but before they show symptoms.

Consequently, this vaccine has a great chance of combatting an outbreak in the context of ring vaccinations, where you give the vaccine only to people in close contact with infected patients. That strategy can be used to break the chains of transmission and reduce the number of cases. It can also be used with first responders and health care workers who need to be protected really quickly.

How to report on Ebola without provoking panic?

IDA JOOSTE, *Internews*, 15 December 2017
South African journalist Ida Jooste has worked widely across Africa on many health issues. In West Africa in 2017, she struggled to find a difficult balance between reassurance and concern, conveying accurate information of risks.

Most of us think we know what a sexually transmitted disease is. But in November 2017, CDC [the US Centers for Disease Control and Prevention] researchers showed that at least twenty-seven different viruses can be found in semen....

It's not known how many of these viruses are sexually transmittable, but it is already clear that Zika and Ebola are. Marburg (which is similar to Ebola), Lassa fever and mumps may be, too. Scientifically, we now can't conclusively say what is sexually transmissible and what is not.

For health writers who spend a lot of time 'in the field', this has raised all sorts of questions....

Ebola, of course, is deadly, but recently things have become more complicated. During the latest outbreak a large number of victims actually survived. The blanket message that 'Ebola kills' was not true for about half of the people who contracted the virus. They are now survivors who have gone on with their lives....

Over the course of 2015 and 2016, scientists started piecing together what sexually transmitted Ebola meant for public health. The first clear case [was] that of a 44-year-old Liberian woman who died in 2015 after contracting the virus from a male partner who had survived Ebola infection nearly six months earlier....

It had only taken a single infection to start the previous epidemic in West Africa. Even if sexual transmission is unlikely, its consequences could be devastating.

Meanwhile, other scientists were altering our understanding of how long Ebola virus remains in semen. We had believed that it could last up to 90 days, and then 180 days – but as time went on, findings...made it clear that vestiges of the virus remained in semen even longer than that. The risk of spreading the disease might linger long after patients had recovered from the infection...

We had a classic science journalist's dilemma: how to communicate uncertainty and risk without making an overstatement that itself would be harmful?

When we spoke with Parker Williams of the Ebola Response Team of the International Committee of the Red Cross, his first concern was for survivors. 'I would be concerned that stigma against survivors may be an issue if this sexual transmission is broadcast,' he said. He was worried that Ebola survivors, already often treated as pariahs, would be further isolated if we publicized what is probably a very small risk of sexual transmission. But he also saw the dilemma, sighing, 'But then, we cannot afford even one case!'...

In late 2016, we interviewed people in Monrovia, setting up focus groups to see what they knew about Ebola's dangers and what information they wanted. Some found it hard to discuss Ebola in an open forum, but the longer we engaged people in conversation, the more animated they became.... 'People are still talking that Ebola is dangerous and can transfer from place to place, and all we can do to prevent ourselves is to put God first,' said one....

We tried to gauge knowledge of sexual transmission.... There was both concern and incredulity about the possibility of sexual transmission. 'I don't believe that a survivor can re-infect another person after 180 days of his post-Ebola life,' said one man, but others, both men and women, said they thought often about the possibility of transmission.

Two people...did not believe Ebola was real. 'Up to now, I believe the virus was not real. It was a man-made virus. It was something that the governments agreed to: the Guinea president, the Sierra Leone president, and the Liberia president in 2012. This meeting was held in Liberia and US $4 million was given for this experiment,' said one.

This spoke to another concern of many who argued that coverage needs to be accurate. 'In Liberia, rumours are strong, and so to defeat rumour you must provide the truth,' otherwise, the speculation will continue to grow on a daily basis, cautioned one man....

Ebola survivors in research programs received safe sex education, aimed at ensuring they did not transmit the virus to their partners, but population-wide safe sex messaging that focused attention on Ebola survivors did not seem appropriate, because the risk was low and too much talk could lead to stigmatizing. Yet for the general population, vagueness or a lack of information could make the risk seem bigger than it is....

Now that we know that many kinds of virus are present in semen, our job as journalists has become easier. We can tell a story about sexual risk in a way that shifts the focus away from Ebola survivors. The story now is about the mystery of these viruses and the need for ongoing research. And of course, it also remains a safe sex story. The simple message is that everyone should be aware of the risk of viral infection from sex.

Frustrations of the humanitarian worker
TRISH NEWPORT, *Médecins Sans Frontières*, 1 August 2019
Médecins Sans Frontières (MSF) has been active in combating Ebola in the DRC, but like others struggled to win popular trust and had to

suspend activity following attacks on its health centres. Trish Newport,
Canadian project manager with MSF, expressed the frustrations in 2019.

I remember 24 July 2018 so clearly. It was the day the ninth Ebola outbreak in DRC was declared over. I had worked during the MSF's vaccination project. It was the first time that the experimental Ebola vaccine was used at the beginning of an outbreak to try and help control the outbreak. The outbreak lasted less than three months, and I remember crying with joy and hope on 24 July when it was declared over.

I naively thought that with this great vaccine the world would never have to face a large Ebola outbreak again. As has happened so many times in my humanitarian life, I was very wrong.

One week after the ninth Ebola outbreak in DRC was officially over, the start of the tenth Ebola outbreak in DRC was declared on 1 August. Today marks the one-year anniversary of the start of that outbreak, and it has become the world's second-largest Ebola outbreak in history.

It has been a long, painful, deadly year for the people living in the Ebola-affected areas in DRC. Ebola treatment centres have been viciously attacked and destroyed, health workers have been murdered because they worked in the Ebola response, security forces 'protecting' Ebola responders have killed civilians and people continue to die of Ebola.

The 'Ebola response' is made up of the Congolese Ministry of Health, the World Health Organization and other international organizations. This response has never gained the trust of the local community. The outbreak is happening in an area that has been plagued in recent years by conflict and massacres of civilians.

I once asked one of our local staff why there was so much anger towards the Ebola response. She answered: 'My husband was killed in a massacre in Beni. All I wanted was some organization to come protect us from the killings, but no international organization came. I have had three children die of malaria. No international organization has come to make sure we have access to health care or clean water. But now Ebola arrives, and all the organizations come because Ebola gives them money. If you cared about us, you would ask us our priorities. My priority is security and making sure my children don't die from malaria or diarrhea. My priority is not Ebola. That is your priority.'

In July, the Ebola outbreak was declared a Public Health Emergency of International Concern. Even more money is being directed towards the Ebola response, but if we don't gain the trust of the population, more money won't do anything. It will just create more problems....

In February 2019, two of MSF's Ebola Treatment Centers were attacked. We didn't know who attacked the centers or why. As we could no longer ensure the security of our staff or our patients, MSF took the painful decision to stop all activities in that area.

We were forced to review the problems we had been facing and how we should change our response to the Ebola outbreak. We determined that we needed to work more closely with the communities, and that we needed to listen to and respond to their health priorities.

We began providing access to free health care for all illnesses that were affecting local communities, like malaria, measles and diarrhea. We began building wells, so that when we told people they needed to wash their hands to prevent the spread of Ebola, they had water to do so. We set up centers for suspected Ebola cases in local health centres, so that people who were possibly infected could be cared for in their community instead of having to travel to other areas for testing, where they would be isolated from their families and communities. By addressing the actual needs and health priorities of the population, we began gaining the trust of the community.

Sadly, this approach has still not been adopted by the overall Ebola response, and there remains overall mistrust as a result. In many areas people still refuse to go to Ebola treatment centres when they are sick, and other people still refuse the vaccine.

One year into the outbreak, more than 2,600 people have gotten sick with Ebola, and more than 1,700 people have died of the disease. When I see families and communities ripped apart by Ebola, it makes me so sad. It didn't have to be like this. Unless a drastic change happens in the management of the Ebola response, the outbreak is not going to end anytime soon.

The only good news from this epidemic is that it can serve as a wake-up call

BILL GATES, *New England Journal of Medicine*, 9 April 2015

US computer entrepreneur and billionaire Bill Gates (b. 1955), together with his wife Melinda, has devoted enormous resources to improving health and education for the world's poorest people through their Foundation, which was launched in 2000. In the New England Journal of Medicine *in April 2015, he warned that the world was not sufficiently organized to face a serious pandemic.*

The ongoing Ebola epidemic in Guinea, Sierra Leone, and Liberia is a huge tragedy. The impact on the people who live in those countries goes far beyond the Ebola deaths. The health systems and the economies have been largely shut down during the outbreak... The only good news from this epidemic is that it can serve as a wake-up call to help us prepare for a future epidemic.

There is a significant chance that a substantially more infectious epidemic will come along over the next twenty years.... Ebola is far from the most infectious disease we know about. During the epidemic, almost all of the secondary infections have taken place after the patient was very sick.... This means there has been very little spread to strangers other than health care workers and those providing emergency transportation. This factor has helped keep the number of cases below 0.5 percent of the general population, and it allowed a few tactics...to slow the epidemic.

I am concerned that...we will miss the opportunity to learn from the Ebola epidemic and be better prepared for the next one. Even if the system we have today worked perfectly, it would not contain a more infectious disease....

Defense budgets and investment in new weapons dwarf investments in epidemic preparation. NATO has a mobile unit that is ready to deploy quickly.... They do joint exercises where they work out basic logistics like how fuel and food will be provided, what language they will speak, what radio frequencies will be used. When soldiers sign up to serve, they know what the risks are and who will take care of them if they're injured or killed. Few of these things exist for an epidemic response. The world does not fund any organization to do the broad set of coordinated activities that are needed for the next epidemic.

The International Health Regulations, adopted by the United Nations after the SARS outbreak of 2002–3, were intended to improve the world's ability to prevent and contain outbreaks. But few countries have met their commitments under the IHR. Nor have most countries established an Emergency Operations Center that can be activated within two hours of identifying an outbreak, a commitment made under the 2014 Global Health Security Agenda. This is a global failure. The world needs a global warning and response system for outbreaks.

The World Bank has estimated that a worldwide flu epidemic would reduce global wealth by $3 trillion, not to mention the immeasurable misery caused by millions of deaths. The world is not nearly as prepared for a massive epidemic as it needs to be....

There is a critical need to reinforce basic public health systems: primary health care facilities, laboratories, surveillance, critical care facilities, etc.... Without a functioning health system – including adequate numbers of trained health workers, good supply chains, disease surveillance, information systems, and policies that enable access by the poor – it is very hard for a country to end the cycle of disease and poverty. Good health is so fundamental to well-being and development that even if there were no chance of another epidemic ever occurring, health care systems would be a worthwhile – and life-saving – investment.

There is no systematic disease-surveillance process in place today in most poor countries.... Even once [the Ebola crisis in West Africa] was recognized, there weren't resources to effectively map where cases were occurring and in what quantity. We need to invest in better disease surveillance and laboratory testing capacity, for normal situations and for epidemics. The data derived from the testing needs to be made public right away. A lot of the laboratories in developing countries have been financed by the polio eradication campaign, so there should be a plan for what capacities we need once that campaign is over....

We need trained personnel ready to deal with an epidemic quickly. One approach is to think of them in three tiers:

1. an incident manager for each Emergency Operations Center, in charge of coordinating efforts by medical care providers, military, volunteers, and others;

2. experts in epidemiology, surveillance, outbreak response, social anthropology, and other areas who can provide surge capacity for the response; and

3. respected community leaders who can lead the local engagement efforts and community workers.

The Ebola epidemic might have been a lot worse if the US and UK governments had not used military resources to help build health centers, manage logistics, and fly people in and out of the affected countries. The militaries also provided command and control capacity to help organize the different groups working on Ebola.... The world should identify trained military resources that will be available for epidemics.... We should have a list of supplies needed to stop an epidemic that reaches 10 million people....

It is critically important to have good data about what's going on... For future epidemics it should be possible to have a system to digitally enter information like suspected cases, locations, survivors, etc. into a database accessible to organizations engaged in the response and the agencies coordinating their work.... Experts will also need computer models to predict what might happen and which interventions should be prioritized.... And we need to improve Internet and cell phone connectivity....

Among the pathogens we know about, flu is the most likely to cause a big epidemic. But we could encounter one we have never seen before. In 2003, no scientist had seen SARS.... Making sure that prophylactics and treatments are available for key personnel...and volunteers could make a gigantic difference in stopping an epidemic and limiting the damage it does.... It should be possible to have general capabilities to make diagnostic tests as well as drugs, and vaccine platforms that could be adapted for use against various pathogens. Today, with the possible exception of flu, we do not have nearly enough capacity to do this.

During the Ebola epidemic there was a lot of discussion about quarantine. Should commercial flights into and out of the affected countries be stopped? Should people returning from the affected region be forced into quarantine? For this epidemic...most of these proposals would have been counterproductive. Banning direct travel from affected areas to the United States, for example, would have forced people to take an indirect route, making them harder to track once they arrived. Forcing people into quarantine would have discouraged volunteers.

But when a far more infectious agent comes along, quarantine will be one of the few tactics in the early stage of the disease that can reduce the spread of contagion. Travel today is so common that an infection can spread across the globe far faster now than in 1918, when the Spanish Flu epidemic swept across the world. During the SARS epidemic, China eventually did a good job of curtailing travel and public gatherings in affected areas. I doubt every country would have handled this aspect as well as China did, because in normal situations the system is designed to avoid abridging individual rights to travel and assemble freely. I worry that in the early stages of an epidemic, democratic countries might be too slow to restrict activities that help spread the contagion.

Part of the process should include a plan for effective public communications.... The ways that people communicate digitally can be used to great advantage, but unless a plan is in place, they will just spread confusion and panic faster than in the past – perhaps at the cost of many lives.

An epidemic could be engineered intentionally.... It is getting easier to create (or re-create) pathogens with only modest effort and technical knowledge. Over the next few decades it will be even more feasible to synthesize, mass-produce, and disseminate pathogens that are highly infectious and largely fatal.... Everything I have described would be worthwhile In preparing for bioterrorism.

The world spends a great deal of money getting ready for war, and... I believe we should build on these efforts so we can be more prepared for a severe epidemic. Some of the capabilities, like transport and some personnel, overlap and can play a dual purpose if properly planned. Other elements will require specific investments.

A serious epidemic would raise a lot of questions about global governance. What body would bring sovereign nations together and ask them to make decisions about limiting travel and allocating scarce resources like vaccines or drugs?... We desperately need processes for making tough decisions fast. One technique that we should borrow from the military is the idea of a war game....

Many people do not think a serious epidemic is a problem for them to worry about. They may think that the United Nations system and WHO has it covered. In fact, WHO has not been clearly chartered or funded to handle most of the things required in an epidemic. Or they may think their government has a plan already in place. While the United States, the United Kingdom, and others are working on many of the things described in this memo, there are still big holes in the world's ability to respond.

There should be a rigorous study of the cost of building a global warning and response system for epidemics.... There would need to be a plan for how much each country would contribute and for coordinating the spending. Other countries need to step up, but they are more likely to do so when they see an overall plan and understand their role in it.... Some global institution needs to be empowered and funded to coordinate a global warning and response system.

In my view, an epidemic is one of the few catastrophes that could set the world back in a huge way in the next few decades. Severe epidemics have struck many times in the past, and they are only more likely as the world becomes more closely connected. By building a global warning and response system, we can prepare for the next epidemic and avoid millions of deaths.

CORONAVIRUS

Until recent times, the coronavirus was a relatively unthreatening virus mostly found in bats, although it can cause a range of respiratory diseases in humans, including the common cold. However, in the 21st century, it has been responsible for two pandemics: the first, SARS (severe acute respiratory syndrome), in 2003, and the second, Covid-19, in late 2019 and 2020. In each case the pandemic resulted from environmental pressures in China that brought city dwellers into more direct contact with bats, allowing the virus not only to jump species but also to spread quickly – a spread that soon became worldwide.

The 2003 SARS pandemic was contained relatively quickly, through comprehensive quarantine and other preventive measures, and because the disease did not become infectious before symptoms emerged. However, although the death toll was relatively low, the secondary economic impact on the affected countries was very high.

The SARS pandemic, the responses to it and its costs, led to a general awareness of the dangers of another, larger pandemic in the future. This emerged in late 2019 and early 2020, with a closely related coronavirus bringing a new disease, known as Covid-19. Sufferers could be infectious for up to a week before symptoms appeared, which made it almost impossible to contain an exponential growth in infection numbers without major disruption. Although the genetic sequence of the virus was fully known within weeks, and many countries began a race to find a vaccine, there was no known cure and even supportive medicine proved difficult. In response, most countries adopted lockdown or shielding policies that severely curtailed human interaction for weeks, at enormous social and economic cost, and causing the world's deepest recession for almost a century.

Faced with these unprecedented issues, political and social tensions surfaced in many countries. Fault lines emerged in some countries between the white population and Black and Asian minorities who appeared more susceptible to the disease; in others, between those with good access to health care and those without. Some of the poorest paid were seen to perform the very jobs that keep society functioning. Questions were raised about access to health care provision for the poor or the elderly, especially where care homes were often starved of resources and likely to be a major source of infection and death. To some, there was an imbalance in the cost of the disruption, which was borne in large part by the young – who were less likely to suffer severely from the virus but whose education was disrupted and employment prospects blighted – and the benefits of shielding, felt mainly by those who were older and/or already had underlying health issues. Above all, some governments chose to work with all communities to protect their populations and provide calm leadership, information and support in unprecedented times, while others preferred to grandstand, pick arguments or challenge the scientific experts. In the long run, the impact of the Covid-19 pandemic may be felt most deeply in resolving these wide tensions, rather than in the narrower issues of epidemiology, preventive medicine and health care. An effective vaccine became available for rolling out a year after the pandemic had begun.

The lessons from SARS

WORLD HEALTH ORGANIZATION, The World Health report, 2003

In 2003, an epidemic of SARS, causing cough, fever and breathing difficulties brought on by a coronavirus, broke out in Guangdong in southern China. No vaccine was available, and the disease could only be contained by quarantine, hygiene and other public health measures; these proved relatively effective as the disease was most infectious during its acute stages. Many of those who caught it were health care workers.

Despite a relatively slow and secretive response from China, the World Health Organization (WHO) was active in alerting the world to the danger and advising on measures against its spread internationally. Nevertheless, a single carrier took it to Hong Kong from where it spread to a number of other countries, including Taiwan, Singapore and Canada, within days; thereafter, however, aggressive containment succeeded in keeping the spread low. By July 2003, WHO declared the epidemic contained; it resulted in 8,000 cases and fewer than 1,000 deaths worldwide. A subsequent WHO report set out the lessons to be learned from the epidemic, and identified the significant social and economic costs of the containment exercise.

The struggle to control the outbreak of severe acute respiratory syndrome (SARS) represents a major victory for public health collaboration. Key lessons emerge that will be invaluable in shaping the future of infectious disease control – and being ready for the day when the next new disease arrives without warning.

- First and most important is the need to report, promptly and openly, cases of any disease with the potential for international spread in a closely interconnected and highly mobile world.
- Second, timely global alerts can prevent imported cases from igniting big outbreaks in new areas.
- Third, travel recommendations, including screening measures at airports, help to contain the international spread of an emerging infection.
- Fourth, the world's best scientists, clinicians and public health experts, aided by electronic communications, can collaborate to

generate rapidly the scientific basis for control measures.

- Fifth, weaknesses in health systems play a key role in permitting emerging infections to spread.
- Sixth, an outbreak can be contained even without a curative drug or a vaccine if existing interventions are tailored to the circumstances and backed by political commitment.
- Finally, risk communication about new and emerging infections is a great challenge, and it is vital to ensure that the most accurate information is successfully and unambiguously communicated to the public.

SARS is a newly identified human infection caused by a coronavirus unlike any other known human or animal virus in its family. Analysis of epidemiological information from the various outbreak sites is still under way, but the overall case fatality ratio, with the fate of most cases now known, approaches 11 per cent, but with much higher rates among elderly people. Transmission occurs mainly from person to person during face-to-face exposure to infected respiratory droplets expelled during coughing or sneezing, or following contact with body fluids during certain medical interventions. Contamination of the environment, arising from faecal shedding of the virus, is thought to play a small role in disease transmission, illustrated by the almost simultaneous infection in late March of more than 300 residents of a housing estate in Hong Kong where faulty sewage disposal was identified. At present, the disease has no vaccine, no curative treatment and no reliable point-of-care diagnostic test, though antibody tests have been developed that can reliably confirm previous infection using acute and convalescent sera. Management of SARS is supportive, and control strategies rely on standard epidemiological interventions: identification of those fitting the case definition, isolation, infection control, contact tracing, active surveillance of contacts and evidence-based recommendations for international travellers. Though demanding and socially disruptive, particularly when large numbers of people were placed in quarantine, these standard interventions, supported by high-level political commitment, proved sufficiently powerful to contain the global outbreak less than four months after the initial alert.

The earliest cases of SARS are now thought to have emerged in mid-November 2002 in the southern Chinese province of Guangdong. Retrospective analysis of patient records, to date incomplete, has identified small clusters of cases, each traced to a different initial case, that occurred independently in at least seven municipalities, with the first case recorded on 16 November 2002 in Foshan City and the largest number of cases concentrated in Guangzhou City. Analysis has uncovered no links among the various initial cases in the clusters. Some cases with no previous known history of exposure also occurred. Early collaborative studies conducted in Guangdong have detected a virus almost identical to the SARS coronavirus in domesticated game animals – the masked palm civet cat and the raccoon dog – sold in Guangdong live markets, suggesting that these animals might play a role in transmission of the virus to humans....

The economic impact of the SARS outbreak has been considerable and illustrates the importance that a severe new disease can assume in a closely interdependent and highly mobile world. Apart from the direct costs of intensive medical care and control interventions, SARS caused widespread social disruption and economic losses. Schools, hospitals and some borders were closed and thousands of people were placed in quarantine. International travel to affected areas fell sharply by 50–70 per cent. Hotel occupancy dropped by more than 60 per cent. Businesses, particularly in tourism-related areas, failed, while some large production facilities were forced to suspend operations when cases appeared among workers. A second impact is more positive: SARS stimulated an emergency response – and a level of media attention – on a scale that has very likely changed public and political perceptions of the risks associated with emerging and epidemic-prone diseases. It also raised the profile of public health to new heights by demonstrating the severity of adverse effects that a health problem can also have on economies and social stability. The resulting high level of political commitment was decisive in the containment of SARS and has much to say about the ability of nations to achieve public health results even when drugs and vaccines are not available to cure or prevent the infection....

SARS will not be the last new disease to take advantage of modern global conditions. In the last two decades of the 20th century, new diseases emerged at the rate of one per year, and this trend is certain to continue. Not all of these emerging infections will transmit easily from person to person as does SARS. Some will emerge, cause illness in humans and then disappear, perhaps to recur at some time in the future. Others will emerge, cause human illness and transmit for a few generations, become attenuated and likewise disappear. And still others will emerge, become endemic and remain important parts of our human infectious disease ecology. The rapid containment of SARS is a success in public health, but also a warning. It is proof of the power of international collaboration supported at the highest political level. It is also proof of the effectiveness of GOARN [Global Outbreak Alert and Response Network] in detecting and responding to emerging infections of international public health importance. At the same time, containment of SARS was aided by good fortune. The most severely affected areas in the SARS outbreak had well-developed health care systems. Had SARS established a foothold in countries where health systems are less well developed, cases might still be occurring, with global containment much more difficult, if not impossible. Although control measures were effective, they were extremely disruptive and consumed enormous resources – resources that might not have been sustainable over time. If SARS reoccurs during an influenza season, health systems worldwide will be put under extreme pressure as they seek to isolate all those who fit the clinical case definition until diagnosis can be ascertained. Continued vigilance is vital.

I suffered an unprecedented and very severe reprimand

DR AI FEN, 'The Wuhan Whistle', *Science Integrity Digest*, March 2020
In late December 2019, Dr Ai Fen, director of the emergency room of Wuhan Central Hospital in China, treated a patient with a serious condition caused by a coronavirus resembling the SARS virus. She passed on this information to colleagues, one of whom, an ophthalmologist named Li Wenliang, posted it on social media channels. Dr Ai's blog setting out her experience was published in China but quickly taken down by the authorities. Both Ai Fen and Li were severely criticized; Li caught the virus when treating patients and died in early February 2020. In an attempt to stop the virus spreading in China, all travel over the Lunar New Year holiday was stopped and Wuhan placed under strict lockdown. Nevertheless, in subsequent months, China was itself

criticized for its secrecy in dealing with the coronavirus in the early stages of the epidemic.

On 16 December, last year, we received a patient at the Nanjing Road emergency department. They had an inexplicably high fever, and they weren't responding to standard medications, their body temperature wasn't going down at all. On the 22nd, the patient was transferred to the respiratory department, a bronchoscopy was done and bronchoalveolar fluid taken and sent out for high-throughput genetic sequencing. Afterwards, the coronavirus result was relayed verbally. At that time, the colleague who was responsible for the patient told me clearly: 'Director Ai, that person's diagnosis is coronavirus.' Later we learned that the patient worked in the Huanan Seafood Market.

Immediately afterwards, 27 December, another patient arrived at Nanjing Road. He was in his forties, without any pre-existing conditions. His lungs were in a terrible state, and his blood oxygen saturation was only 90 per cent. He was under hospital care for almost ten days without any improvement, and was admitted to the respiratory department. A flexible bronchoscopy was also done and the alveolar lavage fluid sent for testing.

At noon on 30 December, an old classmate at Tongji Hospital sent me a screenshot of a WeChat conversation, which said: 'You don't want to go to Huanan Market just now, there are lots of people with high fever...' He asked if it was true. At the time, I was watching a CT scan of a typical patient with pulmonary infection on the computer. I sent him an eleven-second video of the CT and told him it was a patient who had come to our emergency department in the morning, a Huanan Seafood Market case.

Just after 4 p.m. that day, a colleague showed me a diagnostic report that said: 'SARS coronavirus, *Pseudomonas aeruginosa*, 46 strains of bacteria which colonize the oral cavity and/or respiratory tract.' I read the report very carefully many times, and the supplementary information read: 'SARS coronavirus is a single-stranded positive-strand RNA virus. The main mode of transmission of the virus is close-range droplet transmission or contact with respiratory secretions of patients, which can cause an unusual pneumonia that is highly contagious and can affect multiple organ systems, also known as atypical pneumonia.'

At the time, the diagnostic report scared me, I broke into a cold sweat, this was a terrifying thing. The patient was admitted to the respiratory department, and I immediately phoned and reported it to the hospital's public health division and infectious disease division. At that moment, the director of the respiratory department of our hospital happened to be passing my office door, someone who had been involved with SARS. I grabbed the director and said, 'We found this in one of the patients in your department.' The director took one look and said it was worrying.

After calling the hospital, I also circulated this report to my old classmates. I purposely drew a red circle around the words 'SARS coronavirus, *Pseudomonas aeruginosa*, 46 strains of bacteria which colonize the oral cavity and/or respiratory tract' to bring the warning to their attention. I also sent the report to the doctors in the department to warn everyone to take precautions.

That evening, the message was spread widely; the screenshots of the transmission show the photos of the report I'd marked with a red circle, including the ones that I later learned that Li Wenliang passed on to the chat group. At the time, I was thinking it might be bad. At 10.20, the hospital passed on a relayed notification from the city Health Protection Committee. Their main point was that information on the pneumonia of unknown cause should not be arbitrarily released, to avoid causing panic among the public; if panic was caused by information leakage, there would be a thorough investigation.

I was very scared at the time and immediately passed this information on to my classmates. About an hour later, the hospital sent another notice, again stressing that information the group had on this subject could not be leaked. One day later, at 11.46 p.m. on 1 January, the head of the hospital's disciplinary inspection committee sent me a message to come the next morning.

I didn't fall asleep that night, I was worried and thought things through over and over again, but I felt that there are always two sides to everything; even if it had caused adverse effects, it was not necessarily a bad thing to remind medical staff in Wuhan to take precautions. At eight o'clock the next morning, I was called in for the disciplinary review.

In that disciplinary review, I suffered an unprecedented and very severe reprimand.

The leader of the discussion said, 'As the director of the emergency department of Wuhan Central Hospital, you are a professional, how can there be this lack of principle, this lack of organizational discipline, this creating and spreading of false rumours?' This is the original sentence. So I should go back to the 200-odd people in the department to convey the news to them verbally, one by one; we can't send information by WeChat or SMS, we can only talk face-to-face or call, we can't say anything about this pneumonia, 'you can't even tell your own husband', they said...

I was utterly stunned. I hadn't been criticized for not working hard, but made to feel that what I'd done had ruined Wuhan's prospects and its future. I felt strong despair. I am a serious and hard-working person. I felt that everything I had done was in accordance with the rules and well-founded. What did I do wrong? After I read the lab result, I had also reported it to the hospital. My students and my colleagues had communicated among ourselves about how to handle the condition of a patient, we hadn't given out any of the patient's personal information; this is equivalent to discussing a medical case among medical students. As a clinical doctor, I already knew that a very important virus had been found in patients. When other doctors asked, how could you not say so? This is your instinct as a doctor, right? What did I do wrong? I have done what a doctor and a person should normally do. I think anyone would do the same.

I was very emotional at the time, saying that I had done this, and it had nothing to do with the rest of the people; you can just arrest me and jail me. I said that I was not suitable to continue to work in this position, and I wanted to take a break. The leader did not agree, saying that this was the time to test me.

I went home that night, I remember it quite clearly, I told my husband just after I walked in the door, if something goes wrong, you must care for and raise the child — because my second treasure is still very young, only just over 1 year old. At the time, my husband was perplexed by this. I didn't explain.

Be strong and be kind

JACINDA ARDERN, New Zealand, 23 March 2020

As it became clear that a sufferer could be infectious before symptoms of the disease had emerged, and the virus began to spread internationally in February and March 2020, countries saw that complete lockdown – limiting interaction between people, closing workplaces and places of recreation and education – would be the only way to slow reinfection rates and prevent health services from being overwhelmed. With Italy leading the way, having suffered a large and early outbreak, lockdown was introduced even in places where only a few hundred cases had so far been seen. One such was New Zealand, where prime minister Jacinda Ardern (b. 1980) won widespread admiration for her clarity, decisiveness and leadership in announcing lockdown on 23 March, and introducing a 20 per cent pay cut for herself and her ministers. By midsummer, the country declared itself entirely free of the virus, although more cases emerged in Auckland in August.

We currently have 102 cases. But so did Italy once. Now the virus has overwhelmed their health system and hundreds of people are dying every day. The situation here is moving at pace, and so must we....

If community transmission takes off in New Zealand the number of cases will double every five days. If that happens unchecked, our health system will be inundated and tens of thousands of New Zealanders will die.

There is no easy way to say that – but it is the reality we have seen overseas, and the possibility we must now face here....

Right now we have a window of opportunity to break the chain of community transmission – to contain the virus – to stop it multiplying and to protect New Zealanders from the worst.

Our plan is simple. We can stop the spread by staying at home and reducing contact.

Now is the time to act....

Supermarkets, doctors, pharmacies, service stations, access to essential banking services will all be available throughout New Zealand at every alert level. If you do not have immediate needs, do not go to the supermarket.... There will be enough for everyone if we shop normally....

Non-essential businesses in New Zealand must now close. All bars, restaurants, cafes, gyms, cinemas, pools, museums, libraries, playgrounds and any other place where the public congregate must close their face to face function....

Over the next forty-eight hours every workplace must implement alternative ways of working, people must work from home so that interactions with others are limited....

To be absolutely clear, we are now asking all New Zealanders who are outside essential services to stay at home, and to stop all interactions with others outside of those in your household.

I understand that self-isolation is a daunting prospect. So we are being practical. You can leave your home for fresh air, a walk, exercise. To take your children outside. But remember the simple principle. It must be solitary. We are asking that you only spend time with those you are in self-isolation with. And if you are outside, keep your distance from others. That means two metres at all times. This is the single most important thing we can do right now to stop further community transmission....

We will continue to vigorously contact trace every single case. Testing will continue at pace to help us understand the current number of cases in New Zealand and where they are based. If we flush out the cases we already have and see transmission slow, we will potentially be able to move areas out of Level 4 over time.

But for the next wee while, things will look worse before they look better. In the short term the number of cases will likely rise because the virus is already in our community. But these new measures can slow the virus down and prevent our health system from being overwhelmed and ultimately save lives....

The worst-case scenario is simply intolerable. It would represent the greatest loss of New Zealanders' lives in our country's history. I will not take that chance. The Government will do all it can to protect you. Now I'm asking you to do everything you can to protect us all. None of us can do this alone....

I have one final message. Be kind. I know people will want to act as enforcers. And I understand that, people are afraid and anxious. We will play that role for you. What we need from you, is support one another. Go home tonight and check in on your neighbours. Start a phone tree with your street. Plan how you'll keep in touch with one another. We will get through this together, but only if we stick together. Be strong and be kind.

Plague Diaries: April 2020
GONÇALO TAVARES, *Expresso*, May 2020
With people across the world confined to home for months, daily life changed suddenly: those who could both worked and socialized digitally, as did many schoolchildren, using communication tools such as Zoom; home-based hobbies and activities were developed. Many localities developed new self-help groups to support the vulnerable and lonely; nevertheless lockdown added hugely to stress for many, with worries about future employment to add to fears of catching the virus or passing it on to the most vulnerable, and with many families unable to meet even in the face of severe illness or death. Italy was the first Western nation to discover the strange world of lockdown, followed by most others a few weeks later. The Portuguese writer Gonçalo Tavares wrote a blog that captured the strangeness of this time.

7 April
I watch Jean-Luc Godard. Instagram Live.
A cigar between his fingers sometimes, and in his mouth
    almost always.
Around him, masks on some faces.
He talks clearly or semi-clearly, long pauses sometimes.
I imagine Godard's camera pointed at the TV news....
Godard's line: it's not blood, it's red.
What you see on a screen is not blood, it's a colour.
Only off the screen is blood blood.
But this plague has no blood.
One of the rare tragedies where there is no blood.
Hard to understand a tragedy without blood....
When people talk about a tsunami in the hospitals, I say.
It's not a tsunami of water, of course, but of sick bodies.
A solid tsunami.
A tsunami of bodies in a solid state with a total lack of air.

A tsunami of solids that want to breathe.

A tragedy of air.

And also, yes, also a bit of fire.

Pictures from some cities in Latin America: the burning in front of the family home of the dead who are not collected by the state.

So they do not infect....

I'm told about a father who whenever he wants to cry goes out onto the balcony of his apartment so his children don't see.

His children think he's going to get some air....

Maybe the father doesn't know that the children also go out onto the balcony to cry so their father doesn't see.

They say they're going to get some air.

George Kubler once wrote: actuality 'is when the lighthouse is dark between flashes';

'it is the instant between the ticks of the watch'.

...more than ten million newly unemployed people in the United States of America.

Few times are as current and actual as this is now.

Actuality is not a light, it's the opposite.

'it is when the lighthouse is dark between flashes'.

13 April

In Brazil, Christ the Redeemer dressed as a doctor.

Photograph in the *Folha de São Paulo* newspaper.

Christ with overalls and a stethoscope.

We look up and we feel calmer, says an inhabitant of Rio de Janeiro.

Another says: I got scared. It means things are serious.

Christ dressed as a doctor.

A technical Christ, who studied at a school and saves with the help of machines....

In Spain a maximum of two people can attend a funeral.

They say the virus can spread from the lungs to the brain.

The image of a relative beside the coffin, two metres away, in a mask.

And a priest in front of the coffin, also in a mask and two metres away.

The decision. Which two people will say goodbye to the dead person?

The older brother or the younger brother?

The wife or the child?
Sometimes another person approaches. One at the most.
They aren't a relative, they want to pay tribute....
A priest (Spanish) says that many people do not understand these
　　restrictions on funerals, but some do.
Funerals have become dangerous for the living....
'Lockdown in Ireland extended to 5th May', what may be 'an
　　inconvenience for some will be life saving for others'.
The minor nuisance for one, the death of the other.
We have never been so apart.
I'm sorry about the nuisance, but I would rather remain alive.
Each person, an enemy.
Somebody phones me and says they have gone out after three weeks.
And they also say their legs are shaking.
The homeless man on the street is still there and he is certain
　　nothing's going to get him.
I've already gone hungry, he says.
And really, he looks the same.
The president of the European Commission said yesterday that older
　　people might have to stay home until the end of the year.
They are talking about three vaccines and about the impossibility
　　of a vaccine....
I breathe and think: how much time has passed in so little time.
In a month a thousand years or more.
So much time in such a small month....
We cannot bear to stay home any longer.

20 April
Louis Vuitton masks, 199 dollars.
In a yellowish case, really elegant.
And inside, a bag, the same name: Louis Vuitton.
It seems to advertise a jewel, but it is a brown mask, size S.
Size S for small or for Scared?
Imagining size S.
The size of being Scared....
Aníbal Ruão, 93.

He has been to the hospital several times lately: a fall and urinary infections.

On one of those visits they detected Covid-19.

He spent fifteen days in hospital.

He survived, he came back.

When he got back home, his neighbours were on their balconies.

There was applause to welcome him home.

Is it possible by the crooked path to arrive at your destination? Yes.

Can you walk in a straight line to the wrong place? Sure.

Aesthetic applause and applause for somebody who survives.

I think about the clapping at the theatre.

I applaud because it's beautiful, I applaud because it's powerful, I applaud because it made me think, I applaud because you survived....

'Authorities in the Big Apple have released more than 1,400 detainees since the beginning of March.'

In a province in Ecuador, hundreds of deaths have been recorded in the first two weeks of April.

Yesterday, concert: each musician in their home.

Mick Jagger sings: 'You Can't Always Get What You Want'.

A good synthesis.

Another possible synthesis: you are alive, sometimes you get what you want.

The Rolling Stones drummer, Charlie Watts, is at home without a drum kit.

He plays with drumsticks on suitcases he has in front of him.

And on the sofa.

'You Can't Always Get What You Want'.

Close to a hospital in São Paulo there are ambulance sirens.

And also the honking of cars that aren't letting the ambulances past.

The sick are stopped, waiting, in the middle of this political traffic.

Horns and sirens competing to occupy the centre of the air.

You can't always get what you want, darling....

28 April

Boris Johnson interrupted his meeting with the Chancellor of the Exchequer for a minute's silence.

Interrupting the economy with a minute's silence.
A ritual that could be repeated in the middle of every day.
In the middle of the economy: a minute's silence.
'Coronavirus-related syndrome detected in children.'
And a number of doctors, nurses and support staff dead....
In Mexico, some doctors and nurses are being insulted.
They are having water poured over them to clean them.
A doctor is seen as a sick person.
The sickness overtakes the sick person, the doctor, the medical
    instruments, the hospital, the neighbourhood, the city and the
    country.
And your head.
The status of observer disappears.
Sick person or potential sick person. There is no third option.
Clapping, silence and buckets of water....
In Spain, kids are on the street, authorized by decree to leave their homes.
It's like they're seeing the wind for the first time.
It stops being an airy invisible thing and is met with celebration.
Number of dead in Africa rises and there is talk of a possible
    'baby boom'....
In Spain, children discover skateboarding – and all the speed and
    disequilibrium are met by feet that have been still for too long.
The police move forward on horseback, wearing masks, in some
    Italian cities....
Many refuse to wear a mask and people give them sidelong looks.
Many wear masks and people give them sidelong looks.
The sidelong look at another human being has stormed into the
    century, and it won't be leaving anytime soon.
A new species of human who looks sidelong more than they look
    straight ahead.
'Gatherings of more than ten people banned in France.'
Before, when cars stopped at the traffic lights, there would be people
    selling sweets and water on the streets of Latin America.
Now they sell masks at the traffic lights, but in some places the lights
    have turned green and no cars are moving.
And business cannot be good like this.

The spirit of the NHS

DR KIRAN RAHIM, Medic Footprints, 2020

Health services across the world struggled to deal with the unprecedented impact of Covid-19, as large numbers of patients required ventilation in an intensive care unit (ICU or ITU) to help them breathe, and administrators rushed to access sufficient of the unfamiliar and unwieldy personal protective equipment (PPE) to allow health care workers to do their work. In Britain as elsewhere, normal medical services were severely curtailed and staff redeployed to deal with Covid patients. Dr Kiran Rahim, paediatric doctor in the NHS, shared her experience of changing role to be an ITU assistant.

I am home from my first shift as an Intensive Care assistant. A role I have been redeployed to help the nursing staff with their increasing workload. A role for which I hung up my doctor badge and put on a sticker, that simply said 'Kiran "Helper"'.

Last night I barely slept. I turned up, anxious, scared but willing to do what I could in the face of the chaos. I put on three layers of suffocating protective clothing, three pairs of gloves, a face mask that I could barely breathe in and a face shield that made it impossible to know who I was. Despite all of this, nothing could have prepared me for ITU.

The unit that once held eight to ten of the sickest patients in the hospital is now providing life-saving care for thirty. Every single one of them gripping on to the edges of life, sick, on a ventilator and mostly, unstable. Patients who weeks ago were well, probably walking around, sat in their homes, talking with their families, laughing, smiling. People who were now completely unconscious with tubes breathing for them and machines and drugs supporting their heart and body. They lay there, silent and still. The air around them filled with noise from piercing alarms, medications beeps and hissing ventilators.

Today I cared for just two patients, one of whom is unlikely to make it. I prayed for both, silently, as I fought back tears. I prepared their medications, calculated their urine outputs and wrote down their observations. I did what I could.

Today was hard and humbling.

But for me it was *one* day. I am in awe of the ITU staff who work day in day out, often on back-breaking 13-hour shifts. I have no idea how they are coping or how they are processing the trauma around them.

When I walk in my hospital, I find its corridors empty, its cleaners exhausted, its porters drained and its staff broken. But in that ITU today I felt the spirit of the NHS I love so dearly. A spirit that refuses to bow in the face of adversity and sees Herculean efforts from its bone-bear workforce. A spirit that catches the silver lining of very dark days and continues, with grit and grace, to provide compassionate care for all that walk through its doors.

Fake News: Vaccination is a descent into hell

ROBERTO PATRELLA, Italy, 2020

As with many historic pandemics, coronavirus gave rise to panic and a slew of misleading and dangerous rumours that briefly found their way into the mainstream media and flourished in social media channels. These included the suggestions that the virus was released as a biological weapon (some said by the Chinese military, others the US), or that it was a non-existent threat, a hoax dreamed up by billionaires who wished to control us, perhaps by poisoning us with a dangerous vaccine, or a cover for the supposed damage that 5G, the new generation of mobile phone technology, would do to our bodies. The following script, by Roberto Patrella, a de-barred Italian gynaecologist, briefly circulated.

Italians, pay attention.

Covid means 'certificate of identification of vaccination with artificial intelligence', and 19 is the year in which it was created.

Covid-19 is not the name of the virus, it is rather the name of the International plan for the control and reduction of populations which has been developed over the last decades and launched in 2020. What reactivates the virus is the immune ground in which it finds itself weakened by former vaccinations.

What they intend to inject in us is going to be the most terrible vaccines of all. It is literally a descent into hell, with the aim of a massive depopulation of over 80% of the population.

Do not take the tests; the tests are not reliable. They only detect an infinity of small harmless viruses or cell debris which are already naturally part of our microbiota. The people tested will appear increasingly positive in tests (about 90%). This is their goal, and this is why they started the testing process with children.

Once your child gets screened, the whole family, and all immediate contacts, will be forced to be screened.

Pay attention, Italians. Do not listen to the charlatans, the ignorant, who reject the truth.

I remind you, we are not sick. We are, on the contrary, just healthy carriers of this virus. Having the virus does not necessarily mean that you are sick: you are healthy and fine. But everyone will still appear positive in the tests.

All they need to obtain is this: make everyone believe that they are sick. Being positive means being labelled as harmful.

Refusing the detection of the virus is the only key to avoid being vaccinated. Once vaccinated we will all be severely sick, weakened, and we will certainly be led towards our death.

The only solution to save our humanity, but above all to save us Italians, is to make people understand they should not be tested. Do not get yourself tests, do not give them what they lack, do not fall into their trap.

Covid-19 means 'programme of mass extermination'. Don't get tested, it's the only way to save yourself.

Most non-vaccinated people will cease to exist for society. You will not be able to travel without a vaccine, you will not be able to go to the cinema and in the future you won't even be able to leave your own house. This is already happening in some Chinese cities.

Everything has already been set up and activated in all companies and media for mass vaccination.

I will prefer death, absolutely not vaccination.

Fake News: Vaccination or implanting chips?

Sizwe sikaMusi, 25 March 2020

Other conspiracy theories had Bill Gates, long-time proponent of vaccination and global pandemic planning (see page 278), at their heart. The major social media platforms eventually undertook to remove posts promoting such theories, such as this, found on Twitter from a South African with more than 20,000 followers.

Bill Gates is launching implantable chips which will be used to show whether a person has been tested and vaccinated for Corona. These microchips will dissolve under the skin, leaving identification 'quantum dots'. These implants can also be used as a form of ID.

Symptoms come and go, are strange and frightening
Paul Garner, BMJ Opinion blog, 5 May 2020
Paul Garner, professor of infectious diseases at Liverpool School of Tropical Medicine, discussed his experience of having Covid-19, which would not go away, in a BMJ (British Medical Journal) blog.

In mid March I developed Covid-19. For almost seven weeks I have been through a roller coaster of ill health, extreme emotions and utter exhaustion. Although not hospitalized, it has been frightening and long. The illness ebbs and flows, but never goes away. Health professionals, employers, partners and people with the disease need to know that this illness can last for weeks, and the long tail is not some 'post-viral fatigue syndrome' — it is the disease. People who have a more protracted illness need help to understand and cope with the constantly shifting, bizarre symptoms, and their unpredictable course.

Early March seems so far away. I watched Boris [Johnson, British prime minister] introduce social distancing and then shake hands on national television; I talked with epidemiological colleagues about the established effects of austerity increasing mortality in the poor, and how lockdown would worsen this; I advised my 97-year-old father to isolate. I said to myself that years of running and military fitness would protect me from harm. I discounted a runny nose, carefully checked my temperature every day, and examined the CDC/WHO comparison table and decided I did not have Covid-19. Then one afternoon I started feeling strange: I happened to be on a Zoom meeting with David Nabarro [special envoy from the director-general of WHO] who said anyone who felt unwell should isolate instantly, on the spot. I went home early, and then the journey began.

In the first days at home I wasn't sure I had Covid-19. Then I damaged my hands with bleach. It had no smell, I assumed it was old and inactive – but it was just I could not smell the chlorine. The heaviness and malaise became worse, I had a tightness in the chest and realized it could be nothing else. I was mortified that I might have infected the staff I had worked with for over twenty years. I imagined their vulnerable relatives dying and never forgiving myself. My mind was a mess. My condition deteriorated. One afternoon I suddenly developed a tachycardia, tightness in the chest, and felt so unwell I thought I was dying. My mind became foggy. I tried to Google fulminating myocarditis, but couldn't navigate the screen properly. There was nothing to do. I thought, if this is it so be it.

A few hours later I woke up, alive, and the tightness replaced by extreme fatigue. Every day, day after day. Sometimes I felt better and became optimistic; after all, the paralytic state had not recurred; but then the next day I felt as though someone had hit me around the head with a cricket bat. Staff at work criticized me for not being clear 'make up your mind! Are you getting better or not?' I guess they were frightened too, but I really could not understand what was happening.

The illness went on and on. The symptoms changed, it was like an advent calendar, every day there was a surprise, something new. A muggy head; acutely painful calf; upset stomach; tinnitus; pins and needles; aching all over; breathlessness; dizziness; arthritis in my hands; weird sensation in the skin with synthetic materials. Gentle exercise or walking made me worse – I would feel absolutely dreadful the next day. I started talking to others. I found a marathon runner who had tried 8 km in her second week, which caused her to collapse with rigors and sleep for 24 hours. I spoke to others experiencing weird symptoms, which were often discounted by those around them as anxiety, making them doubt themselves.

The internet described recovery times of about two weeks for people that had not been hospitalized. I had not had severe disease, yet here I was after four weeks still unwell. My doctor neighbour and GP were concerned. I consulted with friends who were consultants in infectious diseases by email and they wondered if I had more lung involvement than I had estimated. My tenant had friends who were still ill at four weeks and this helped a lot.

The least helpful comments were from people who explained to me that I had post viral fatigue. I knew this was wrong. There was a pattern in that period from two weeks to six weeks: feeling absolutely dreadful during the day; sleep heavily, waking with the bed drenched in sweat; getting up with a blinding headache, receding during the day, turning me into a battered ragdoll in the evening.

I joined a Facebook page (Covid-19 Support Group) full of people with these stories, some from the UK, some from the US. People suffering from the disease, but not believing their symptoms were real; their families thinking the symptoms were anxiety; employers telling people they had to return to work, as the two weeks for the illness was up. And the posts reflect this: 'I thought I was going crazy for not getting better in their time frame'; 'the doctor said there is zero reason to believe it lasts this long'. And too, people report that their families do not believe their ever-changing symptoms, that it is psychological, it is the stress.

Over the weeks, I have been touched by the people that have quietly stepped in to help me cope, appropriate, unobtrusive, timely. Family, friends, colleagues and neighbours. Our local yoga studio's motto is 'a community building strength in mind, body and heart'. This love and support gives us a direction for our future. And today the disease has lifted. For the first time, I do not feel awful.

The aim of this piece is to get this message out: for some people the illness goes on for a few weeks. Symptoms come and go, are strange and frightening. The exhaustion is severe, real and part of the illness. And we all need support and love from the community around us.

The path to herd immunity

THE GREAT BARRINGTON DECLARATION, 4 October 2020

As the pandemic continued into the final months of 2020, governments across the world, reluctant to enter a second – and economically dev- astating – full lockdown, chose instead to reintroduce increasingly complex measures to limit interaction in order to reduce infection rates. Many populations became increasingly restive at what were perceived as illogical, illiberal and ineffective rules; the scientific consensus also began to fracture. Some experts – led by Professor Martin Kulldorff at Harvard University, Professor Sunetra Gupta at Oxford and Professor Jay Bhattacharya at Stanford – lent their names to a declaration of a different policy, one that aimed at achieving 'herd immunity' with the minimum of human and economic disruption.

As infectious disease epidemiologists and public health scientists we have grave concerns about the damaging physical and mental health impacts of the prevailing Covid-19 policies, and recommend an approach we call Focused Protection.

Coming from both the left and right, and around the world, we have devoted our careers to protecting people. Current lockdown policies are producing devastating effects on short- and long-term public health. The results (to name a few) include lower childhood vaccination rates, worsening cardiovascular disease outcomes, fewer cancer screenings and deteriorating mental health – leading to greater excess mortality in years to come, with the working class and younger members of society carrying the heaviest burden. Keeping students out of school is a grave injustice.

Keeping these measures in place until a vaccine is available will cause irreparable damage, with the underprivileged disproportionately harmed.

Fortunately, our understanding of the virus is growing. We know that vulnerability to death from Covid-19 is more than a thousand-fold higher in the old and infirm than the young. Indeed, for children, Covid-19 is less dangerous than many other harms, including influenza.

As immunity builds in the population, the risk of infection to all – including the vulnerable – falls. We know that all populations will eventually reach herd immunity – i.e. the point at which the rate of new infections is stable – and that this can be assisted by (but is not dependent upon) a vaccine. Our goal should therefore be to minimize mortality and social harm until we reach herd immunity.

The most compassionate approach that balances the risks and benefits of reaching herd immunity, is to allow those who are at minimal risk of death to live their lives normally to build up immunity to the virus through natural infection, while better protecting those who are at highest risk. We call this Focused Protection.

Adopting measures to protect the vulnerable should be the central aim of public health responses to Covid-19. By way of example, nursing homes should use staff with acquired immunity and perform frequent PCR testing of other staff and all visitors. Staff rotation should be minimized. Retired people living at home should have groceries and other essentials delivered to their home. When possible, they should meet family members outside rather than inside. A comprehensive and detailed list of measures, including approaches to multi-generational households, can be implemented, and is well within the scope and capability of public health professionals.

Those who are not vulnerable should immediately be allowed to resume life as normal. Simple hygiene measures, such as hand washing and staying home when sick should be practiced by everyone to reduce the herd immunity threshold. Schools and universities should be open for in-person teaching. Extracurricular activities, such as sports, should be resumed. Young low-risk adults should work normally, rather than from home. Restaurants and other businesses should open. Arts, music, sport and other cultural activities should resume. People who are more at risk may participate if they wish, while society as a whole enjoys the protection conferred upon the vulnerable by those who have built up herd immunity.

We are a significant step closer

Dr Albert Bourla, Pfizer Chairman and CEO, 9 November 2020

In late 2020 highly encouraging results in trials for a vaccine were reported by several companies, giving rise to hope for a global vaccine rollout in 2021. The first to be announced was a joint venture by the American pharma giant Pfizer and a German startup, BioNTech, and the first person to receive this vaccine was ninety-year-old Briton Margaret Keenan, on 8 December 2020.

Today is a great day for science and humanity. The first set of results from our Phase 3 Covid-19 vaccine trial provides the initial evidence of our vaccine's ability to prevent Covid-19. We are reaching this critical milestone in our vaccine development program at a time when the world needs it most with infection rates setting new records, hospitals nearing over-capacity and economies struggling to reopen. With today's news, we are a significant step closer to providing people around the world with a much-needed breakthrough to help bring an end to this global health crisis.

Citizens of Venice celebrate the Festa del Redontore,
first held in 1576 to give thanks for the ending of the plague.

POSTSCRIPT

In 2020, with the world in lockdown, normal life was put in abeyance. With the skies clear of aircraft, oil consumption in freefall and town centres deserted by all other than flocks of deer, monkeys or ducks, it seemed momentarily as if the Covid-19 pandemic could bring some lasting changes – even benefits – to the world. It was described by some as the world's best chance to slow the galloping climate chaos, to rebuild a sense of community and to address social injustices that had become glaring.

But this was a passing dream, just as Covid-19 itself was a passing nightmare. Though lockdown was ended in cautious fits and starts, and some behaviours – like remote working for office workers – appeared to have become more widely entrenched, the passing of the first wave of the pandemic saw a return to something approaching the old ways of life. Businesses and schools reopened and consumption, including international travel, took off once again. Governments inevitably focused on addressing the huge costs of the pandemic response, the recession and unemployment it caused, the services lost and the town centres decimated by the sudden shift to online shopping. The appetite for systemic change dissolved into a desire to 'move on'. Only in the area of racial inequality, where the Black Lives Matter movement coincided with the end of lockdown, was the pandemic obviously linked to a longer-lasting political movement.

The second wave that hit the Northern Hemisphere in the last three months of 2020 saw a decline in compliance and a rise in tensions around the world as the public tired of restrictions, questioned the logic of their governments' sometimes complex rules, and doubted the explanations and sometimes confusing statistics presented by the experts. But before the tensions boiled over, the news that a vaccine would be widely available early in 2021 held out a promise – seized upon by governments and public alike – that the coronavirus crisis would soon be a thing of the past. An orgy of consumerism was anticipated. In this amnesiac future, the prime legacy of 2020 would be sky-high taxes, and hidden pain in the hearts of millions of parents, spouses, siblings, children and friends.

It was ever thus. Throughout the ages, pandemics have arrived, been endured and eventually passed on, leaving survivors to grieve and to pick up the pieces of their lives. Yet they never leave history unchanged. On the most obvious level, the Covid-19 pandemic was credited with influencing the result of the US presidential election in November 2020, as voters tired of the incumbent's chaotic response to the virus. Even a pandemic has winners, like Joe Biden, as well as losers, like Trump: it takes away the lives of some and wrecks the life chances of many more, but can create opportunities for others to prosper. For most, though, such crises bring disruption that needs urgently to be cleared away so that 'normality' can return.

On a Sunday in July for more than 400 years, Venice has celebrated the passing of the plague in 1575 with a feast, fireworks and a bridge of barges. This sense of communal relief at the lifting of a terrible natural affliction is yet another connection with historical experience that the world is learning from the Covid-19 pandemic.

But as a historical rather than a purely epidemiological event, a pandemic is never completely 'over', and the questions it raises will re-emerge in coming years and decades. We all – scientists, governments, families – will have to find ways to learn the lessons from this one, partly because we can live better than we have done in the past, and partly because another pandemic will surely arrive when we least expect it.

As Albert Camus wrote in *The Plague* (1947), probably the best-known work of imaginative literature about epidemics: 'As he listened to the cries of joy that arose above the town, Rieux recalled that this joy was always under threat. He knew that this happy crowd was unaware of something that one can read in books, which is that the plague bacillus never dies or vanishes entirely, that it can remain dormant for dozens of years in furniture or clothing, that it waits patiently in bedrooms, cellars, trunks, handkerchiefs and old papers, and that perhaps the day will come when, for the instruction or misfortune of mankind, the plague will rouse its rats and send them to die in some well-contented city.'

SOURCES

Athenian Plague

Thucydides: *The History of the Peloponnesian War*, translated by Richard Crawley (London, 1866)

Sophocles: in *Sophocles I*, translated by David Grene, Richmond Lattimore, Mark Griffith and Glenn W. Most (Chicago, 1991)

Antonine Plague

Ammianus Marcellinus: in *Roman History*, Volume II (Cambridge, MA, 1940)

Aelius Aristides: *Sacred Tales II*, edited by C. A. Behr (Amsterdam, 1968)

Galen: in 'Galen and the Antonine Plague' by Littman, R. J. and M. L. Littman, *American Journal of Philology*, Vol. 94, No. 3 (Autumn 1973), pp. 243–55

Paulus Orosius: *Seven Books of History Against the Pagans*, Book VII, Chapter XV, translated by Roy Deferrari (Washington DC, 1964)

Lucian of Samosata: in *The Works of Lucian* (Volume IV), translated by A. R. Harmon (London, 1925)

Plague of Justinian

Procopius: *History of the Wars*, *Volume II*, Chapters 22–23, edited by T. E. Page and W. H. U. Rouse (Cambridge, MA, 1964)

Procopius: *Secret History*, Chapter 6, translated by Richard Atwater (Ann Arbor, 1961)

Evagrius Scholasticus: *Ecclesiastical History*, Chapter 28, translated by E. Walford (London, 1946)

John of Ephesus: Chronicle, Part 2; quoted in *Pseudo-Dionysius of Tel-Mahre, Chronicle*, translated by Witold Witakowski (Liverpool, 1996)

John of Ephesus: *Lives of the Eastern Saints* 17, 1; quoted in *Pseudo-Dionysius of Tel-Mahre, Chronicle*, translated by Witold Witakowski (Liverpool, 1996)

Michael the Syrian: quoted in *Pseudo-Dionysius of Tel-Mahre, Chronicle*, translated by Witold Witakowski (Liverpool, 1996)

Gregory of Tours: *History of the Franks*, Book 4, Chapter 31, and Book 9, Chapter 22, translated by Earnest Brehaut (London, 1916)

The Venerable Bede: *Ecclesiastical History of the English People*, Chapter XXVII, translated by A. M. Sellar (London, 1907)

Leprosy

Gregory of Nazianzus: in *St Gregory of Nazianzos, Selected Orations*, translated by Martha Vinson (Washington, DC, 2003)

William of Tyre: *A History of Deeds Done Beyond the Sea*, Book XXI, Chapter 1, and Book XXII, Chapter 1, translated by Emily Atwater Babcock and A. C. Krey (New York, 1943)

Alice of Schaerbeek: Edmond Martène's *De Antiquis Ecclesiae Ritibus*, in *Alice the Leper: Life of St Alice of Schaerbeek*, edited by Martinus Cawley (Lafayette, OR, 2000)

Bernard de Gordon: *Lilium Medicinae*, translated by Richmond C. Holcomb in 'Antiquity of congential syphilis', *Bulletin of History of Medicine* 10, 1941

Jordan of Turre: in *A Source Book of Medieval Science*, edited by Edward Grant (Cambridge, MA, 1974)

Enköping Hospital: in *The Medieval Leper and His Northern Heirs*, Peter Richards (Woodbridge, 2000)

The Black Death

Gabriele de' Mussi: in *The Black Death*, Rosemary Horrox (Manchester, 1994)

Jean de Venette: in *The Chronicles of Jean de Venette,* edited by Richard A. Newhall (New York, 1953)

Rochester Priory: *Chronicle of Rochester Priory*, British Library, Cotton MS Faustina BV

Giovanni Boccaccio: *The Decameron*, translated by Mark Musa and Peter Bondanella (New York, 2010)

Francesco Petrarch: in *The Black Death: 1347*, George Deaux (London and New York, 1969)

Tommaso del Garbo: *Consiglio Contro a Pistolenza* (Bologna, 1866)

Henry Knighton: *Chronicon*, in *Chaucer's World*, edited by E. Rickert, C. C. Olson and M. M. Crow (Oxford, 1948)

Robert of Avesbury: *Robertus de Avesbury de Gestis Mirabilibus Regis Edwardi Tertii*, edited by E. Maunde Thompson (Cambridge, 1889)

Ibn Battuta: *Travels in Asia and Africa 1325–1354,* translated and edited by H.A.R. Gibb (London, 1929)

Ibn Khaldun: *Prolegomenon or Muqqadimah*, translated by Frank Rosenthal (Princeton, NJ, 1969)

St Roch: *The Golden Legend,* Book V, translated by William Caxton in 1483, edited by F.S. Ellis (London, 1900)

Taqi al-Din al-Maqrizi: *Histoire des sultans mamlouks, de l'Égypte*, translated by Étienne Marc Quatremère (Paris, 1845)

Martin Luther: in *Martin Luther, Luther's Works, Vol. 43: Devotional Writings II*, edited by Jaroslav Jan Pelikan, Hilton C. Oswald and Helmut T. Lehmann (Philadelphia, 1999)

Sweating Sickness

Edward Hall: in *Hall's Chronicle* (London, 1548)

Thomas le Forestier: *Treatise on the Venyms Fever of Pestilens* (London, 1485)

Francis Bacon: *The History of King Henry VII*, in *The Works of Francis Bacon, Lord Chancellor of England*, Volume 1, Basil Montagu (London, 1844)

Sebastian Giustiniano: in *Calendar of State Papers Relating To English Affairs in the Archives of Venice, Volume 2, 1509–1519* (London, 1867)

Thomas More: in 'England, the "sweating sickness", and the continent', John L. Flood, *Renaissance Studies*, Vol. 17, No. 2 (June 2003)

Jean du Bellay: in *Preuves de l'Histoire du Divorce de Henry VIII* by J. LeGrand, Vol. III (1688)

William Roper: *Life of Sir Thomas More* (London, 1894)

Henry Machyn: *The Diary of Henry Machyn* (Camden Society, 1847–48)

John Caius: *A Boke, or Counseill against the Disease Commonly Called the Sweate or the Sweating Sickness* (London, 1552).

George Thomson: quoted in *The Lord Bacons Relation to the Sweating-Sickness Examined*, Henry Stubbe (London, 1670)

Syphilis

Marcello Cumano: in *Calamities and the Economy in Renaissance Italy: The Grand Tour of the Horsemen of the Apocalypse*, G. Alfani (London, 2013)

Francesco Guicciardini: *History of Italy*, Volume I (Princeton, NJ, 1984)

Gonzalo Fernández de Oviedo: in

'The Early History of Syphilis: a Reappraisal', Alfred Crosby, *American Anthropologist New Series*, Vol. 71, No. 2 (April 1969), pp. 218–27

Joseph Grünpeck von Bürckhausen: *Neat Treatise on the French Evil*, translated by Merrill Moore and Harry C. Solomon, *British Journal of Venereal Diseases* (1935)

Ulrich von Hutten: *De Morbo Gallico: A Treatise on the French Disease* (London, 1730)

Desiderius Erasmus: 'The Unequal Marriage', in *The Colloquies of Erasmus*, Volume II, translated by N. Bailey (London, 1878)

Girolamo Fracastoro: *Syphilis, or A Poetical History of the French Disease*, translated by Nahum Tate (London, 1686)

Thomas Sydenham: in *The Entire Works of Dr Thomas Sydenham*, edited by John Swan (London, 1763)

New World Smallpox

Rhazes: *Treatise on Smallpox and Measles,* quoted in 'The Air of History (Part IV): Great Muslim Physicians Al Rhazes' Rachel Hajar, *Heart Views* (April–June 2013)

Bernardino de Sahagún: *General History of the Things of New Spain*, or *Florentine Codex* (1576)

Native Mexican annals: in 'Spanish and Nahuatl Views on Smallpox and Demographic Catastrophe in Mexico' Robert McCaa, *Journal of Interdisciplinary History*, Vol. 25, No. 3 (Winter 1995)

Toribio de Benavente Motolinía: *Motolinía's History of the Indians of the New Spain*, edited and translated by Elizabeth Andros Foster (Westport, Conn., 1973)

Mayan annals: in *The Annals of the Cakchiquels*, translated by Adrián Recinos and Delia Goetz (Norman, OK, 1953)

Pedro de Cieza de León: *The Second Part of the Chronicle of Peru*, translated by Clements Markham (New York, 1883)

Guaman Poma: *The First New Chronicle and Good Government* (Austin, TX, 2010)

William Bradford: *Of Plymouth Plantation*, edited by William Davis (New York, 1979)

The Great Plague

Daniel Defoe: *A Journal of the Plague Year* (London, 1722)

Plague in Marseilles: in *The Great Bill of Mortality or, The late dreadful Plague at Marseilles* (Bristol, 1721)

Cholera

Tibetan manuscript: in 'Cholera Studies: The History of the Disease I', R. Pollitzer, *Bulletin of the World Health Organization* (1954) 10(3), pp. 421–61

Gaspar Correa: in 'Cholera: molecular basis for emergence and pathogenesis', John J. Mekalanos, Eric J. Rubin and Matthew K. Waldor, *Pathogens and Disease,* Volume 18, Issue 4, August 1997, pp. 241–48

H. H. Wilson: *History of British India 1805–1835*, Volume II (London, 1846)

James Jameson: *Report on the Epidemick Cholera Morbus as it Visited the Territories Subject to the Presidency of Bengal, In the years 1817, 1818, and 1819* (London, 1820)

James Copland: *Of Pestilential Cholera: Its Nature, Prevention, and Curative Treatment* (London, 1832)

Liverpool Chronicle: in 'The Liverpool Cholera Epidemic of 1832 and Anatomical Dissection: Medical Mistrust and Civil Unrest', Sean Burrell and Geoffrey Gill, *Journal of the History of Medicine and Allied Sciences,* Volume 60, Issue 4, October 2005, pp. 478–98

James Newland: in 'Kitty Wilkinson: A Civic Myth?', John Dobie, *The Journal of the Institute of Baths Management Incorporated* (1972)

John Snow: *On the Mode of Communication of Cholera* (London, 1855)

Robert Koch: *Cholera in Germany During the Winter of 1892–1893*, translated by George Duncan (Edinburgh, 1894)

Toronto Evening News: in 'Fearing Future Epidemics: the Cholera Crisis of 1892', Paul S. B. Jackson, *Cultural Geographies* (2012)

Aly Tewfik Shousha: *Cholera Epidemic in Egypt in 1947: A Preliminary Report* (1947)

Charles Wheeler: *American Journal of Public Health*, Volume 36 (February 1946)

William Budd: in *Typhoid fever: its nature, mode of spreading, and prevention,* William Budd (London, 1870)

George Soper: 'The Curious Career of Typhoid Mary', in *The Bulletin of the New York Academy of Medicine,* 1 October 1939, 15(10), pp. 698–712

Third Plague Pandemic

C. A. Gordon: in *An Epitome of the Reports of the Medical*

Officers to the Chinese Imperial Maritime Customs Service, from 1871 to 1882 (London, 1884)

James Lowson: *Indian Medical Gazette* (February 1897), p. 45

Waldemar Haffkine: *British Medical Journal* (12 June 1897), 1(1902), pp. 1461–62

W. G. Liston: in *Reports on Plague Investigations in India* (Cambridge 1911), p. 217

Smallpox: From Treatment to Eradication

Thomas Sydenham: *Medical Observations,* Section III, Chapter II (London, 1669)

Thomas Dover: *The Ancient Physician's Legacy to His Country* (London, 1732)

Lady Mary Wortley Montagu: in *The Letters of Lady Mary Wortley Montagu*, edited by Mrs Hale (Boston, 1884)

Giacomo Casanova: *Story of My Life*, translated by Arthur Machen (London, 1894)

Benjamin Franklin: *Autobiography*, edited by Frank Woodworth Pine (New York, 1916)

William Heberden: *Some Account of the Success of Inoculation for the Small-Pox in England and America* (London, 1759)

John Ferdinand Dalziel Smith: in *Eyewitness Accounts of the American Revolution* (New York, 1968)

Caleb Haskell: *Caleb Haskell's Diary,* edited by Lothrop Withington (New York, 1922)

Edward Jenner: *An Inquiry into the Causes and Effects of the Variolae Vaccinae* (London, 1798)

Edward Jenner: *On the Origin of the Vaccine Inoculation* (London, 1801)

Anti-vaccination society: The Historical Medical Library of The College of Physicians of Philadelphia (https://www.historyofvaccines.org/content/broadside-3) [accessed 1 October 2020]

William H. Foege: *House on Fire: The Fight to Eradicate Smallpox* (Berkeley, CA, 2011) © William Foege 2011

Declaration of Eradication: World Health Organization (Switzerland, 1980)

'Spanish Flu'

'The Spanish Epidemic': *The Times*, 3 June 1918

Pfieffer's bacillus: quoted in *Pandemic 1918*, Catherine Arnold (London, 2018)

Wilfred Owen: 'Letter to Susan

Owen, 24 June 1918', in *Wilfred Owen Collected Letters*, edited by H. Owen and J. Bell (Oxford, 1967)

'Influenza Spreading in Germany': *The Times*, 3 July 1918

N. Roy Grist: in 'What We Can learn from 1918 Influenza Diaries', Meilan Solly, *Smithsonian Magazine*, 13 April 2020

Lutiant Van Wert: https://www.archives.gov/exhibits/influenza-epidemic/records/volunteer-nurse-letter.pdf [accessed 1 October 2020]

'Wear a mask': in 'Lessons Learned from the 1918–1919 Influenza Pandemic in Minneapolis and St Paul, Minnesota' Miles Ott, Shelly F. Shaw, Richard N. Danila and Ruth Lynfield, *Public Health Report*, Nov–Dec 2007, 122(6), pp. 803–10.

Imtale Grillo: in *Influenza Pandemic Storybook*, Centers for Disease and Control and Prevention, https://www.cdc.gov/publications/panflu/stories/imtale_grillo.html [accessed 1 October 2020]

Blaise Cendrars: *Oeuvres Completes*, vol. VIII, p. 662 (Paris, 1964)

Government of New South Wales: 'To the People of New South Wales', *Sydney Morning Herald*: https://www.records.nsw.gov.au/archives/collections-and-research/guides-and-indexes/stories/pneumonic-influenza-1919# [accessed 1 October 2020]

'Dying by Hundreds': *The Times*, 6 January 1919

George Soper: *Science Magazine*, 31 May 1919

Edwin O. Jordan: *American Journal of Public Health*, November 1925, 15(11), pp. 943–47

Poliomyelitis

Michael Underwood: in *A Treatise on the Diseases of Children, Volume II* (London, 1784)

Wade H. Frost: 'Poliomyelitis (Infantile Paralysis): What is Known of its Causes and Modes of Transmission', *Public Health Reports*, 14 July 1916, Vol. 31, No. 28.

Wade H. Frost: 'Do children have greater exposure or greater susceptibility?', *Public Health Reports*, 14 July 1916

Richard Lloyd Daggett: *Not Just Polio* (Bloomington, IN, 2010)

Islamic Advisory Group for Polio Eradication: http://polioeradication.org/wp-content/uploads/2016/07/

Jeddah_Declaration_EN-1.pdf [accessed 1 October 2020]

Judith Shaw Beatty: https://shotofprevention.com/2016/06/08/my-polio-story-is-an-inconvenient-truth-to-those-who-refuse-vaccines/ [accessed 1 October 2020]

Asian Flu and Hong Kong Flu

Harvey Morris and Maria Morandini: https://news-decoder.com/asian-flu-coronavirus/ [accessed 1 October 2020]

H. V. Reeves: *British Medical Journal,* 9 November 1957, quoted in https://www.ncbi.nlm.nih.gov/pmc/articles/PMC1962748/pdf/brmedj03128-0065a.pdf [accessed 1 October 2020]

Clark Whelton: 'Say Your Prayers and Take Your Chances', https://www.city-journal.org/1957-asian-flu-pandemic [accessed 1 October 2020]

J. Corbett McDonald: RCGP Archives. Between Ourselves. ACE G3–4, Dec 1957, quoted in 'History Lessons: The Asian Flu Pandemic', *British Journal of General Practice*, August 2009, 59 (565), pp. 622–23

W. K. Chang: *Bulletin of the World Health Organization*, 1969, 41 (3-4-5), pp. 349–51

Roger McNeill: 'I survived the Hong Kong flu of 1968', *North Shore News*, 26 April 2020

Alexander D. Langmuir and Jere Housworth: 'A Critical Evaluation of Influenza Surveillance', *Bulletin of the World Health Organization*, 1969, 41(3-4-5): 393–398

AIDS

Michael Gottlieb: 'Kaposis's sarcoma and pneumocystis among homosexual men', *CDC Morbidity and Mortality Weekly Report*, 3 July 1981

Larry Kramer: '1,112 and Counting', *New York Native*, March 1983, quoted by Karen Ocamb, Bileroco project on LGBTQ Nation, 14 June 2011

AIDS in gay men: San Francisco Department of Public Health leaflet, May 1983, http://s3-us-west-2.amazonaws.com/ucldc-nuxeo-ref-media/7bd18019-fa2e-458f-8ea0-ed63eabe20d5 [accessed 1 October 2020]

'All we have is memories and pictures': in 'Survivors of 1980s AIDS crisis reveal what happened to them', *Gay Star News,* 2 February 2015

Jean White-Ginder: https://hab.

hrsa.gov/about-ryan-white-hivaids-program/who-was-ryan-white [accessed 1 October 2020]

Castro Hlongwane, Caravans, Cats, Geese, Foot & Mouth and Statistics: http://www.virusmyth.com/aids/hiv/ancdoc.htm [accessed 1 October 2020]

'There is so much more to life': https://www.avert.org/living-with-hiv/stories/elizabeth [accessed 1 October 2020]

Ebola

Garrett Ingoglia: 'A Firsthand Account of Life at the Epicenter of the Ebola Outbreak in Monrovia, Liberia', *Huffington Post*, 10 September 2014

Gillian McKay: 'First-hand reflections on supporting Ebola outbreak response in DRC', London School of Hygiene and Tropical Medicine, 4 September 2019, https://www.lshtm.ac.uk/newsevents/expert-opinion/first-hand-reflections-supporting-ebola-outbreak-response-drc [accessed 1 October 2020]. This was first published by the Pierre Elliott Trudeau Foundation.

Thomas Geisbert: 'Ebola Aftermath: Three Personal Stories', *Discover* magazine, 30 November 2015, https://www.discovermagazine.com/health/ebola-aftermath-three-personal-stories [accessed 1 October 2020]

Ida Jooste: 'My Struggle to Report on Ebola Without Provoking Panic—or Complacency', 15 December 2017, *Internews*, https://internews.org/news/my-struggle-report-ebola-without-provoking-panic-or-complacency [accessed 1 October 2020]

Trish Newport: 'Ebola Outbreak Still Rages One Year on after Declaration', 1 August 2019, Doctors Without Frontiers, https://www.doctorswithoutborders.org/what-we-do/news-stories/story/ebola-outbreak-still-rages-one-year-after-declaration [accessed 1 October 2020]

Bill Gates: 'The next epidemic – lessons from Ebola', *New England Journal of Medicine*, 9 April 2015, 372, pp. 1381–84

Coronavirus

WHO report: *The World Health Report 2003: Shaping the Future*, https://www.who.int/

whr/2003/en/ [accessed
1 October 2020]

Ai Fen: https://
scienceintegritydigest.
com/2020/03/11/dr-ai-fen-the-
wuhan-whistle/ [accessed
1 October 2020]

Jacinda Ardern: 'Coronavirus:
Prime Minister Jacinda
Ardern's full COVID-19
speech', Newshub, 23 March
2020, https://www.newshub.
co.nz/home/politics/2020/03/
coronavirus-prime-minister-
jacinda-ardern-s-full-covid-19-
speech.html [accessed
1 October 2020]

Goncalo Tavares: in *Plague
Diaries 2020*. Published by
arrangement with Literarische
Agentur Mertin Witt. This text
was originally published in
Portuguese in the *Expresso*.
All rights reserved by the
author and translator, Daniel
Hahn.

Dr Kiran Rahim: 'The Spirit of the
NHS', *Medic Footprints, 2020*,
https://medicfootprints.org/
the-spirit-of-the-nhs/ [accessed
1 October 2020]

Roberto Patrella: 'The
Depopulation Agenda:
Don't Get Tested', https://
www.bitchute.com/video/

OQHz9Fz6spJ3/ [accessed
1 October 2020]

Paul Garner: 'For 7 weeks
I have been through a
roller coaster of ill health,
extreme emotions, and utter
exhaustion', *BMJ Opinion*,
5 May 2020 [accessed
1 October 2020]

Great Barrington Declaration:
https://gbdeclaration.org/
[accessed 17 October 2020]

Albert Bourla: 'Pfizer and
BioNTech Announce Vaccine
Candidate Against COVID-
19 Achieved Success in First
Interim Analysis from Phase
3 Study', https://biontechse.
gcs-web.com/news-releases/
news-release-details/pfizer-
and-biontech-announce-
vaccine-candidate-against-
covid-19 [accessed 10
November 2020]

Postscript

Albert Camus: *The Plague* (1947),
translated by Robin Buss
(London, 1962).

FURTHER READING

Alfani, G. *Calamities and the Economy in Renaissance Italy* (London, 2013)

Arnold, Catharine. *Pandemic 1918: The Story of the Deadliest Influenza in History* (London, 2018)

Arnold, David. *Colonizing the Body: State Medicine and Epidemic Disease in Nineteenth-Century India* (Berkeley, CA, 1993)

Baldwin, Peter. *Contagion and the State in Europe: 1830–1930* (Cambridge, 1999)

Baldwin, Peter. *Disease and Democracy: The Industrialized World Faces AIDS* (Berkeley, CA, 2005)

Barry, John M. *The Great Influenza: The Story of the Deadliest Plague in History* (New York, 2004)

Behrman, Greg. *The Invisible People: How the U.S. Has Slept through the Global AIDS Pandemic, the Greatest Humanitarian Catastrophe of Our Time* (New York, 2004)

Benedict, Carol. *Bubonic Plague in Nineteenth-Century China* (Stanford, CA, 1996)

Benedictow, Ole. *The Black Death 1346–1353: The Complete History* (Woodbridge, 2004)

Bhattacharya, Sanjoy, Mark Harrison and Michael Worboys. *Fractured States: Smallpox, Public Health and Vaccination Policy in British India, 1800–1947* (New Delhi, 2005)

Cantor, Norman F. *In the Wake of the Plague: The Black Death and the World it Made* (New York, 2001)

Crosby, Alfred W. *America's Forgotten Pandemic: The Influenza of 1918* (Cambridge, 2003)

Defoe, Daniel. *A journal of the Plague Year* (London, 1722)

Diamond, Jared. *Guns, Germs and Steel* (London, 1988)

Dobson, Mary. *Murderous Contagion: A Human History of Disease* (London, 2015)

Echenberg, Myron. *Plague Ports: The Global Urban Impact of Bubonic Plague, 1894–1901* (New York, 2007)

Engel, Jonathan. *The Epidemic: A Global History of AIDS* (New York, 2006)

Espinosa, Mariola. *Epidemic Invasions: Yellow Fever and the Limits of Cuban Independence, 1878–1930* (Chicago and London, 2009)

Evans, Richard J. *Death in Hamburg: Society and Politics in the Cholera Years* (New York, 2005)

Fenn, Elizabeth A. *Pox Americana: The Great Smallpox Epidemic of 1775–82* (New York, 2001)

Foege, William M. *House of Fire: The Fight to Eradicate Smallpox* (Berkeley, CA, 2011)

Hamlin, Christopher. *Cholera: The Biography* (Oxford, 2009)

Harper, Kyle. *The Fate of Rome: Climate, Disease, and the End of an Empire* (Princeton, NJ, 2017)

Hayden, Deborah. *Pox: Genius, Madness and the Mysteries of Syphilis* (New York, 2003)

Hays, J. N. *Epidemics and Pandemics: Their Impacts on Human History* (Santa Barbara, CA, 2005)

Holmburg, Christine, Stuart Blume and Paul Greenough. *The Politics of Vaccination: A Global History* (Manchester, 2017)

Honigsbaum, Mark. *The Pandemic Century: One Hundred Years of Panic, Hysteria and Hubris* (London, 2019)

Hopkins, Donald. *The Greatest Killer: Smallpox in History* (Chicago, 2002)

Horrox, Rosemary. *The Black Death* (Manchester, 1994)

Humphreys, Margaret. *Yellow Fever and the South* (Baltimore, 1992)

Iliffe, John. *The African AIDS Epidemic: A History* (Athens, OH, 2006)

Jones, David S. *Rationalizing Epidemics: Meanings and Uses of American Indian Mortality since 1600* (Cambridge, MA, 2004)

Kiple, Kenneth, ed. *The Cambridge World History of Human Disease* (Cambridge, 1993)

Kiple, Kenneth, ed. *Plague, Pox and Pestilence: Disease in History* (London, 1997)

Kohn, George C., ed. *Encyclopedia of Plague and Pestilence: From Ancient Times to the Present* (New York, 2008)

Kohn, Samuel K. *Epidemics: Hate and Compassion from the Plague of Athens to AIDS* (Oxford, 2018)

Kolata, Gina. *Flu: The Story of the Great Influenza Pandemic of 1918 and the Search for the Virus that Caused It* (New York, 1999)

Little, Lester K., ed. *Plague and the End of Antiquity: The Pandemic of 541–750* (Cambridge, 2007)

Lord, Evelyn. *The Great Plague: A People's History* (London, 2014)

MacKenzie, Debora. *Covid-19: The Pandemic That Never Should Have Happened, and How to Stop the Next One* (London, 2020)

Markel, Howard. *Quarantine! East European Jewish immigrants and the New York City epidemics of 1892* (Baltimore, 1997)

Martin, Sean. *A Short History of Disease: Plagues, Poxes and Civilisations* (Harpenden, 2015)

McNeill, J. R. *Mosquito Empires: Ecology and War in the Greater Caribbean, 1620–1914* (Cambridge, 2010)

McNeill, William. *Plagues and Peoples* (Harmondsworth and New York, 1976)

Oldstone, Michael B. A. *Viruses,*

Plagues and History (New York, 2010)

Oppenheimer, Gerald M. and Ronald Bayer. *Shattered Dreams? An Oral History of the South African AIDS Epidemic* (Oxford and New York, 2007)

Oshinsky, David M. *Polio: an American story* (Oxford and New York, 2005)

Porter, Roy. *Bodies Politic: Disease, Death and Doctors in Britain, 1650–1900* (London and Ithaca, NY, 2001)

Porter, Roy, ed. *Cambridge Illustrated History of Medicine* (Cambridge and New York, 2001)

Powell, J. H. *Bring Out Your Dead: The Great Plague of Yellow Fever in Philadelphia in 1793* (Philadelphia, 1993)

Ranger, Terence and Paul Slack. *Epidemics and Ideas: Essays on the Historical Perception of Pestilence* (Cambridge, 1992)

Rosenberg, Charles E. *The Cholera Years: The United States in 1832, 1849, and 1866* (Chicago, 1962)

Rothman, David J., Steven Marcus, and Stephanie A. Kiceluk (eds). *Medicine and Western Civilization* (New Brunswick, 1995)

Shilts, Randy. *And the Band Played On: Politics, People, and the AIDS Epidemic* (New York, 1987)

Slack, Paul. *Plague: A Very Short Introduction* (Oxford and New York, 2012)

Snowden, Frank M. *Epidemics and Society: From the Black Death to the Present* (New Haven, 2020)

Spinney, Laura. *Pale Rider: The Spanish Flu of 1918 and How it Changed the World* (London, 2018)

Wain, Harry. *A History of Preventive Medicine* (New York, 1970)

Watts, Sheldon. *Epidemics and History: Disease, Power, and Imperialism* (New Haven, 1997)

Willrich, Michael. *Pox: An American History* (New York, 2011)

Wolfe, Nathan. *The Viral Storm: The Dawn of a New Pandemic Age* (London, 2011)

Zinnsser, Hans. *Rats, Lice and History: Being a Study in Biography, Which, After Twelve Preliminary Chapters Indispensable for the Preparation of the Lay Reader, Deals With the Life History of Typhus Fever* (New York, 1935)

SOURCES OF ILLUSTRATIONS

2 Metropolitan Museum of Art, New York. Rogers Fund, 1919;
6 Wellcome Collection, London; 18 Chronicle/Alamy; 32 Metropolitan
Museum of Art, New York. Rogers Fund, 1919; 86 Wellcome Collection,
London; 142 Institute of Experimental Medicine, St. Petersburg;
212 Photo George Konig/Keystone Features/Getty Images; 252 © Stuart
Franklin/Magnum Photos; 306 Photo Touring Club Italiano/Marka/
Universal Images Group via Getty Images

ACKNOWLEDGMENTS

I would like to thank the following for their invaluable
assistance in preparing this book: Lawrence Clarke,
David Cox, Ben Hayes, Joanne Murray, Colin Ridler,
Jen Moore, Craig Thorn, Melanie Winterbotham,
plus of course Ann Furtado.

INDEX

Peter Furtado is the former editor of *History Today*. His publications include the *Sunday Times* bestselling *Histories of Nations*, as well as *Revolutions: How They Changed History and What They Mean Today* and *Great Cities Through Travellers' Eyes*.

Plague, Pestilence and Pandemic © 2021
Thames & Hudson Ltd, London

Introduction, editorial material and its
arrangement © 2021 Peter Furtado
For details of other copyright material see
Sources and *Sources of Illustrations*

Typeset by Mark Bracey

First published in 2021 in the United States of
America by Thames & Hudson Inc., 500 Fifth Avenue,
New York, New York 10110

Library of Congress Control Number 2020951764

ISBN 978-0-500-29613-4

Printed and bound in the UK by CPI (UK) Ltd

Be the first to know about our new releases,
exclusive content and author events by visiting
thamesandhudson.com
thamesandhudsonusa.com
thamesandhudson.com.au